T0293605

ROUTLEDGE LIBRARY EDITIONS:
MANAGEMENT

Volume 5

YOUR ORGANIZATION:
WHAT IS IT FOR?

YOUR ORGANIZATION: WHAT IS IT FOR?

Challenging traditional organizational aims

JOHN ARGENTI

Routledge
Taylor & Francis Group

LONDON AND NEW YORK

First published in 1993 by McGraw-Hill Book Company Europe

This edition first published in 2018
by Routledge
2 Park Square, Milton Park, Abingdon, Oxon OX14 4RN

and by Routledge
711 Third Avenue, New York, NY 10017

Routledge is an imprint of the Taylor & Francis Group, an informa business

British Library Cataloguing in Publication Data
A catalogue record for this book is available from the British Library

ISBN: 978-1-138-55938-7 (Set)
ISBN: 978-1-351-05538-3 (Set) (ebk)
ISBN: 978-0-8153-6679-9 (Volume 5) (hbk)
ISBN: 978-1-351-25860-9 (Volume 5) (ebk)

Publisher's Note
The publisher has gone to great lengths to ensure the quality of this reprint but points out that some imperfections in the original copies may be apparent.

Disclaimer
The publisher has made every effort to trace copyright holders and would welcome correspondence from those they have been unable to trace.

Your organization: What is it for?

Challenging traditional organizational aims

JOHN ARGENTI

Published by

McGRAW-HILL Book Company Europe
Shoppenhangers Road, Maidenhead, Berkshire, SL6 2QL, England

Telephone   0628 23432
Fax   0628 770224

British Library Cataloguing in Publication Data

Argenti, John.
   Your organization: What is it for? —
   Challenging Traditional Organizational Aims
   I. Title
   658.401
   ISBN 0 07 707799 7

Library of Congress Cataloguing-in-Publication Data

Argenti, John.
   Your organization: What is it for?: challenging traditional
   organizational aims / John Argenti.
       p.   cm.
   Includes bibliographical references and index.
   ISBN 0 07 707799 7
   1. Organization. 2. Corporate governance. 3. Directors of corporations.
   I. Title.
   HD31.A6463   1993
   658.4—dc20   92–43398 CIP

1234   CUP   9543

Typeset by Computape (Pickering) Ltd, North Yorkshire
and printed and bound in Great Britain at the University Press, Cambridge

Contents

Preface

$\mathbf{T}$his is a book about your organization. But it is *not* about its management—there have been far too many books on management in the past two or three decades and the last thing we need now is another one of those. And it is not just about companies either; it concerns all types of organization including non-profitmaking organizations.

It is mainly about the *governance* of your organization, that is the regulating, supervising or overseeing of its performance and conduct. Governance is the activity that takes place above management, one step up from it.

Or, rather, it should. Most organizations have no system of governance at all; many that have find it ineffective. It is, I believe, this lack of an effectual system of governance, rather than any defect of management, that accounts for the poor performance of most organizations.

I define governance as 'setting standards of corporate performance and of corporate conduct, and ensuring that these are attained'. Of these three tasks, that of deciding corporate objectives is the most important—it is *infinitely* more important than most people have yet understood. If you get its corporate objective right your organization will soar to heights undreamed; get it wrong and it will languish and decline—and not even the most vigorous and imaginative management can rescue it from its wilderness. Choosing a suitable corporate aim is the organizational kiss of life—it turns frogs into princes!

This subject is the last unconquered peak of organizational theory and practice, and by far the most momentous. In spite of the critical importance of getting it right, I believe most organizations—certainly most non-profit-making organizations—have got it wrong. I describe, in blunt practical detail, how to determine these objectives and set corporate targets.

The second task of governance, deciding how an organization should behave in the community, is becoming increasingly significant as society matures and becomes less tolerant of wayward corporate conduct. And, I believe, most organizations have got this wrong too! Certainly many companies have.

Why have so many organizations adopted defective aims and debatable morals? It is because, having swallowed all those overweening books on management, we have empowered managers to determine these things for us; if we let them do that we must not be astonished when they resolve them to their own advantage rather than in favour of their organization. The job of a manager is to *achieve* corporate goals, surely, not to set them? I want someone who is *not* a manager to lay down standards of corporate performance and corporate conduct and to make sure that the management attains them.

I therefore want to see the appearance of a whole new profession, that of *'governing director'*, to be set above the management in all socially significant companies and non-profitmaking organizations. I want them to use a highly systematic approach to selecting corporate objectives, and to foster an updated definition of corporate morality, one that will be appropriate over the next few decades. And then they should supervise their organization's performance and conduct methodically and professionally.

So I am proposing three entirely new ideas in this book: a new methodology for setting corporate objectives (called the 'purpose sequence'); a fresh formula for socially attractive corporate conduct (including the novel 'principle of engagement'); and a new breed of 'governing director' (quite unlike present-day so-called governors and non-executives) to take these top decisions out of the hands of managers. I have rolled these three notions into one coherent concept which I have called 'the 'beneficiary doctrine'.

This, then, is the aim of this book: to introduce the 'beneficiary doctrine' with its three interrelated components: corporate performance, corporate conduct and a system of corporate governance.

Why have I written it? Because I am distressed at the pathetic performance of so many non-profit organizations and at the unattractive behaviour of so many companies around the world, and I believe that this doctrine will massively improve organizational effectiveness and conduct to the lasting benefit of society. I believe that, although it may take many years, these proposals will have a major impact on the performance of all types of human organization. Many of my conclusions run diametrically opposite to currently accepted dogma; I wish I could claim to have solved all the problems that such an approach inevitably raises.

I have tried to write so that everyone who supervises or manages an organization, whatever its size or form, can follow my argument with ease (I know how busy these people are). I have not written it for the academic so it is not full of minutely detailed and learned references and footnotes; on the contrary, I have tried to keep it simple and straightforward.

I explain where I think we have gone wrong and what the general principles are by which we can put all our organizations on to a more steadfast track and keep them there. While this is not strictly a 'practical guide', I believe readers will quickly recognize the practical implications for their own organizations.

Note: Your organization: what is it for? was written between February 1989 and July 1992.

CHAPTER ONE

The problem

In this chapter I shall explain why I believe that something has gone very seriously wrong with some of our organizations, why it matters so much and why we need a completely new approach.

The unanswered question

Imagine you are walking down the street and you bump into one of your friends who runs his own business—let us suppose he is your local builder. 'How are you getting on?' you ask. 'Oh, fine, thanks', he replies. 'We have just had our latest annual accounts which confirm that we have almost doubled profits over the past five years.' No doubt you congratulate him and wish him continued good fortune.

A few yards further on you meet another friend; this one is a very senior civil servant in the Department of Health. 'How are you getting on?' you ask. 'Oh, fine, thanks. We have just had our latest annual report which confirms that we now employ 40 000 more nurses than five years ago, the bed/patient ratio has fallen to 0.54321 and I am delighted to tell you that 21 per cent more hip replacement operations were performed by 11 per cent fewer surgeons. Moreover', she continues proudly, 'breast cancer has fallen by 8.4 per cent—although, curiously, lung cancer has increased by the same amount—8.4 per cent. However, ... '

'Hold on, hold on', you cry. 'I did not ask for the medical case-history of the entire population! I only wanted to know how well your employer, the Department of Health, has performed over the past five years.'

'Er, ... ' she replies, and changes the subject.

Do you see the problem? It strikes me as absolutely extraordinary that your local builder, who probably employs ten men and whose business is not exactly the central pillar of the national economy, knows to the nearest penny how well it has performed, while the Department of Health (which, in Britain has a million employees—the largest civilian organization in Europe!), apparently has no idea.

What they do is not what they are for

If you exclaim, 'But it does have an idea—dozens of them; look at all the figures my friend had at her fingertips', then all I can say is that you have missed the point. The point is that your builder was able to give you a figure which described the achievements of his business as an *organization*, as a corporate whole, while by contrast *none* of the figures the civil servant gave you said anything at all about the Department of Health. They told you all about nurses, beds and hip replacements, but nothing about the overall performance for the past five years of that corporate entity known as the Department of Health of which your friend is a senior executive.

The builder could have given you a similar exuberance of figures; he could have recounted that, compared with five years ago, he now employs four extra bricklayers, that the ratio of ladders per employee is down to only 0.54321, and that 21 per cent more drain-pipes have been replaced by 11 per cent fewer labourers. Moreover dry rot has fallen by 8.4 per cent—although, curiously, wet rot has increased by the same amount— 8.4 per cent. However, ... ' and on and on with the same infectious enthusiasm as the civil servant. But while the builder has also told you how well his organization has performed, as a corporate whole (it has doubled its profits), the civil servant has not. Her top figure is missing— *the top one* please note, the one that matters above all the others. Now do you see the problem?

We know what each of these organizations *do*—broadly, the building company repairs houses and the government department manages health services—that is what they *do*; and we have little difficulty in measuring any of the myriad activities, tasks and projects in either of them. We can easily see, for example, how long it took the builder to build a house and for a Department of Health hospital to perform a hysterectomy. We can easily measure what they *do* and how efficiently they do it. But can we measure what these organizations are *for*? We know what the company is for, it is to make a profit for the owner, and we can see quite clearly, in the annual report, whether it has done so. But what is the Department for? We do not know, and the civil servant has not been able to tell us either what that is, or how to measure it or whether it has done it.

Not very scientific

I will conjure up another friend for you; this one is a Fellow of the Royal Society—arguably Britain's most prestigious scientific institution. Ask him how his Society is getting on and he will take you through their annual report from which you see that there have been a number of meetings of COPUS (Committee on the Public Understanding of Science), that advice has been given to the government on embryo research, how 200 people attended a conference on water acidification, and so on, including (even) how many pages its members had published in various learned journals during that year.

But all this is what they *do*; what I want to know is whether the public understands science any better today than, say, a decade ago—that, after all, is the principal aim of the Royal Society; that is what it is *for*. My impression is that the average Briton's understanding of science remains utterly abysmal, but, because there are no figures for this in the report we are left in ignorance (not only no figures, it is not even mentioned!). It is a bit ironic that our leading scientific institution can show us no verifiable outcomes of any kind while it presumably demands confirmation to many places of decimals for the work of its illustrious members.

But perhaps you would prefer to have a friend on the Arts Council. I am sure she can recount for us many fascinating stories of how a few thousand pounds of government subsidy rescued a splendid troupe of ethnic players or delivered a magnificent opera to the good people of Northtown. These are some of the things it did last year and there are masses of figures, all carefully audited, to tell us how much they have spent; but that is what it *did*; what is it *for*? Well, their charter says it is to 'develop and improve the understanding and practice of the arts and to increase their accessibility to the British public'.

Now, I am sure you already know the question I want to ask her: 'How is the Arts Council, as a corporate whole, getting on?' by which I mean do we in Britain understand the arts better today and are they more accessible to us than, say, a decade ago—and so it is us, the British public, not those ethnic players and opera singers, who are the true intended beneficiaries of this organization, and it is an estimate of the benefit to us that I really want to hear—and I want the answer as sharp and as meaningful as the one we got from your builder friend. Will we get it? I do not think so.

Not good enough

What on earth is the point of organizations like these? It is not just the Royal Society and the Arts Council whose performance we cannot judge. We cannot assess Oxford University, the Trades Union Congress, the Salvation Army, the Football Association, the Commonwealth, the Milk Marketing Board, and on and on endlessly. There must be a couple of thousand of these socially significant organizations in every country of the world—the New York Police Department, the Arab League, the Paris Chamber of Commerce, the Singapore Institute of Management, NATO, the World Health Organization, the Indonesian Farmers Union ....

All I want from them is an answer to the query 'how are you getting on?'. It would be very difficult to think of a question of greater simplicity or gravity, but neither you, nor I, nor they, can answer it—certainly not with anything approaching the assurance of your little builder. No one, not even the managers themselves, know which figures would answer the question and indeed the answer is literally unknowable for most of them.

But surely we ought to be able to ascertain, with considerable confidence, what these organizations are supposed to be doing, for whom, and whether they are doing it or not. After all, we can usually tell whether something works, even quite complex things: which was the most effective economic system over the past four decades, the one in East Germany, or the one in the West? It is unarguable. Does aspirin alleviate headaches? Incontroverti- ble. Did ICI have a good year? No, its profits are down 12 per cent. You can actually analyse, inspect, examine, investigate—and measure, *with figures*—all these artefacts, some simple, others unbelievably complex, and see for yourself. But 'did the Legal Aid Board have a good year?'; we have no idea. How is the Southtown Women's Institute getting on these days? Don't know. Where are the performance figures for Christian Aid? Er, how do you mean? What is the score for the Commission for Racial Equality since it began work in 1977? What score?

Futile annual reports

Scan through any annual report, what does it tell you? Absolutely nothing! Take a children's charity, such as Barnardo's, whose annual report tells us about Tom who kept stealing cars; but after attending one of their centres is now a normal youth happily working in a garage. They show a picture of this bustling, smiling young man to prove it. They tell us about Tracey, who kept absconding from school; but after they took her in hand she is now a contented hairdresser in Croydon. Fine. Marvellous. But a charity like Barnardo's helps 20 000 children every year. What happened to all the others? How many are homeless, roaming the streets of London? Or did they all become astronauts? We have no idea.

Where is the evidence that these charities have the slightest effect on their clients' lives? If there is any evidence why is it not in their report? Even if we knew that, we still cannot say if Barnardo's is more worth while than, say, the National Trust (which preserves Britain's historic houses). All we can say is that they both spend about the same volume of cash each year; whether they do equal 'good'—or any good at all—we have no idea.

By contrast, consider the trouble and expense companies go to to learn how their products are doing in the market-place. A manufacturer of mint jelly can now tell, from computerized supermarket print-outs, how many shoppers bought the product immediately after buying a leg of lamb at the meat counter. How many schools, for example (or children's charities), take such trouble to follow the careers of their ex-students? I suppose students *are* more important than mint jelly?

Or take arms agreements: the one thing that matters, above everything else, is that they must be verifiable. To sign an arms agreement without an on-site verification process is utterly useless—difficult, expensive, time-consuming though it inevitably is, without this the agreement is void, barren, hollow, worthless; the system of verification *is* the agreement. Or the law: you cannot just accuse someone of theft and he goes directly to jail. You have to get some evidence. It is sometimes rather a nuisance to get it, and it costs a lot of money, but without it . . . . And on and on, through the whole vast gamut of human experience; if you cannot verify, if you cannot authenticate, corroborate, substantiate, confirm, ratify, prove, ascertain, establish, determine, demonstrate, certify, test, and do so empirically, realistically, pragmatically, practically, in the real, physical, material, solid, tangible, substantial, actual, palpable world—then you might as well not bother.

Yet here are all these organizations, beavering busily away, and we have not the slightest idea what effect they are having. Some of them have plainly become self-perpetuating and self-serving and have long since given up beavering. Many of them survive only by consuming the reserves of finance they have built up over past decades. Some do not seem to have any measurable output or any discernible effect on anything at all, or so little that we have to get a Royal Commission to study them for four years to tell us what it is.

Two different worlds

I expect you noticed that all of these were 'non-profitmaking organizations' (NPOs, as I will call them), both governmental and non-governmental. By contrast, virtually every company knows how well it is performing almost continuously; most of them know what their profits are every month compared with the same month for the past many years and compared to every one of their significant competitors. Some know this daily, for every single product in every single theatre of operations anywhere in the world! In general, then, companies know what they are doing and how well they are doing it. Non-profitmaking organizations do not.

Companies have a speedometer on the dashboard which you can read whenever you like; you cannot read the speedometer in most NPOs. They do not have one.

I find this dichotomy perfectly outrageous and profoundly disturbing. We have two quite discrete standards of organization here: the profitmaking and the non-profitmaking. We all accept this as a perfectly normal phenomenon; we refer to the notable disparity in 'culture' between the two types, implying that NPOs are not in the same league as companies. Of course it is not quite as clear-cut and black and white as this—some companies do wallow uselessly for years, living off their fat; some non-profitmaking organizations, on the other hand, know exactly what they are doing and can provide a stack of evidence for the superb results they are achieving (I give some sparkling examples later)—but it is not a bad generalization; few people, on reflection, will quarrel with it.

Indeed, a view accepted all round the globe today is that if you want to learn how to run an organization, you should go and study a business; and if you want to get things done, you had best ask a company to do them. The last thing you should study—and the last thing you need if you want results—is an NPO. If you wish to shake it up, privatize it! If you want it properly managed, recruit your executive team from business, not from an NPO. If you want service with a smile, avoid government offices and council houses like the plague.

It is incredible to think that all this used to be the other way round! A century ago the Foreign Office, Birmingham City Council and the Church of England would surely have been voted 'Most Effective Organizations of the 1890s' and any young person who wanted to get on in the world would have sought a career in them; the one thing an ambitious Victorian gentleman would not have thought of going into was a company! But today, when managers move from the private sector to the public, they suffer a culture shock; they find that they must abandon tight, goal-directed decision-making and systematic, methodical project appraisal, and adapt instead to personal prejudice, huge bumbling committees, great rambling management hierarchies, and tonnes of warm fudge. A vice versa shock is suffered when managers move in the other direction.

Bleak expectations

The modern world is full of NPOs letting us down: 16 per cent more police officers over the past decade, 65 per cent increase in the police budget, the number of patrol cars up by 38 per cent and so on and so on. Meanwhile, year after year, for as far back as most of us can remember, the crime rate rises relentlessly every year and the clear-up rate falls. And then we hear the police telling us that the crime rate is not a valid indicator of their performance (see page 164). Really? If protecting you and me from crime is not what the police are for, what are they for; and who is supposed to be doing it if they are not?

School budgets up by this, the number of teachers per pupil up by that, cost per student up by something else. Meanwhile what has happened to the standard of education? It has gone down. Homelessness in Britain has apparently doubled in the past decade; what have the government, and those many dozens of charities devoted to housing the homeless, been doing? Cruelty to children and animals has gone up; what have all the children and animal charities been doing for the past few decades?

Our system of justice, once the finest in the world, has descended into dismal, Dickensian, disrepute. What have all those organizations devoted to upholding this system—dozens of them, governmental and non-governmental alike—been doing for the past few decades? Was pay any better in unionized firms than in non-union ones over the past five years? No, it was not, so what have the unions been doing all this time? The population of our prisons rises relentlessly every year, decade by decade; what a ghastly indictment of all those organizations who strive to bring it down (including supposedly the Home Office, which actually *runs* the prisons!). Women's pay is 10 per cent lower here, compared to men's, than on the continent; what has the Equal Opportunities Commission been up to for the past couple of decades?

The examples are endlessly repeated through every aspect of our lives. If anything like any of this had happened in the private sector the chief executive would have been sacked long ago, the company just a bitter memory in the shareholders' cheque-books.

The huge importance of this

I believe all this matters *enormously*. Something like half of all the activities in the world are carried out by NPOs, half the people in the world are employed in them. And so, approximately, half of all the human beings in the world work for organizations which either do not know what they are doing, or cannot demonstrate that they are doing it, or are making such a palpable mess of it that it is quite clear that they are not doing it at all. Moreover, a $10m charity for children, say, is of far greater social significance than any $10m company; in terms of their effect on society most NPOs far outweigh most companies, size for size.

It is simply not tolerable for the performance of these organizations, so vital to our quality of life, to be so desolate. It is not just that we cannot evaluate these NPOs; what is worse is that, on the rare occasions when we can, so many of them do not seem to work at all. We may have the whole balance of society completely wrong; we may have far too many NPOs, perhaps a hundred times too many, perhaps almost none of the services we use throughout our lives should be in public hands. Do you know? Does anyone? We know when we have too many companies in any given sector—the marginal ones go bust. But NPOs?

But this is not just a battle between companies and NPOs; what about the various types of NPO? Would crime, disablement, poverty, our inner cities be tackled best by a government NPO, or one run by the Church, or a secular charity, or a self-help cooperative? We have no idea. Is voluntary contribution the best source of succour for those millions starving in Africa? We do not know. Why not? Because we cannot measure, and therefore cannot compare, the performance of any of the various types of NPO.

Progressive decline

And so we go on lowering our sights and making excuses for them so that now we have come to *expect* the police not to catch your burglar; we *expect* our state schools to turn out oiks; we *expect* justice not to be done in our courts; and we *expect* our laws to be grotesquely outdated (in spite of the Law Commission, specifically set up back in 1965 to comb through and modernize them. What on earth have *they* been doing?).

Why did it take our government 15 years to discover that all those billions it spent on our inner cities have had no effect whatever, and about 50 years to grasp that those grim Victorian mental institutions were not providing the best available treatment for their inmates? Because no one was measuring their performance.

My personal belief is that well over half of Britain's top NPOs, right through the alphabet starting with the Arts Council, the British Institute of Management, the Church of England ... currently make no worthwhile contribution to our national life. But it is not just Britain. Although we do seem to be near the bottom of the class these days, NPOs all over the world are plainly less effective than companies are. The Americans spend one-third more on state education than a decade ago; what has happened to the results of the Scholastic Aptitude Test? They have gone down. What has happened to their crime rate, drugs, race, inner cities ...? It is the same story all around the globe.

If we cannot measure the performance of NPOs we cannot know if we need them at all or whether we would be better off without them—perhaps they are, indeed, just an outmoded form of human organization left over from Queen Victoria's golden age. We cannot arrange them in a meaningful performance league table as we can with companies. We cannot tell whether they are being managed well or badly—or not at all. Even when they have plainly lost their way no one seems to grasp what has happened or do anything about it for decades, and even when they do it takes five years for an official report to determine what to do and another five to do it. Can you imagine any company, even your amateurish little builder, tackling their problems like this?

The role of the corporate objective

But it is not only that many NPOs do not seem to know what they are doing, some of them are plainly going in entirely the wrong direction because they have been saddled with corporate objectives precisely contrary to what is required! Impossible? Don't believe me?

Take any perfectly ordinary NPO such as the Northtown College of Adult Education. Now the young people of Northtown are presumably saying to it,

'No thank you, we do not want to train to be mere electrical repairers—we can earn far more as electronics engineers.' So, should the college offer them a new added-value course in this high-level subject?

This college has been told by its Local Education Authority that they will judge it by two criteria: the student/staff ratio and examination passes per student. Very well, let us do the sums. What will happen to the student/staff ratio if the college offers its students this new upgraded course in electronics? Answer: it will deteriorate (the more rigorous the subject the smaller the class is likely to be and the greater the teaching content; so, fewer students per staff, maybe far fewer). And the second yardstick—the exam passes per student? This ratio will also fall—fewer students will pass a higher course with its inevitably more difficult exams. So what does the college decide to do? Well, both these indicators will deteriorate if they offer the higher course so the management decides not to offer it.

What a disaster! No wonder we are so short of skills in Britain. But note this, it was not the fault of the management; they did not make this decision. The college's corporate objectives have been set in such terms that it cannot respond to any demand for added-value. *Any* attempt to move *any* of the college's courses up-market will lead to a fall in the ratios on which it is judged. (Actually it is judged on seven other insane 'performance indicators' as well—I funked showing you these here but see page 135.)

A vast contagion

Does it matter if Northtown College is moving in a direction exactly opposite to the one its community obviously wants it to? Frankly, no, not much. It employs a mere 200 graduate teachers; it educates only a few thousand students each year. So, no, it is small and not very important. There are, however, 500 other such colleges in Britain, employing collectively a significant proportion of all the graduates that all our universities turn out, and all using the same daft criteria. How much has it cost the nation do you suppose, employing the wrong corporate objectives for all these colleges, over all these years? There are 25 000 schools and dozens of polytechnics and universities. There are many thousands of local governments, government agencies, institutions, charities, societies, voluntary organizations and so on. All, or nearly all, have no better idea of what they are supposed to be doing, or how to measure it, than Northtown College. What has it cost us, do you imagine, over all the past decades, for all these organizations to have been using defective corporate aims?

The plight of our education system is not a result of poor teaching, outdated curricula, mouldering buildings, large classes, progressive teaching methods, obstructive unions; it is because we have no idea what we want the system to do and no means of measuring whether it is doing it. Two decades ago we abolished most of our grammar schools; are the comprehensive schools that replaced them any better? The answer is we still, after all these years, have not the slightest idea because we do not know by which criteria to judge a school, and there are no figures even if we did. (You might think universities would have more sense and would have skilfully devised some intellectually scintillating technique for judging their performance, so see page 141 where I describe Oxford's Norrington Table which is even *more* misleading than anything Northtown College was told to use!)

No, it is no good; until we know exactly what we want our education system to do it is impossible to decide which method of teaching, which textbooks, which technique for training teachers, which anything, is best. All these debates, of which countless thousands are held every day in schools, at home, in Parliament, in the press and on television, are utterly sterile without 'question number one': *What is it for?* Yet never, *never*, do you hear anyone preface their opinion with a definition of the aim.

If you do not know where you are going any road will do, runs the uncannily accurate cliché.

Most have the wrong objectives

As I say, it is not just schools and colleges; I could have chosen any NPO. *Most* of them have been given the wrong top criteria—the wrong 'corporate objectives'. These are not occasional lapses. Setting the wrong objectives to organizations, or not setting any at all, is the norm. Not only our schools, colleges and universities, but also local governments, agencies, charities, institutions—virtually every component of our organized lives (except companies). They are not failing the nation because of lack of capital investment or ageing computer systems; not because this or that government cut their budget; not because of management incompetence or poor technology training; not because of our class structure or because we lost an empire a lifetime ago; but because these organizations have not taken the trouble to identify exactly what they are trying to do for whom and so have no idea whether they are doing it.

Read any article in a serious newspaper or journal; study the reports of commissions and inquiries. All they ever offer is suggested treatments for defects in *management*. They go on and on about cutting costs and improving efficiency. As I write, the Woolf Report on prisons has just been published. It contains 208 recommendations relating to the detailed management of prisons; 600 pages of advice, no doubt all very sensible, on how to manage a prison right down to the sort of trivia that, in a company, a fifth-rank charge-hand would decide every day of the week on his or her own initiative.

But 'What is a prison for?' Do not ask—in most official inquiries such top questions are explicitly excluded by the terms of reference. 'How do you measure the performance of a prison?' Do not ask. It is much, much easier to answer 208 simple, practical questions than one cardinal, pivotal one like 'What should be the corporate objective of a prison?'. Why must we not ask? Because the government has already decided (see page 148 for their nonsensical definition) and it is not up for further discussion. As for efficiency, how can you improve the efficiency of a prison if you do not know what it is for?

How many books and articles are published every year on such management topics as say, total quality, human resource development or strategy formulation? Infinite. Measureless. Incalculable. And on corporate objectives? This one!

Stark simplicity

Why does everyone go on and on answering the second-level questions— the management ones? One of the main themes in this book will be that corporate objectives must be extremely simple, that one should be able to express them in just a few concrete, ordinary words—if you cannot do that then you have got it wrong. Now imagine the reaction if a Royal Commission into the purpose of the police, say, came out with an official report consisting of just one paragraph! Screams of laughter from the press. Cabinet resigns. Britain sinks into North Sea. But this is precisely what I am saying: that corporate objectives must be brutally blunt. One paragraph is far too much. A single short sentence is quite enough.

The last thing we need is pages of abstruse logico-philosophical, labyrinthine formulae (see page 95 for a preposterous piece of gibberish given to British Airports plc as an objective). The people who run large, important organizations, love large important sentences. They suppose that when stating corporate objectives they must put on a display of intellectual and philosophical prowess. But it is quite the contrary; corporate objectives have to be simple. Childishly. Without clear, unadorned, *quantified*, objectives the modern processes of management cannot even start; none of the techniques of modern professional management, developed in such abundance over the past few decades, can work without figures—that is why they work superbly in companies where simple, quantified corporate targets are available but not in NPOs where they are not.

Today's managers are target-hitting warriors; give them a target and they will reach into their copious quivers for the most effective up-to-date arrow; without that target they are impotent. Yet no one ever sets targets for corporate wholes. That is why so many of our NPOs perform so poorly: it is because the top managers have not been given a single, simple, quantified, *corporate* target to hit. Of course, you can go one step further and set the wrong aim altogether; then, obedient servants that they are, they will select the wrong arrows.

11

Cui bono? (Who benefits?)

And so, as will be seen in detail later, efficiency is not seen as a useful indicator in this book. What an organization does—its undertakings, its activities, its operations, however efficiently or excellently they are run—is not what it is for. Colleges teach, that is what they do (and let us hope they are efficient at it) but teaching is not what they are for; they are for ... you will have to wait until Chapter 10 to find out! By then the distinction between efficiency and performance, between what an organization *does*, its projects, its functions, its ventures, its activities, its operations, and what it is *for*, its corporate objective, its aim, its purpose, will have become abundantly clear.

It is small wonder that companies are streaking away with all the prizes; they know what they are for. Not only are NPOs being privatized apace but the average company is growing twice as rapidly as the average NPO (see page 173). There are now dozens of companies whose turnover is greater than the GNP of many nations. Companies dominate society. If it were true that they are the most effective form of organization known to humanity then all these trends would be welcome, and we should indeed let all our NPOs slide into the waste-bin of history, as a useless and outdated form of human activity, and entrust everything—everything—to companies; but not many people want that sort of new world order.

In any case not all companies *are* more effective than all NPOs. It is significant that the Automobile Association has very few competitors. Why? Because, over the past several decades, it has done its job as well as any company could have done it. Some state schools get better results than some private ones. It is hard to imagine any company cherishing our historic buildings more devotedly than the National Trust. So where direct comparison is possible it is not always the profit-maker that beats the NPO.

What is it, then, which marks the successful organization out from the normal run?

CHAPTER TWO

The solution

In this chapter I shall suggest that the solution to the problem of all those under-performing organizations is the 'beneficiary doctrine'. I shall briefly describe its three interlocking parts: its new methodology for determining corporate objectives; its fresh definition of corporate conduct; and its distinctive system of governance. I shall also explain what practical effects I hope it will have on organizations and on society.

Single-mindedness

At the end of the first chapter I asked what it was that distinguished the successful organization from the normal run. I believe it all boils down to the way their corporate objectives are set. Companies know what they are doing for whom and so can go at it single-mindedly. *That* is the explanation of their success, not, as most people believe, the profit motive, competition or market forces, self-interest or superior management ability. Their secret is that, unlike other types of organization, they actually have a clear aim; they know what they are trying to achieve. It is not *what* your aim is, it is *whether you know what it is*! It is not that they are profitmaking that does the trick; it is that they *know* they are profitmaking. Most NPOs know they are not profitmaking, but alas, have no clear idea what they *are* trying to do. Those that do know, do it very well indeed—as well as any company,

Single-mindedness is the ultimate corporate advantage.

Is that so? Can it be as simple as that? Well, why do you think NASA's project to put a man on the moon was so successful? Was it because NASA was a profitmaking organization? It was not, of course. And did you think that Band Aid's triumph resulted from its carefully selected, expensively trained business-school executives? (In case you have forgotten, Bob Geldof is a long-haired pop star with no more idea of formal management than a rabbit ; yet look what he did!). Was the BBC the world's best radio station for 50 years because of competition (there was none) or its advanced technology (absurdly crude)? And Britain in the war—winning a war is all due to market forces, is it?

Greenpeace—the leader of the eighties

Take Greenpeace. Was its extraordinary influence on world affairs in the eighties all because of profits and financial incentives to its management (they were mostly unpaid volunteers)? Or maybe you thought it was their comfortable air-conditioned offices and you failed to notice them bobbing about in rubber dinghies under the bows of a supertanker? Greenpeace was founded in 1971 and grew from 80 000 members in 1980 to 2 000 000 in 1990—a growth rate of about 40 per cent per annum throughout the decade (during which other environmental groups grew at around 15–25 per cent). Note this well; no other organization, not even any company, beat this rate of growth over such a period of time.

So it is not profits. It is not free-market forces. It is not the spur of competition. It is not conditions of work. It is certainly not professional management. Nor advanced technology. It is not better training. It is not even self-interest or the lure of becoming a millionaire. It is not communism or socialism versus capitalism. All these factors are in vain and inadequate without the essential component. What drove these organizations to their soaring success was their single-minded, dedicated, committed, devoted, service to one, single, clear-cut, compelling, cause. This is what gave the management and employees their focal point; this is what wound these organizations up tight, taut, like a crossbow aimed at the bull's-eye. Hundreds of people, thousands of them—millions even—caught in a whirlwind of energy and driven towards a single, agreed, essential goal. *They knew exactly what they were supposed to be doing.*

The one item common to all success is single-mindedness; that is true for individuals, for teams, for companies, for NPOs, for athletes, for managers, for governments, for nations. The key to organizational success is for the organization to act like an individual person driven by one single aim. All the sticks and all the carrots in the world will fail if the organization does not have a single clear-cut aim.

'Restless ambition, never at an end'

But we must beware; the more passionately single-minded an organization becomes the more its people may be tempted to cheat. This is true of anyone, whether individually or in an organization. It is not only single-minded business people, driven by profit and greed, who cheat: police officers who fabricate evidence to obtain a conviction; politicians who tell us one thing to get elected ('no new taxes') and then do the opposite; priests whose fervour leads them to the brutal persecution of heretics; athletes who take performance-enhancing drugs; scientists who cook their experiments; all of us—we all bend the rules in order to hit ambitious performance targets. Performance and conduct are two sides of the same coin.

Now I want all our organizations, especially NPOs, to perform better, far better, better by miles; that is what part one of the beneficiary doctrine demands. But if we intend to spur them to higher levels of performance we must be sure that in part two we look to the morals of these organizations to constrain any excesses and, in part three of the doctrine, we must furnish them with a powerful system of governance to make sure they stay under proper control. To strive for maximum possible achievement always results in excess; to seek ethical behaviour alone yields merely self-righteous mediocrity; to demand effective control over organizations brings stifling bureaucracy. It has to be a balanced trilogy. It is precisely because they have failed to provide this triple balance that all previous attempts, stretching back over the centuries, to improve the performance of organizations, have failed.

The paramount corporate advantage

Part one of the beneficiary doctrine suggests that, contrary to Adam Smith's dictum (and Thatcherism), not every successful person, and not every successful organization, is motivated by profit and wealth or even self-interest. Notice that while companies, which *are* driven by profits and self-interest, are today's leading organizations, this was not always so (I mentioned the Church and public service in Chapter 1) and it is not always so today (Greenpeace was quite categorically *not* motivated by profit or self-interest). Or to be more accurate, while self-interest is a major motivating engine for companies, especially proprietorial ones, it is not a major one, indeed it is negligible, in such organizations as Barnardo's, Save the Children or Greenpeace.

No. You do not have to be self-centred or a company to be a highly successful, vibrantly motivated, organization. But you do need to be single-minded. Note this please:

> The most successful organization of the eighties was **not** profitmaking, did not owe its success to free markets, to competition, to professional management, to knowledge-workers or advanced technology and was not motivated by self-interest.
>
> However, it knew what it was supposed to be doing and went at it single-mindedly.

We should hold this up to the light for a minute and think about it.

Do they know what they are doing?

The huge advantage that companies have, then, is that they pursue their aims single-mindedly—they know what they are doing, for whom, and how well they are doing it. Companies can answer that simple question I started the previous chapter with: 'How are you getting on?' Most NPOs cannot.

Or rather, they say they cannot. I do not believe them.

I am convinced that all, or virtually all, organizations could say what they are for and whether they are any good at it. I believe there are powerful reasons, many of them psychological, why so many NPOs pretend they cannot.

Whether that is so or not (see 'spoilers' in Chapter 8), if any organization cannot answer this elemental question—How are you getting on?—then the beneficiary doctrine says it should be re-formed until it can. We really should not be wasting society's resources on organizations which cannot prove that they are making a worthwhile contribution to the community. When I say 'prove' I mean with figures, as companies do. It is time to apply the same harsh rules to NPOs that shareholders apply to companies. It is time that NPOs equipped themselves with a 'bottom line'. If we told them that they must clearly define what they are trying to do *and* demonstrate to us, with figures, that they are doing it, or else lose their funding, they would very soon put their minds to the problem.

I am suggesting that the vast majority of NPOs, who say they cannot measure their performance, could actually do so if they dropped their self-indulgent pretence and took some trouble to do so. When you found an organization you have an absolutely clear idea of how you want it to change the world. OK, then say so in words of one syllable and, better still, with figures.

What is it for?

Suppose you are forming an organization to 'reduce poverty in Southtown', then you must define what you mean by 'poverty in Southtown' and measure it now and measure it again next year and the next to see if it has declined. If you want to 'help children' you must say exactly what you want to do for which children and measure whether you have achieved it year after year.

If Northtown Council decides to launch a 'health improvement unit' then they must define 'health in Northtown' and measure it before and after to see if the health of these citizens has actually improved—and it is no use whatever telling us that they have increased cervical screening by 10 per cent, for instance, or have installed some miraculous medical device costing $10m; what matters, and it is *all* that matters, is whether the North-townians are more healthy than they were and more healthy than Southtown-ians who cannot boast a health improvement unit.

If you found a charity to help the suicidally depressed then you had better show that the suicide rate in those towns in which you operate is significantly lower than where you do not. Similarly, if you form an organization to help young offenders not to do it again, all that matters is: did they?

What I am demanding here is no more rigorous than what is accepted practice in the private sector. If a cement company builds a new factory, the fact that it turns out a million tons of cement is of trivial significance. That is only what it does. The key question, in a different logical category of significance for the company, is: did it make the desired level of profit? *That* was what the factory was for, not to make cement. If it failed to make a million tons but made a profit—result, happiness! If it made a million tons but failed to make a profit—result, misery!

We run our NPOs on the unique metaphysical rule that even if you cannot see any useful result it does not matter; it is bound to be there really, only it is invisible. Time after time we do it. Within the past year the government has set up two new agencies: Training and Enterprise Councils (TECs) and Scottish Enterprise; neither has meaningful objectives (see pages 54–55). We will never have the faintest idea whether the billions of pounds that they will collectively spend each year are having the slightest effect on anything. No company would dream of launching a project without installing a mechanism for monitoring its performance against a specific profit target. NPOs are gaily launched without even the remotest idea of how to tell if they are working. We even have a new ministry (as if there are not already far too many)—the Ministry of National Heritage. And how, pray, are we to judge the success of that?

The world is full of dreadful, heart-wrenching problems. We could, if we really tried to do so, ameliorate some of the worst of these. To waste our resources on organizations like these, whose effectiveness is unknown and unknowable, utterly outrages my sense of humanity.

Targets: the hallmark of modern management

So that is the theme of part one of the beneficiary doctrine. I want to know, not just in words, but with figures, what each socially significant organization thinks it is doing for whom and how well it is doing it and, of course, I mean over a substantial period of time; it would be preposterous to try to judge the performance of a socially significant organization over just a year or two. I describe in the following chapters how these questions may be answered. But notice what this central message really is: if an organization cannot express its aims numerically then there is something fundamentally wrong with its aims, so much so that it cannot be considered a viable entity in the modern world. It is going to have to re-form. If it still cannot, then it would seem a suitable case for closure.

Now, since this is plainly a very testing demand on all these organizations, half of which will not be able to meet it, I must repeat why I think it is so necessary:

1 I want to be sure we are not wasting society's resources on organizations which are not working and so I want to see the figures which demonstrate that they are.

2 I want to be able to compare one NPO's performance with any other NPO—and with companies (*then* we shall see what should be privatized and what should not, and how we wish to balance our society).

3 I want to know how well they are being managed—and you cannot begin to see this if you do not even know how well the organization itself is performing.

Finally—and this is the positive drive behind the beneficiary doctrine, far more important than those three rather defensive reasons:

4 Organizations achieve a massive boost in performance from knowing two things; first, in just a few simple words, what they are trying to do for whom, and second by setting quantified targets for this aim. These are tremendous incentives—far in excess of anything that even the most inspirational and visionary managers can bring them. Something almost supernatural.

And *two* of them! One boost from a few simple words, a further one from a few simple figures.

Figures: the managerial imperative

We all know how setting targets and deadlines can galvanize managers and employees; everyone has grasped how strongly these can motivate. We build elaborate hierarchies of target-related rewards and bonuses all the way up the hierarchy of managers. And then we stop, in a dead fright, just before we get to the target at the top, the *corporate* aim, the one that matters more than all the rest because all of them flow from it! None of these incentives work without a clear corporate aim; conversely a clear corporate aim frequently works just on its own, even when all these material motivations are entirely missing—as with Greenpeace, Band Aid, or a nation at war, where they were, quite simply, and highly significantly, entirely absent. The only thing not absent in these cases was that these organizations knew *exactly* what they were trying to do and could express it in words of one syllable: save the planet, feed the starving, win the war.

But I am going further. Organizations need to know not only what they are doing in words but also, in this modern, numerate world, in figures. Does that assume it is possible to measure everything that organizations do? Could we measure child care, for example? Well, one of our most professionally run children's charities, Barnardo's, repeatedly stresses in its annual reports that it evaluates all its projects. So, even activities in this apparently unquantifiable area can be measured, it seems. Be that as it may, the beneficiary doctrine says that by far the most important feature of any organization is whether its performance can be evaluated. If it cannot, that organization should redefine its aims so that it can.

Am I really suggesting that we should measure the performance of the Church of England, for example? What, with *figures*? Is that not just obscene? Utterly Orwellian? Positively offensive? I do not know and I do not care whether it is ethical or not; I only care whether society is well served by its organizations. I am not merely revolted by the litany of failure by which our nation is disfigured, I am positively fearful of its consequences for our future; *I want it reversed.*

So that is part one of the beneficiary doctrine: modern organizations must have a verifiable, quantified, corporate performance target.

Corporate conduct

Part two of the beneficiary doctrine refers to corporate ethics. Just as you and I must behave reasonably in society, so must organizations, whether they are trying to make a profit, protecting wildlife, overthrowing a tyrant, relieving famine or whatever. So there is a code of corporate ethics, which all civilized communities lay down for all organizations and made manifest to them by the law, custom and practice, example, peer pressure and ordinary common decency.

In practice some organizations behave themselves rather less well than others. Companies, as noted above, have a dreadful reputation (even our staid British high street banks are now seen by the public as crooks and rogues). The notorious greed of modern companies drives them to misleading advertising, strong-arm competition, pollution, high-pressure selling, dangerous products, fraudulent financing, soulless sackings: a thoroughly unattractive record—'the unacceptable face of capitalism'. Indeed, there is every reason to believe that some companies cause such distress that their overall effect on society is totally negative; where is the gain if a company makes a profit of $10m for its shareholders if it does $11m of damage to society? And most people would not dream of trusting the average company to run the BBC, for example, and certainly not a hospice or a mental home—nor indeed any public service where a caring attitude and consideration for others is required.

No, market forces are fine for some things but can also lead to a type of society that most of us would find thoroughly distasteful. It is not for nothing that, in many nations even today, 'profit' is the corporate objective that dare not speak its name.

But the problem goes far wider than companies; our whole code of corporate ethics is defective. We set our organizations a model of behaviour that is so riddled with anomalies that if they try to follow it they either fail to thrive or they have to cheat. The theory we all seem to accept without question is that an organization should benefit everyone: ICI should benefit the whole community, for example, not just its shareholders. A local hospital should not just benefit patients: the whole community should gain. I am sure this is an error, well-meaning though it may be.

The 'stakeholders'

This 'stakeholder' concept has evolved over many decades. Some people even insist that the benefits from any organization should be distributed to all the stakeholders in *equal proportions*. Thus, in a company, its workers, its managers, its bankers, its shareholders, its suppliers, its customers, the state, the local community, the environment, should all benefit equally. It has become accepted that it is the task of the management of a company to 'hold the balance' of benefit as between its several stakeholders.

The same is said of many NPOs: a school should benefit the local community, the teachers, the state, the pupils, their parents, the publishers of textbooks, the caterers, the janitors; they are all, according to this seductive theory, stakeholders, deemed to hold a stake in the future of the organization and therefore entitled to a benefit from it and, in the 'equity' version, they should all be favoured equally; and it is the job of the managers to see fair play between these groups. (And, did you notice, these managers who are to hold the balance always turn out to be one of the stakeholders!)

The beneficiary doctrine rejects very decisively this lavish philosophy and insists that organizations should be single-minded, not multi-purpose. Multi-purpose organizations are unmanageable. An organization, according to this doctrine, should aim to generate a designated benefit to its 'intended beneficiaries' (that single group of people for whose benefit the organization exists) and that is that—it should not even attempt to satisfy anyone else's needs. A school has one intended beneficiary only—its students; a company one only—its shareholders; a hospital—its patients. Good heavens, do you suppose a surgeon would halt his operation half-way through because he had just been informed that *only* his patient was going to benefit? ('I'm not going to waste my time on this fellow, not unless the community is going to benefit', he says, sewing the wound up again, in a fit of self-righteous indignation.)

The beneficiary doctrine does not recognize the name 'stakeholder' at all and rejects the idea that they have any 'stake' in, or claims upon, or rights (other than those under the law) over the organization or its resources. It does recognize that many of these people have a profound interest in it and so describes them with the well-known, but neutral, phrase 'interest groups'.

Two ethical principles

How, then, does the beneficiary doctrine suggest organizations should behave towards these important people? It recognizes two precepts which all organizations must observe. The first is the 'no harm principle' which states that in pursuing their corporate objectives, organizations must not cause significant harm to any member of any interest group. As will be seen in Chapter 14, it is a very stringent rule and leads to a regime of corporate conduct that is far more ethical than that adopted by most organizations today. A number of organizations would disappear if it was correctly applied—and these would not be just those hated chemical companies who so flagrantly damage our environment; a wide variety of others would be on the danger list, including some of our religions.

The second rule is called the 'principle of engagement'. As has been made very clear, the beneficiary doctrine requires organizations to concentrate on yielding benefits to the intended beneficiaries only and to refrain from attempting to benefit any of the stakeholders or interest groups. On the contrary, the question every organization should ask is not 'what should we be giving the stakeholders?' but 'how can we best engage the enthusiastic cooperation of our interest groups to enhance the benefit we deliver to our intended beneficiaries?' In other words *it turns the stakeholder theory on its head*. Organizations should misquote President Kennedy: 'Ask not what we can do for the stakeholders, but what they can do for our beneficiaries.'

I want organizations to dedicate their every effort, and to channel the spirited assistance of all concerned, towards the intended beneficiary. I do *not* want managers acting like Father Christmas to anyone who claims to be a 'stakeholder'. The Automobile Association does not go round building low-cost housing for the poor, deliberately recruiting surplus staff to reduce local unemployment, granting aid to the Nigerian economy, campaigning for brighter architecture: the AA helps motorists—period! That is all it does. It does it extremely well, so well that it has remained almost immune from competition, even from companies, for decade after decade. One reason for its success is that it skilfully engages the copious support of all its relevant influential interest groups—its own employees, motorists themselves, the government, the public, relevant companies, road research institutions and so on—in its dedicated pursuit of helping the motorist.

Engaging all the interest groups

If only all managers could enlist the aid of relevant interest groups with such relish as Barnardo's does; it employs 4000 people but it also calls upon 26 000 volunteers! Even if they are only part-timers, their enthusiasm must be worth another two entire work-forces. Just think how much more effective our police, for instance, might be, if they applied the principle of engagement as convincingly as that.

Here is a deep neglected well of fortune—overlooked for decades because most managements see their official employees as the sole motive power of their organization and everyone else as mere bystanders—no, worse than that; as diners at the same table as the beneficiaries, allowed to share the meal because they are so-called stakeholders. But, I insist, the meal is for the customers, not for the cooks and waiters.

The beneficiary doctrine, then, demands two high ideals: it requires each organization to achieve an exacting level of performance for its intended beneficiaries and, to the same end, to enlist the enthusiastic and even delighted cooperation and approbation of everyone concerned. Higher performance and, in order to attract their endorsement and support, better behaviour towards the interest groups.

The governing directors

This brings us to part three of the beneficiary doctrine which calls for a new kind of supervision at the top of each socially significant organization. Each such organization should elect a small governing board, completely separate and aloof from the executive directors and management, whose duties would be to set performance and conduct standards for their organization and ensure that these are maintained.

I want each significant organization to elect a few mature, sensible people as 'governing directors'. Their task is entirely distinct from that of the members of a European company's supervisory board, for example, or school governors in Britain, or charity trustees, or typical British or American non-executive company directors. All these examples of 'corporate supervisors' are utterly unlike the role I wish to ascribe to my governing directors and are, in my view, travesties of what is required—why, we have even got it wrong in Parliament where, when we carefully 'separated the powers' several centuries ago we separated the wrong powers, thus rendering most contemporary governments unworkable as systems for managing a modern nation. Moreover, all these systems of governance appear to be entirely ineffective in protecting either the interests of the intended beneficiaries or of the interest groups (why is it so often an outsider, such as a journalist, rather than the governors, who uncovers the abuse of its beneficiaries by an organization?).

What I am proposing has almost nothing in common with any of these misguided machinations. For a start, my governing directors will not represent the stakeholders as do the European supervisory boards; they will represent only the intended beneficiaries.

Their three duties

The duties of these governing directors (described in detail in Chapter 16) include these three key tasks: first, to set performance standards for their organization—that is, as foreshadowed above, to lay down what benefits the intended beneficiaries may expect from their organization and to specify what target level of delivery they deem to be satisfactory. But note, 'target level of benefit to the beneficiaries', not targets for activities; what an organization does is not what it is for, remember; managers measure the activities, governing directors must measure the results, the outcomes, *to the beneficiaries*. It would be their job to set sensible targets, neither too low nor too ambitious, and then make sure that the beneficiaries were actually getting what they were supposed to be getting.

Second, they must define the organization's code of corporate conduct based on the two ethical principles outlined above: no harm and engagement. And third, having set these standards for corporate performance and corporate conduct they should monitor their organization's compliance with them; these governing directors would, in other words, be the final arbiters, the internal watchdogs, who keep their organization up to scratch. Note that they do not supervise the management, they monitor the performance of their organization, a completely different task to that ascribed to them by other writers. They should publish their organization's performance each year in a special, brutally revealing format not seen anywhere at present.

All organizations, after a time, tend to lose their way, let their standards slip and begin to serve themselves instead of their intended beneficiaries; the governing directors are there to prevent this happening. Moreover, they would do so continuously; we would not have to witness a decade or two of decline and then have to set up an official inquiry lasting another half-decade to get it put right

Stifling the managers

But would not this clumsy supervisory apparatus foisted upon the managers enrage, discourage, stifle and impede them? Well, do you imagine the top executives in BMW are cowed by their supervisory board? I doubt it, and in any case my version is far less intrusive than that European practice, which I find quite overbearing. My governing directors will be far less meddlesome than the British school governors whose job specification (in the 1988 Education Reform Act) is, in my opinion, absurdly onerous and interventionist; a ludicrous misunderstanding of the word 'governor'. My governing directors would also be infinitely less interfering than the ethical committees who scrutinize closely the work of scientists, who, nevertheless, manage to get on with their research into human embryos or whatever. Governing directors would, however, be somewhat more assertive and more effective than the typical supine, sycophantic, British or American company non-executive director (they could hardly be less!).

Governing directors will be a new profession with their own 'Institute of Governing Directors' wholly distinct from, and much superior to, the actual

Institute of Directors, whose narrow self-serving concept of the non-executive director has distorted the role of these valuable people for years.

Manager and supermanager

But surely, you will complain again, it is the management who should determine corporate objectives and corporate conduct, why do you want a special over-person, a supermanager to do this? Well, first, these governing directors are not managers in any sense whatever; they are entirely non-executive; the last thing they should do is any management. And second, managers have no business taking these decisions; the role of a manager is to achieve corporate targets, not to set them. It is not only that managers tend to set short-term targets; worse, they actually set the wrong sort of targets altogether—they set targets that reflect their own ambitions and interests in the organization, rather than the aims of the beneficiaries. They also habitually select strategies which suit their ends, rather than those of the organization. 'Oh, come on', you will be saying (especially if you are a manager), 'the amount of damage that does is just tiny—no managers could get away with anything very significant'.

Oh, really? If you want a rough estimate of the extent to which company managers run away with their organizations think of ICI, generally accepted as one of the 'best managed' companies in Britain. Recently the question of the 'break-up value' of ICI has been vigorously discussed in the financial press; a widely-held view is that, in its present form, ICI is worth about £12bn, but that it would be worth £16bn if it was split asunder into separate enterprises. The difference is the extent to which its managers have expanded ICI beyond its optimum value—that is by about a third. Thus their deliberate empire-building has cost their shareholders £4bn. An even more blatant case was the Imperial Group; a predator (the Hanson Group) bought it for £2.5bn, promptly sold off half of it for £2.4bn and kept the other half for virtually nothing, suggesting again that its previous managers had expanded and diversified it far beyond its economic limits.

This phenomenon is not rare; it is routine. De-mergers are still uncommon because managers hate seeing their empires being dismantled and fight like alley cats to stop it (strictly in the interests of the shareholders, you understand), but, where they do occur, shareholders nearly always see substantial gains in value. In whose interests have all these companies been managed over all these decades, do you suppose?

Managers: whose side are they on?

But the problem exists not just in companies; this same managerial self-service is endemic in NPOs as well, even in the 'caring' professions right up to the point where managers render their organization useless to everyone except themselves. Can anyone doubt that some hospitals are run for the vainglory of their consultants, rather than the patients? Are the regimes in some childrens' homes for the good of the children—or the convenience of the staff? Do 'progressive' teachers apply their techniques for the advancement of their students—or to satisfy their own social prejudices?

Why is it illegal to conduct research into the efficacy of some aspects of our legal system—jury decisions, for example; for whose benefit was this ordained; to improve its efficiency, or protect its administrators? When the civil servants in Brussels are exhorted to be '*communautaire*' does it mean they should show more concern for the people of Europe? Of course not. What an absurd suggestion. It means they should show greater loyalty to the European bureaucratic hierarchy. Why do we have a 'stop–go' economy? Is it to improve the standard of living for the citizen? No, of course not, it is because the politicians let things rip at election time to buy our votes and have to rein them back immediately after—it happens every time in every democracy especially those without an independent central bank.

Do all managers, universally, 'go for growth' for the welfare of the beneficiaries of their organization—or to advance their own empires? (Actually, and not surprisingly, we will see evidence in Chapter 12 that growth significantly damages beneficiaries' interests.)

Back in the bottle

And so when I say that managers aim at objectives for their own ends, rather than for the beneficiaries, I am not thinking of mere peccadilloes, but of a systematic misapplication of their skills—skills of remarkable potency today. We have become so inured to managers acting in their own interests that we have completely failed to comprehend the extent to which they have despoiled the aims and resources of their organizations—sorry, of *our* organizations (they have even got me at it). Far from the concept of managers as corporate heroes, this book sees them as a foremost cause of the degeneracy of our organizations.

No, I want governing directors to decide the corporate aims on behalf of the beneficiaries. I want managers to achieve them. No one should ever be asked to do both, to be judge and jury in his or her own case. Surely we have been on this planet long enough to know all about conflicts of interest. Give someone power and they will use it; we should not blame them for doing so, but we most certainly need to keep our eye on them. I do not go all the way with Lord Acton, but I certainly see why he said 'Power tends to corrupt, and absolute power corrupts absolutely. Great men are almost always bad men.'

I want the management genie back in the bottle—yet still delighting in their powers. The key to this trick? The special technique of setting corporate objectives described in Chapter 6.

25

Government as watchdog

Or you may say, 'Why do we want governing directors as watchdogs? Surely it is the task of government to supervise the behaviour of organizations in society?' But governments everywhere, from Sweden to Brazil, are (at last, and thank heaven) spinning off, deregulating and devolving more and more of their functions to autonomous bodies, a trend that wonderfully enhances the responsiveness of these organizations and, at the same time, amplifies our personal freedoms and choices. The modern, professional, responsible organization should be truly self-governing; the last thing I want is for government to set up more watchdogs with more teeth, thus eroding our liberties (in fact the last thing I want is for government to do more of anything, least of all to lay down moral standards).

I personally do not want to be told by my government (and certainly not by the European one) what I may buy in a shop on Sundays, nor what time of day I may drink a glass of beer, how many hours I may work, nor the age at which I may retire. And I certainly do not want a return of state-run do-gooders like the Board of Film Censors which snipped the rude bits out of films for 60 years and which, now it has gone, is not mourned by anyone on earth. Just as I do not want the government to tell me how to live my life so I do not want them to tell organizations how to behave; surely it is better to leave all these ethical decisions to each organization's governing directors who will know, to the nearest millimetre and to the latest split second, what sort of behaviour public opinion does and does not demand from their own particular organization.

These governing directors, then, are there to represent the intended beneficiaries, not to manage; they will uphold their organization for the benefit of these beneficiaries; they are to be the leading experts on the 'How are you getting on?' question which, in the beneficiary doctrine, is question number one. They are the keepers of the *cui bono*; the key-holders of the 'Why are we here?' conundrum. And guardians of their organization's morals.

An ultimate form of democracy

I see these governing directors as the last step in a three-stage voyage from autocracy to democracy that so far has taken humanity several millenniums. This trend is manifest not only in politics but in companies, NPOs, in every field of human activity. Power, like wealth, has moved relentlessly from the few to the many. First came the tyrants, reigning over their organizations without hindrance, often as their own personal fief as did the kings and barons of yore and as do their inheritors, the autocrats and dictators of today. This was executive management without any governance at all, a system of dominion which, in certain circumstances (see page 225) is unbeatable in getting results even today, but which is now in rapid decline as the ruled have become better educated and demand to have their views heard by the rulers.

Hence the rise of democracy—rule by the people for the people. Yet what we have today is only a hybrid system where the roles of governance and management are fused and confused because it is the managers who both represent the beneficiaries and, at the same time, manage the organization. As a result, it is still common for managers to be able to pervert their charges. (How often, for example, when you have complained to an organization has the management responded, not with careful consideration of your complaint, but with a spirited defence of their organization? How often have you then asked, with irritation, 'Whose side are they on?'—and then realized, with a rueful smile, whose it was!)

I wish to move from this transitional half-way house to the uncompromising and clear-cut separation of powers into governance on the one hand and management on the other, in which beneficiaries achieve a voice through their elected representatives that cannot be gainsaid by the managers, and where organizations—companies, charities, trade unions, colleges, even governments of nations—are, at last, run by their managers solely and unequivocally for the intended beneficiaries. This would be true, universal democracy, the ultimate version; we have waited a long time for it. I call it 'corporate democracy': a society in which the leading organizations, including government, accept the right of beneficiaries to elect a governing board, entirely distinct from the managers, and to have their organizations managed in their interests—only then will we have reached 'the end of history'.

The consequences

I am convinced that something quite remarkable will come from the application of the beneficiary doctrine with its three mutually reinforcing parts—performance, conduct and governance. I look for a vast improvement in our standard of living *and* our quality of life.

Let us assume that about half the world's organizations are companies and half are NPOs. Take companies first: I hope that many of them, which do not at present explicitly set long-term profit targets (and most do not), will begin to do so at the insistence of their new governing directors. My experience suggests that this single action—identifying a long-term, quantified profit target to aim at—has an electric effect on company performance, and so I anticipate a notable increase in the profitability of all those that adopt this concept.

But note this well: I am not calling for the aggressively ambitious targets that all those belligerent management books extol, because that would just exacerbate the levels of ruthlessness and greed that are already excessive in the private sector, thanks to the overweening position given to 'macho' managers in organizations. No. As will be seen in Chapter 6, I want something much more attractive than that. And I also want companies to behave far better under the new principles outlined above.

But the most substantial gains would come from the public sector, from NPOs. Not only would their performance improve enormously as a result of setting single-minded corporate objectives and quantified, verifiable targets (virtually none of them set any now), but I foresee further remarkable and highly positive effects on NPOs from the introduction of both the principle of engagement and the no harm principle. The mere act of lifting the onerous terms of the stakeholder theory, which many NPOs presently embrace, will itself result in a substantial additional improvement in performance.

NPOs reaching up to companies

I thus expect a massive increase in NPO efficacy resulting in a momentous growth in their numbers and influence—and in their impact on society. NPOs will, at last, be able to look companies in the face, as they did a century ago. But this re-found buoyancy will also generate exciting new flexible styles and forms of NPO, each adapted to its own specialist niche (as described in Chapter 18 where I review the wide variety of consequences of the beneficiary doctrine). Among the other significant suggestions there will be a description of how federations, composed of autonomous specialist organizations, will blossom, together with a profound change in our parliamentary system.

And so I hope for a major improvement from the private sector and a huge one from NPOs—a significant overall escalation in world benefit. I mean *significant*; I mean another 1 per cent per annum on the standard of living, 4 per cent growth for OECD countries, not 3. You consider that absurd? But a single, clear objective galvanizes organizations, it inspires them. From top to bottom, everything improves to an extent that has to be seen to be believed. Look at the bounding, innovative Greenpeace in the eighties and compare it with the lame and pedestrian Church of England. Judge the contrast for yourself; is the former 5 per cent more successful than the latter? Twenty per cent? Two hundred?

Give your organization a convincing corporate objective and it will soar beyond your wildest dreams; give it a defective one, or none at all, and it will languish and decline. Let us not draw the wrong conclusion from experience. The reason companies are so effective is *not* because they are profitmaking but because they know what they are trying to do for whom, can measure whether they are doing it, and, consequently, their management can go at their tasks single-mindedly and be rewarded appropriately.

I want NPOs to become just as single-minded as companies so that their performance is lifted nearer their level, a giant step upwards. And if we can achieve this, then we can look forward to a miracle; there is an order-of-magnitude improvement that we can make, starting now, to the Western way of life.

Summary

We are increasingly dependent on organizations today for everything we value most. Yet most NPOs have not defined what they are trying to do for whom, nor have they been able to measure or monitor their results (or they say they cannot; mercifully, though, as a rule, they do behave with consideration for others).

And in remarkable contrast, most companies do know what results they are supposed to be achieving and they monitor their performance closely and continuously, but alas, they often behave with scant concern for others and frequently and casually debase so many aspects of our quality of life.

It really does matter to us that so many companies behave so badly—the face of capitalism really is unacceptable today. And it really does matter that the performance of all those non-profitmaking organizations is either unknown, unknowable or downright useless.

The beneficiary doctrine says three things about all this:

1 That every organization, whether company or NPO, should set out to benefit one clearly identified group of beneficiaries, and that a single, long-term, verifiable, target figure should be set to reflect what it is trying to do for them. If it cannot set such a target it should be re-formed until this becomes possible.

2 That companies and NPOs—indeed all of us—are ill-served by the stakeholder theory. The no harm principle and the principle of engagement should be adopted in its place.

3 That a separate board of non-executive governing directors be appointed to socially significant organizations to set explicit standards of long-term corporate performance and corporate conduct for them, and to monitor their performance against these. In view of the failure of all our current systems of governance to restrain the power of the modern manager, an explicit recognition of the distinction between elected governance and executive management is required to safeguard all our more vital organizations; then the goal of true corporate democracy would be in sight.

29

The application of this three-part doctrine will result in a kaleidoscope of new types of NPO together with a most spectacular improvement in their performance, and, taken with enhanced performance and behaviour from companies, will lead to a greatly enriched standard of living and quality of life.

CHAPTER THREE

Organizations: what are they for?

Chapter 2 contained a brief, complete, summary of the beneficiary doctrine. In this chapter I want to start at the very beginning again in order to build a more explicit foundation for the rest of the book. First I shall have to define what organizations are and describe the various forms they may take.

I shall then ask 'what are organizations for?', which leads directly to the central conundrum of setting corporate objectives. I shall outline a new approach to solving this age-old riddle featuring a sequence of steps which all organizations should follow in order to identify and quantify their aims. I call this the 'purpose sequence' and I shall describe it in detail in both this chapter and the next two. I hope it is a sufficiently practical approach for the reader to apply each step to his or her own organization.

Although this sequence is the same for all organizations it is much more difficult for NPOs than it is for companies and so, while I shall be able to demonstrate how companies may move through it in just one chapter (Chapter 7), it will take a further four chapters to illustrate how it may be used by NPOs.

Thus almost the entire first half of the book is devoted to selecting corporate objectives. This is the first of the three parts of the beneficiary doctrine. It is the most significant and it is the factor which will have the greatest impact on the performance of organizations.

Organizations: what are they?

Most definitions of the term 'organization' begin with the words, 'a group of people acting together'. Those words 'group of people' imply that there has to be more than just one person to form an organization. One person is not, fairly obviously, an organization, but two may be.

Then there are the words 'acting together'. If there was just one person acting alone he or she would have a very clear idea in mind as to the task in hand without having to communicate with anyone—he or she would, literally, be 'single-minded'. For many tasks, especially where coherence and consistency are essential, this is a very real advantage (thank goodness Beethoven did not form an organization to write his Fifth Symphony). But for some things we just have to construct an organization, even if it takes a massive effort to ensure that everyone is 'acting together'. For example, you need an organization to perform the Fifth Symphony. Now, the more coherently the conductor explains how it should sound the better will be the performance: 'all moving to the same beat', 'all playing the same tune' and 'on the same wavelength' are the clichés typically used to describe an organization that is behaving single-mindedly.

The whole point of forming an organization, then, is to achieve something that one person alone cannot do, but to do it as nearly as single-mindedly as a single person would. It is obvious that there are an increasing number of tasks that we want to perform in the modern world where the organization wins hands down. The number of individuals working on their own in rugged isolation is surely in decline today, while organizations play a growing role in all our lives.

So, that is what an organization is: a group of people acting together.

Imagine there is a car crash; a number of motorists would stop and hurry to the scene bearing coats, tool-kits, tow-ropes—anything they thought might help. Someone would phone the ambulance, another would drag out a victim, a third would bind a wound. This is obviously an organization: it is 'a group of people acting together'.

Now imagine a gathering of friends arranging a birthday party; is that an organization? Both of these—the party and the car crash organizations—will break up and disappear as soon as their task is completed and, furthermore, neither has any formal management, so it could be argued that they are not 'proper' organizations. In my view, however, they are just as legitimate as one that lasts a thousand years, and has a whole galaxy of managers all toiling away in a stately, traditional, formal hierarchy.

Six types of organization

An organization, then, can be 'permanent' or 'project', as I will call them, the latter version dissolving as soon as its aims have been achieved. It is of interest that some of these project organizations are astonishingly effective even though they have no management at all. This is probably because, like the rescue organization, everyone can see perfectly well what the aim is and how they can best 'act together' to attain it; both the aims and the means are so obvious, and so compelling, that single-mindedness is thrust upon them by the circumstances, and a high level of effectiveness is achieved without any formal management at all.

There is another pair of contrasting organizations in the examples above; the group of friends were acting in their own interests—the birthday party was for their own enjoyment. But the rescuers in the car crash were acting, not for themselves, but for the victims. I call these organizations 'introvert' and 'extrovert'. Introvert organizations act to benefit the members of the organization themselves. These would include a health club, a trade union, a cooperative and all companies. Among the extroverts, which aim to benefit persons other than the members, are a government, a hospital, a school and all charities. This contrast, which I believe has not been adequately noted before, is important because we view the conduct of extrovert organizations rather more leniently than introvert ones and, I suspect, Adam Smith's observation that self-interest is the key to organizational success is valid only, or mainly, for such introvert organizations as companies and is much less applicable, and perhaps negligible, in extrovert ones.

This brings us to the third pair of organizations, the most distinctive of all: profitmaking and non-profitmaking. I shall call these simply 'companies' and 'NPOs'. (The Americans refer to the latter as 'not for profit organizations'; luckily the initials still fit.)

So, for the purposes of this book, I want to note three pairs of types of organization: project and permanent; introvert and extrovert; and, most important, company and NPO.

Companies are always introvert (companies are formed by the shareholders for their own benefit), so there can be no such thing as an extrovert company. NPOs, on the other hand, can be either—but I think I am right in saying that all NPOs run by or sponsored by governments (quangos, agencies, corporations, institutions and the like) are extrovert and that no democratic government likes to be seen running an introvert organization. All types of organization can be permanent or project. No organization can be both a company and an NPO, nor introvert and extrovert at the same time, nor of course, project and permanent.

I return to all this later—and there are full definitions in the Glossary for all the key words I am using here and throughout the book.

Organizations: what are they for?

I now want to ask what organizations are for. It is an odd-sounding question and it requires a brief explanation of its own.

You can ask 'what is a knife for?' and receive a very simple answer: 'for cutting'. But you cannot ask 'what is a crow for?' because, while a knife is an artefact, fashioned by humans for a specific human purpose, a crow is not made for a specific human purpose; it is not *for* anything, so far as we know, except perhaps for the continuation of its species. So you can have an 'excellent' knife and a 'useless' one, meaning that the average human would judge that it is good or bad at performing its designed function, but you cannot have an 'excellent' crow or a 'useless' one. The question 'what is it for?' is meaningless for objects not used for a human purpose. Conversely, objects for our use must be 'for' something.

The reason for this brief diversion into the deeper reaches of linguistic philosophy is that we keep confusing the word 'organization' with 'organism'. Management textbooks tell us that the purpose of any organization is 'to survive'. But an organization is not an organism, it is an artefact and was brought into being to do something quite specific and useful. Organizations are teleological (to use the jargon), they have a purpose. Mere 'survival' is fine for crows but hardly relevant for one of society's artefacts such as a knife or an organization. No one founds an organization with its mere survival in mind; what they have in mind is that it should, like the knife, do something useful.

But what? We know what organizations *are*—they are groups of people acting together—but what are they *for*?

To answer this we must return to those definitions. The one most frequently seen usually ends in the words, 'group of people acting together for a common purpose', or I have seen 'acting together to solve a problem'. But I suspect the former is a mere tautology: if people are 'acting together' they are obviously working 'for a common purpose' so this widely accepted definition is in fact rather useless. What about 'to solve a problem'? Well, it is true that organizations are usually formed with quite a serious intention, people do not usually form them just for fun. However, they do sometimes—where is the 'problem' when someone forms a country and western club, for example (other than their taste in music)?

Deliberate, considered, pointed

I believe that organizations are not there 'to achieve a common purpose' or 'to solve a problem'. These definitions are far too weak and general. When someone forms an organization they *always* have something absolutely definite in mind. No one wakes up in the morning and says to their spouse, 'I think I'll form an organization today, dear'. No, it is usually a very deliberate, considered act; one that is pointed, focused, aimed, purposeful; not vague, indistinct and unbounded. Not only are founders' intentions usually very definitive, they are sometimes passionately so, as when, angered and ashamed at the sight of so many starving children in Ethiopia, and no one doing anything to help, Bob Geldof forms Band Aid (a highly effective project organization, please note).

I believe all organizations are formed to do something quite specific—to benefit *specific people*. If you found a hospital for blind sailors it is to benefit blind sailors. If you form a government of the United Kingdom it is to benefit the people of the United Kingdom. If you form a golf club it is for golfers.

To benefit certain specific, nameable, human beings.
Organizations are for people.

Definitive. Unequivocal. Positive. And, did you notice, beneficial, benevolent, benign? Unusually for rapacious society, here is an artefact which specializes in doing good for the people for whom it is formed. Organizations are 'A Good Thing'.

So, organizations are formed to benefit *specific people* — no organization in the history of the human race has ever, I believe, been formed for any other purpose. This anthropocentric view extends even to charities for animals; these too are really for people. Save the whale? *Cui bono?* Would you join an organization to save the rabies virus? (If you say, 'yes, but only for scientific purposes, of course' — *touché*, I think).

Most people would claim that a school should benefit not only the children, for whom it is founded, but also the teachers, the parents, the local community, the state, local employers, those who built and who maintain the school, the caterers, the publishers of textbooks, and even the janitors. Similarly with a children's care charity: the stakeholders are not only the children but their families, the charity's staff, its managers and planners, professional specialists, politicians and the local community. A golf club is for the golfers, the caddies, the local community . . . .

So, you will demand, the full definition of an organization should read as follows: 'An organization is a group of people acting together to benefit everyone concerned'. My view is, categorically, no, that is not correct. *That is the popular belief — and it is completely wrong*!

The intended beneficiaries

I said earlier that when a charity to help starving Ethiopians is set up, the founders have but one single aim in mind — to relieve the plight of starving Ethiopians. But the founders would go further; they most certainly do not expect their charity to care for the suppliers of the food in any way whatever. Nor to help the transport contractors. The founders do not set up their charity to 'serve the community'. They do not have the Ethiopian government as an object of their benefactions. Very definitely not. Absolutely, categorically and emphatically not. No, the sole intended beneficiaries — the *sole* intended beneficiaries — are starving Ethiopians.

Are children's charities really for the planners and professionals and politicians? In my ignorance I thought they might have something nice up their sleeves for children.

And surely a school is for its pupils. Weightwatchers is for slimmers. The Boy Scouts is for boys. And if you set up a company you would, if you were honest, declare its aims as 'to make a profit for myself'. You would not have the suppliers, workers, local community or the state at the forefront of your mind — in fact, they would be nowhere in your mind. Does that mean that you would be able to ignore, or actually aim to dis-benefit all these people? Well, you would not be making profits for long if you took that attitude. 'Exactly', you will exclaim triumphantly, 'and so that means you *do* intend to benefit them, after all!' My response is, 'No, you do not. What you intend is to treat all these people in such a way that they will allow you, and even assist you, to make a profit. The organization, however, is for you.'

This is the relationship, not that of deliberately generating a benefit for all these people in the same way as you deliberately intend to generate one for yourself; to pretend any other relationship is pure hypocrisy. There are two quite distinct groups of people who benefit from any given organization: the intended beneficiaries and the incidental beneficiaries. These latter are often referred to as 'the stakeholders'. But 'stakeholders' is a word I expressly wish to avoid because the very name implies that all these people may be deemed to have a stake in the organization and are therefore in some way *entitled* to a benefit from it. This is the argument put forward in the stakeholder theory, which I will discuss at length in Chapter 13. For now I will just say that, although it has come to be almost universally accepted, I believe the stakeholder theory is nothing but a curse upon society for it demands a code of corporate conduct that deflects organizations from their true role.

The final definition

In my opinion the correct definition of an organization is:

An organization is a group of people acting together to generate a satisfactory benefit for its intended beneficiaries.

The intended beneficiary is anyone for whose benefit any given organization is formed and for whom it exists. That person is the *raison d'être*. Thus a school is formed to benefit children—and for no other reason, not even for a hint of another reason. Even if a school was built and run entirely by the pupils (assisted, if you like by robots from Mars thus ensuring that no Earth-person could derive even a scintilla of benefit), that school would still be a valid organization so long as it benefits the pupils. A hospital is to benefit the sick. The British Medical Association is for doctors. The Automobile Association is for motorists. The European Community is for Europeans. The variety of the aims and objectives of human organizations are a spectacular tribute to human ingenuity—and yet they are all the same! They are there to benefit their intended beneficiaries.

You see why I have called it the beneficiary doctrine. It says that organizations should be utterly single-minded towards these people. The key to corporate success is assiduous, diligent, unceasing commitment to the intended beneficiaries. I believe that multi-purpose organizations, those that try to be all things to all people, those which attempt to 'serve the community', or that believe they are there 'for the good of all' or to 'benefit the stakeholders', or who 'wish to balance the aims of everyone concerned' are not only at a huge competitive disadvantage in the modern world, they are also the result of a universal but ridiculous misunderstanding. Worse; I believe they are literally unmanageable. They cannot be managed in the sense that their corporate objectives will be unattainable.

I hope in Chapter 14 to describe a code of corporate conduct that is much more appropriate to the world we live in than the stakeholder theory, a code which describes how organizations should act towards all their incidental beneficiaries (or interest groups as I prefer to call them) in a manner which actually enhances the way organizations behave in society.

Meanwhile my view is categoric: as soon as an organization turns its mind to benefiting people other than its intended beneficiaries it starts upon the road to degeneration and decay.

The corporate purpose

It seems to me, then, that no organization will be able to answer the question I posed in Chapter 1, 'How are you getting on?' (or its close relative, 'Why are we here?'), unless it knows who its intended beneficiaries are, what it is trying to do for them and whether they think it is doing it. Moreover, this question should not be addressed to the organization at all but to the intended beneficiaries. They, uniquely, are the people who can say how well it is doing; neither the organization itself, nor its management, is entitled to make this judgement.

If that is so, it becomes necessary to move through a whole sequence of questions before we reach the 'How are you getting on?' one. We have to know who the intended beneficiaries are, what the organization is supposed to be doing for them, what level in the provision of this the intended beneficiaries consider satisfactory and, finally, we have to be able to measure whether that level is actually being attained and whether the intended beneficiaries are, in fact, satisfied. And so that simple 'How are you getting on?' question turns out to be more like 'What are you trying to do for whom and how well are you doing it?' which in turn becomes a five-part formal catechism which I call the 'purpose sequence'.

THE PURPOSE SEQUENCE
A catechism for organizations

1 Who are your intended beneficiaries—who are the people for whose benefit your organization exists?

2 Exactly what benefit are they expecting from you?

3 How do you measure this *with figures*?

4 What level of performance do the beneficiaries consider satisfactory, and, even more important, what level would they say is unsatisfactory?

5 What level of performance did you actually deliver to them over the past five or ten years?

It is a far cry from 'How are you getting on?' but this is what that informal little question actually means and this is what I was getting at in Chapter 1 when I was testing out the Department of Health, the Arts Council and all the others. They could not answer this simple, informal question because they cannot answer the five formal ones of the purpose sequence.

Words and figures

While making clear that these five questions form a continuous sequence — organizations wishing to establish their credibility have to move through all five of them — I am now going to break them into two groups: words first then figures. Questions 1 and 2, which require brief verbal answers, relate to what I call the 'corporate purpose' (the 'what are you doing for whom?' bit) while the latter three, which must be expressed numerically, relate to setting targets and monitoring results; I call this the 'target sequence' (the 'how well are you doing it?' part), and thus the corporate purpose and the target sequence fit together to form the purpose sequence.

I shall deal with the corporate purpose in this chapter, the target sequence in the next two, and then I shall put them together again to move through all five questions, in sequence, first for companies in Chapter 7 and then NPOs in Chapters 9 to 12.

As will be seen, for some organizations all these questions may be answered in a trice. In others none of them. The beneficiary doctrine says that if an organization finds it impossible to answer any one of them then its aims should be redefined until it can do so. Moreover, we should demand strict, unequivocal answers that are capable of being objectively verified, in practice, in the real world, 'on the street'. It is not acceptable in the twentieth century, and still less in the next one, for an organization to consume society's valuable resources without yielding a demonstrable return to someone and, moreover, unless that return can be stated in a form that is empirically verifiable, then it must be assumed that it is not being provided at all. Guilty unless proven innocent.

I now wish to describe the items in this questionnaire, starting with identifying the intended beneficiaries. But alas, first I have to clear out of the way yet another confusion that stalks through almost all the textbooks on this subject.

Another fine mess

A major cause of the absurd bewilderment that reigns throughout any discussion of this topic is that the words 'corporate objective' are commonly used with three entirely different meanings. Consider this simplified, but otherwise typical, statement of objectives frequently found in textbooks or at the start of a corporate plan for any company or NPO:

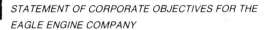

STATEMENT OF CORPORATE OBJECTIVES FOR THE
EAGLE ENGINE COMPANY

1 We propose to increase our share of the market by providing superior quality and value for money to our customers.

2 We aim to be excellent employers and to offer our staff outstanding opportunities in career development.

3 We intend to make satisfactory profits for the shareholders.

4 We wish to lead the engine industry in technology.

5 Our objective is to contribute to the public good and to the quality of life in the community.

These five statements may all appear to be 'objectives', and indeed, in the sense that they are all 'things we aim to do', that is what they are; the words 'aim', 'goal', 'charter', 'vision', 'mandate', 'strategy', 'values', 'policy', 'mission', 'target' are all commonly used in the sense of 'something we intend to do'. But in fact they fall into three entirely different logical categories. Only statement 3 represents the genuine corporate objective; for a company to aim to make a satisfactory profit for its shareholders is, I believe, its only true purpose. Every company that was ever formed was formed to do that; every company that ever failed did because it did not make a satisfactory profit. Profit is the *raison d'être* of every company; any organization which is not aiming to make a satisfactory profit is quite simply not a company; any that is, is.

You can imagine a company saying 'OK, we now have enough employees (or market share, factories, etc.), we do not want any more', but they would *never* say that about profits. By the same token no road safety organization would ever say 'OK, that's enough safety', while they might say 'OK, that's enough barriers, motorways, legislation, underpasses'. No, profitmaking is what the word 'company' means (confusingly lawyers use the word 'company' to mean any organization 'limited by guarantee'; I am using the word as ordinary people do—to mean an organization having a share capital owned by its shareholders).

So the only true corporate objective in the above list is that profit aim. If that is so, what is the standing of the other four 'corporate objectives'? Two of them turn out to be possible corporate *strategies*; two of them are statements about corporate *conduct*.

A corporate conduct statement is any general rule intended to regulate an organization's actions on moral or ethical grounds. The company above, for example, aims to be an excellent employer and wishes to play a liberal role in the local community. 'Conduct' is how one behaves. It is neither ends nor means. It says nothing about what one is going to do, a lot about the manner of doing it.

A corporate strategy, on the other hand, is what one does: it is any line of *action* which management believes will help to achieve the corporate objective. Eagle Engines evidently consider that increasing market share and becoming a leader in technology will help their profits; if they discovered that these actions were not improving their profits, or worse still, damaging them, they would stop doing them. These strategies are selected for one reason only: that they are expected to contribute to the corporate objective. In other words, strategies are means designed to achieve the end, which is profits.

Aims, means, conduct

Let me summarize these three entirely different uses of the words 'corporate objective' and then, for the rest of this book, I will use the words 'corporate objective' with one meaning only—as the 'corporate purpose'.

Corporate purpose

Corporate purpose is the reason why any organization was formed and why it continues to exist. It is the justification for its very existence, its *raison d'être*. It is the sole criterion by which one may judge whether the organization, as a corporate body, is a success or a failure. It is the aims or ends as opposed to the means—it will never, in all its life-history, cease to try to achieve its aims while it may, and frequently will, change the means. It is 'why we are here'; it is what it is for, as opposed to what it does. An organization's corporate purpose is unalterable; if it is changed, the organization itself would have to be reconstituted as a new legal entity. The purpose of every organization is to deliver a satisfactory benefit to its intended beneficiaries.

Corporate conduct

Corporate conduct is how organizations behave, it is any action taken (or deliberately *not* taken) because it is felt to be morally, aesthetically, socially or personally desirable (or repugnant). Actions taken for these reasons would be taken *regardless* of whether they increased or *decreased* the organization's ability to achieve its corporate purpose or even if they made it impossible; they are taken because they are 'the right thing to do'. Conduct is largely independent of purpose. (My words 'corporate conduct' embrace all synonymous concepts: ethos; values; morals; vision; culture; code of ethics; standards of behaviour; social responsibilities; etc.)

Corporate strategies

These are actions, or categories of action, taken because, and *only* because, the management believe they would improve the organization's ability to achieve its purpose or its standards of conduct. If they believed such actions would not help to achieve these they would not take them. Strategies are means, not ends. Strategies are actions, they are what an organization *does*, not what it is *for*. The *sole* justification for a strategy is its effect on achieving the purpose or conduct.

Although all three of these meanings are used in textbooks, articles and memoranda of association and mission statements more or less interchangeably, I trust they are now seen as wholly different and distinct. So different and distinct are they, indeed, that the first two, purpose and conduct, are plainly corporate desiderata and so should be determined by the intended beneficiaries; these are the input into the management process, while the strategies to achieve them are the output of that process and so should be selected by the management. The sole justification for a strategy (or, indeed, for any action that any organization ever takes or decides not to take) is that it helps to achieve purpose or conduct, and the sole justification for management is whether it successfully finds strategies capable of doing this.

Why does it matter?

Consider this example of the severe practical consequences an organization would face if it confuses aims with means, purpose with strategy. Imagine a company which believes its top corporate aim is 'to increase turnover'. Faithfully, the management will search for any strategy that will increase turnover, and even if some of this extra income is obtained at nil margin or *even at a loss* they will go on increasing turnover because that is what they have been told is the top aim. It sounds silly, it *is* silly, yet many companies, having set themselves this aim, do increase turnover right up to the point where they actually go bust (there is even a technical term for this mad phenomenon: it is called 'overtrading').

What has gone wrong here? The fault this company made was to promote a strategy ('increase turnover') to the status of a corporate aim in spite of the fact, which you and I can now see clearly, that this is a means not an aim, a second-level item not a top-level one; it is a corporate strategy to achieve a corporate purpose, not the purpose itself. And notice how, by adopting 'increase turnover' as an aim the management had no idea when to stop increasing it! As soon as they realize that the real aim was to make a profit, they would stop increasing turnover when it no longer generates any additional profit. Why would they suddenly recognize when to stop? Because the test of a strategy is 'is it helping to hit the top aim?' As soon as they realized that it was not doing this they would desist. You can easily tell which is an aim and which a means—the means is the one you stop doing when the two are in conflict.

Aims confused with means

If you adopt a means as an aim, then you not only get saddled with a dangerous strategy, as above, you also preclude the selection of all other strategies! Try it. Imagine a company placing 'lead our industry in technological advances' as its top corporate aim (many companies do actually select this). What will its management do now? Answer, they will obediently select any strategy that places their company in the technological lead, but they will not select (indeed they will give no thought at all to) a strategy to cut costs, for instance, or reduce bank borrowing. Why not? Because neither of these strategies helps to achieve the top aim they have selected. Cutting costs and reducing bank loans can contribute to improving profits which, of course, they have stupidly not selected as the top aim. (Serves them right if they go bust too!).

Choose the wrong aim and you automatically choose the wrong means. Select a dud corporate purpose and you inevitably select a dud corporate strategy. Britain chose the wrong 'objective' in the sixties and seventies when we aimed for 'full employment'; all that happened was that we got inflation. Why did it go wrong? Because full employment is not the top aim of any national economy; growth of GNP is. Aim for that and employment, inflation, exchange rates, interest rates, money supply—and all the other phenomena that make up a nation's economy—fall into place as either causes or effects of that growth.

Did we choose the wrong aim for the National Health Service (NHS); to deliver treatment 'free at the point of demand'? Surely no one would ever aim to do that for its own sake; there must be a higher level of justification for such a pursuit. I presume it is to improve the health of the British people—that is the aim. 'Free at the point of demand' is only a means (what an organization does is not what it is for). What the NHS *does* is give us free health treatment. What it is *for* is to improve our health (or so I surmise, for no one ever spells this out). And notice again what happens if you think 'free at the point of demand' is the aim—you do not even consider looking for another means of achieving it. But put 'health improvement' at the top and you instantly see that, in addition to free treatment there are all sorts of other ways and means to improve the health of a nation such as preventative medicine, paid-for treatment and public health measures.

What is the Church of England for? Judging by the emphasis it places on their work with them, it is to help the poor and underprivileged—the clergy is a sort of social worker. Or is that only a means, a strategy? If so, what is the aim behind it? If this was clearly spelt out might some new strategies, perhaps more effective in the modern world, become evident?

So, a vital step for any organization is to distinguish between corporate aims and means; one way to differentiate purpose and strategy is to reiterate the question 'why are you doing that?' until you reach the top. Imagine a labourer carrying furniture out of an office into the street. What for? Because the organization is moving to a new office. Why is it doing that? Because it is trying to save money. Why? To improve profits. Why? Because this is a company and that is what it is for.

The hierarchy of aims and means

Each action is a means to achieve an aim in the level above it in a whole hierarchy of aims and means, until you get to the top one which is in a logically different category simply because it *is* the top one—the *corporate* objective. The validity or wisdom or the innovative content of any of the lower aims or means could be challenged (it might have been better to have sold their factory rather than the offices, for example) but the one thing you cannot challenge is the aim of the company itself, as a corporate body, which is to improve its profits; a company can *never* aim not to make a satisfactory profit. It will never be right to do that, not so long as it is still a company. Making a profit is what the word 'company' means; it is what a company *is* just as a knife is for cutting.

Here, then, is a hierarchy of aims and means where the aims of the junior managers are the means of their seniors, all the way up the ladder until you get to the top aim which is different to all the others, because it *is* the top one. Just as the link at the end of a chain is logically different to all the others because, and solely because, it is the end one. A key distinction between ordinary, run-of-the-mill objectives and *the one at the top*, the corporate objective, is that managers should set all the targets for their juniors all the way down the hierarchy, but the top one, the corporate target, should not be set by a manager at all but by the beneficiaries of the organization.

The top aim cannot be changed without altering the very nature and purpose of the organization, while all the others can be changed as often as circumstances demand; no imagination whatever is required to set the top one, because it is in the innermost nature of the organization itself, while all the others demand the vigorous use of innovation if the top one is to be attained in the current competitive world.

All the other synonyms for 'corporate purpose' one sees in management textbooks—mission, goal, aims, objective, vision, plan—are also so ill-defined that they can, and are, used interchangeably in all three senses (purpose, conduct, strategy) thus rendering the statements in which they appear—and sometimes an entire book—meaningless and even ludicrous. One frequently sees, 'We aim to be the leading organization in our field' as a company mission statement. For whose benefit? If being the leader really does improve profits for the shareholders then that is fine but my impression is that, for most organizations, it merely boosts the ego of the managers. It is a means, not an aim. Indeed, the whole of this absurd muddle between top aims and second-level means results from managers having been allowed to set the top ones as well as the middle ones and, naturally, they select whatever aims best suit them—going for leadership, for instance, is an exhilarating experience for managers.

Make cars or make profits

To argue that companies make profits in order to continue to make cars (or whatever) rather than make cars to make profits appears to be another circular argument like the celebrated chicken and the egg. But no circular arguments exist; if you ask, 'whose egg?' in response to the question, 'which came first, the chicken or the egg?' that will reveal that either it was the chicken's egg—in which case, rather obviously, the chicken came first—or it was someone else's egg, in which case the question is seen to be invalid; the circle is broken. Volvo, for example, might deliberately stop making cars but they would never intentionally stop making profits. If they stopped making cars they would make something else (in fact, they have just bought a pharmaceutical company). If they stopped making profits they would cease to exist as a company. It is not circular; it is aims on the one hand and means on the other. Separate and distinct.

So extensive are all these misunderstandings and convolutions in this area that most companies and many NPOs *never* discuss their corporate objectives. When they do the confusion is so acute and so ineffably embarrassing that it takes them several days locked away in a top management seminar to find out what they are supposed to be doing for whom, and often come away more confused than when they went in.

Summary

I offered this definition:

> An organization is a group of people acting together to generate a satisfactory benefit for its intended beneficiaries.

The beneficiary doctrine draws very special attention to the unique duty that organizations have towards their intended beneficiaries and, contrary to the well-known and widely accepted stakeholder theory, denies that any other group of people has any rights or 'stake' in organizations.

Organizations may be classified as either project or permanent, extrovert or introvert and company or NPO. All government organizations are extrovert, all companies are introvert; many project organizations know their corporate objectives much more accurately than some permanent organizations, especially large and ancient ones.

The widespread tendency to confuse aims with means and both with 'conduct' does not help the identification of a true corporate objective and often leads to ridiculous strategic decisions.

Any organization wishing to identify how well it is getting on needs to clarify the answers to five questions, the first two of which require an accurate verbal definition of their intended beneficiaries and the benefit to which they are entitled.

CHAPTER FOUR

The purpose sequence

I explained in the previous chapter that an organization is there to benefit its intended beneficiaries and no one else; they are its sole *raison d'être*. I proposed a catechism of five questions—the purpose sequence—designed to identify who the beneficiaries are and what benefit they should receive, and I now wish to move through the first two questions of this sequence: who are they and what do they want? I shall discuss the target sequence, where we try to place figures on these verbal answers, in the next two chapters.

The intended beneficiaries

In most cases it is very obvious who the beneficiaries are of any given organization: Help the Aged is for the elderly; the Consumer Association is for consumers: the Northtown Milk Cooperative is for dairy farmers in Northtown, and so on endlessly. Very often there is, then, not the slightest doubt as to who they are. Moreover, they can often be described with considerable precision: Northtown Primary School might identify their beneficiaries as 'children aged 5 to 11 from within the Northtown District Council boundaries excluding the severely handicapped and those below IQ 85' or whatever.

But alas, it is not always so easy. After a number of years, when an organization has become very large and complex, when the original aims have been achieved, or overgrown with tradition and bureaucracy (and pompous mission statements), doubts begin to creep in. Is the Ministry of Agriculture, Fisheries and Food (MAFF) for the farming and fishing industries or is it for consumers? My impression is that it is for farmers but they are only 3 per cent of the population, so can that be right? Does it matter? Why do we have to know? Because no one can judge how well this ministry has been run over the past few years if we do not know who it is for. Who can judge, farmers or consumers? (and if both, who gets the casting vote?)

Who are the intended beneficiaries of the Law Society? Is it there to benefit solicitors or to enhance the British legal system for the benefit of the public? Are building societies working for savers or borrowers, or for both? If for both by what right do the managers decide what balance should be struck between them? By whose mandate, for example, did they give savers a real return of *minus* 6 per cent per annum throughout the seventies while the mortgagees saw their house prices soar? Many building societies now accept profits or 'surpluses' as their top aim. While this is acceptable as a benefit it does not reveal who are the beneficiaries and, according to the beneficiary doctrine, it is therefore useless; what is the point of deliberately tucking away millions of surplus pounds year after year, decade after decade, unless someone owns it? What on earth for? *Cui bono*? An organization without beneficiaries is not valid (and invariably becomes the private plaything of its managers).

It is interesting that most of the organizations which cannot answer this elementary question are large or ancient; small organizations (and project organizations) have less difficulty. Indeed I believe that, of all the many reasons why 'small is beautiful', the chief attraction of small organizations is the clarity with which their employees know who their intended beneficiaries are; their aims are so much more brightly focused than in large ones. Of course there are some organizations—the Freemasons, for example—who seem happy to keep us in perpetual ignorance of who the beneficiaries really are.

The elusive beneficiary

What about RIBA (the Royal Institute of British Architects)? Its charter (dated 1837) says it exists, 'for the general advancement of Civil Architecture', and senior RIBA executives carefully explained to me that the organisation is *not* for architects but for *architecture*; 'we are not a trade union like the British Medical Association', they added, sniffily. So it appears that, contrary to my fundamental rule that organizations benefit *people*, here is one that benefits *things*. But surely, just as the National Trust preserves buildings for you and me and our grandchildren, so RIBA is enhancing the 'built environment' (as architects like to call it) for you, me and our grandchildren. So it *is* for people, after all. (Actually, I think we have still got it wrong; I see RIBA strictly as a trade union for architects just like all the other professional bodies including the BMA. Sorry!)

So this first question in the purpose sequence (Who are your intended beneficiaries?) is, astonishingly, not as simple as it looks; sometimes there is doubt about the exact identity of the intended beneficiaries, sometimes they are simply misstated, and sometimes there appear not to be any at all!

But worse is to come. 'No man can serve two masters' says Matthew's gospel (6:24). I believe that every organization should serve just one person or one group of similar people. The intended beneficiaries should, in other words, be strictly homogeneous. Many NPOs break this rule.

The reason why nationalization failed our nation so comprehensively in the middle decades of this century was nothing to do with poor management (they were no worse than those in private companies, indeed they often came and went between the sectors), it was because no single beneficiary was ever ascribed to any of the corporations. Sometimes it was the workers who were to benefit (as when, in areas of high unemployment, state-owned corporations were instructed to recruit employees they did not need), sometimes it was the customers (when prices were artificially held down), sometimes the British economy was the designated beneficiary (as when the government cut much-needed capital investment to effect a Keynesian deflation). Occasionally these corporations were invited to make a profit. Or told to hit several of these aims at once (as the notorious Ryder Report suggested for the doomed British Leyland in the sixties). Sooner or later the burden of acting as Father Christmas to all and sundry will cripple any mortal organization.

Double beneficiaries

Again, joint projects, which should on the face of it provide abundant advantages to the partners, are notoriously short-lived for the same reason: they break the 'one master' rule. Imagine an American conglomerate and the Chinese government forming a joint company in China. Everything would be fine for a while but as soon as there was a recession the American owners would want to cut the labour force, but, of course, the host government would not, and the project would collapse amid recriminations.

This applies to cooperatives too. What a powerful concept they should be: the intended beneficiaries are customers (or suppliers or employees) who are also shareholders; each member thus has not one, but two, profound and hugely motivating stakes in the success of their organization. Such a concept should have swept the world by now. Why has it not? Because the needs of a customer (keeping prices down, for example) sometimes actually conflict with the needs of a shareholder (raising prices to boost the dividend). We should learn the lesson well: give an organization two 'masters' and you will cripple it for life.

How about this idea: let us merge Save the Children with Help the Aged! The reason this is such a stupid idea (in spite of the cost savings it would surely yield) is that we could never measure its performance, and even if we could we would have no idea whose opinion of its effectiveness we should pay the most attention to—the children or the aged.

So what are we to say of the Natural History Museum which actually has two such flagrantly conflicting beneficiaries: scientists and children! Here are the exact words in its charter:

*1. ... to discover and make available to the scientific
community the information contained within its
collection of natural objects ...*

*2. ... to entertain, interest and educate children and
adults in natural history.*

Half its budget is devoted to the former and 10 per cent to the latter (the rest is overheads). No, *not* the other way round! Unseen by visitors, 400 scientists are working away in offices and laboratories, advising governments, preparing reports for companies, classifying species and so forth. So it is the scientific community that wins, not the children.

But by whose mandate was that decision made? How can any human being, including the museum's governors and management, decide how to allocate resources to two such disparate beneficiaries? By what rational precepts can this trade-off be made? Who decided, and on what grounds, that so much of the budget should be devoted to taxonomy and only 10 per cent to children and not the other way round?

And who shall declare whether the Natural History Museum is a success or a failure — the scientific community or the children? Which of them has the prior demand upon its resources? Which of them calls for the dismissal of the chief executive — and for what transgression against whose interests? And, finally, which of the intended beneficiaries should be forsaken if the organization finds it cannot serve them both?

It is no good answering that 'the government' will make these decisions; how are they going to do that? They do not know any better than you or I how to trade off scientists against children. Politicians love to pretend they are omniscient, or possess the judgemental powers of Solomon, but what do they know that we do not? And what about all the other organizations with double beneficiaries who are not answerable to a government? Such as the BMA.

Further attempts to face two ways

The British Medical Association (BMA) also has two targets. Its charter states its purpose as 'To promote the medical and allied sciences and to maintain the honour and interests of the medical profession'. It is to achieve *two* aims apparently: the promotion of medical science *and* the interests of doctors. But who decides when it has done a good job? Do we, the public, as beneficiaries of advances in medical science, or do the doctors, as beneficiaries of the enhanced position of the medical profession? Or both of us (in which case does my vote count the same as one of their members)?

Or take the Southtown College of Adult Education. It serves school leavers (aged 16 to 19) who need to pass vocational exams to further their careers, and older adults (such as retired people) who simply wish to learn about the history of art, say, or home cooking. How can the performance of this college possibly be measured? We cannot add exam results to roast pork, bricklayers to Rembrandt. Nor do the adults need the same classroom equipment, the same teachers or teaching methods (and certainly not the same boisterous ambience) as the youngsters, so the saving in the cost of facilities is low—yet most of our adult colleges try to serve these two disparate clients.

Surely it is clear that the Ministry of Agriculture, Fisheries and Food is not there to satisfy both farmers and consumers and that the Arts Council is not there to serve both dancers and public? Helping farmers and dancers are what these organizations *do*; serving the citizen is what they are *for*. And yet, year after year, the discussion rages inside and outside these and all other similar organizations as to who are their 'customers' and what is their 'true purpose'.

Why is this 'two masters' lesson of thousands of years' standing so little regarded? I believe it is because most of us simply do not comprehend how organizations work. Organizations are very concrete things, they conform to rigid rules just like engineering structures do; there are burdens and loads you can and cannot heap upon them, lest they break down and collapse. You have to *design* them according to certain laws. Just as a combined hair dryer and bicycle saddle would be a ridiculous product concept (even though it could be made far more cheaply than the two products separately), so all dual-purpose and multi-purpose organizations are defective and quite simply unmanageable; all of them should be re-formed to meet the needs of just one homogeneous group of people.

Multi-purpose organizations might have been viable in Victorian times when our industrial revolution had given us an overwhelming pile of wealth to spend on our social welfare, but in the highly specialized world of today any organization that attempts to benefit more than one beneficiary is at a monstrous competitive disadvantage; today it is like trying to do two impossible things before breakfast.

You can no more drive an organization in two directions at once than you can a bus.

The single-minded organization

The chief conclusion emerging from this discussion is that every organization should adopt just one homogeneous group of people as their intended beneficiaries. Moreover, as we have seen earlier, none of the so-called stakeholders qualify as intended beneficiaries either for, while no organization should ever dis-benefit any of these interest groups, neither should they be assumed to have any legitimate claims on the resources of the organization.

These rules may be summarized as follows:

RULES FOR DEFINING THE INTENDED BENEFICIARIES

1 No organization should serve more than one homogeneous set of intended beneficiaries—that is, the person or persons for whose benefit the

organization was originally formed or for whom it now exists should be unequivocally defined and limited to one set, class or category of people.

2 No organization should include any incidental beneficiary, or stakeholder, or interest group among its intended beneficiaries.

3 The more unambiguous and consistently its intended beneficiaries are identified the more effective an organization is likely to be seen to be.

And so, as the conclusion of this first question in the purpose sequence, every organization should identify just one set of homogeneous intended beneficiaries. If the definition is not absolutely unequivocal, or if it contains more than one set, then the question has not been correctly addressed, the organization will be unmanageable, and it should be re-formed until a valid answer can be obtained. I am a dedicated follower of the principle underlying Occam's Razor which might be summarized as, 'Don't have two if one will do'.

I have to add that the view that organizations should benefit just one group of people is entirely contrary to accepted wisdom. Virtually every textbook rejects this as 'simplistic'; senior executives decry the idea, even going so far as to say that they would not consider it challenging enough to run a single-purpose organization; managers frequently describe their task as 'balancing the needs of the stakeholders'. I consider this view to be just another in the 'spoiler' series (page 112). Peter Drucker, the great management guru, has said that, whether one likes it or not, all modern organizations are multi-purpose. I do not like it and I do not believe it. I thoroughly resent all these clever people who claim they can manage multi-purpose organizations while casually admitting to anyone who asks that, no, actually, it is not possible to measure their performance. I believe multi-purpose organizations are ineffective, a curse upon society and should be ruthlessly re-formed (see page 246 for some of the methods).

But will not this rule lead to twice as many organizations, each twice as specialized but half the size? Yes, exactly so. But will they not then be twice as vulnerable in this world of giants? Not if they regroup into federations and adopt the principles of mall-management (but for details of all this we will have to wait until Chapter 17).

Finally, I mentioned the word 'spoilers'. Managers in the public sector spend much of their time persuading us that it is not possible to measure performance 'in their particular case'. 'We have no bottom line', 'We are not like a company, you know', 'My organization is far too complex to be measured'. I believe all this is a myth. In one thing they are correct: you cannot measure an organization with more than one beneficiary. And that is precisely why so many NPOs have more than one. It is a deliberate spoiler. We will meet a number of these comforting managerial concoctions throughout the book and in Chapter 8 I list and describe all the common ones.

Defining the benefit

Now we turn to the second of the two questions in the purpose sequence: 'Exactly what benefit are the beneficiaries expecting?'. Just as with the beneficiaries, it is sometimes easy to see what benefit some organizations are generating for their beneficiaries—and sometimes it is not.

Among the easy ones are: companies 'make profits for shareholders'; the Scottish Youth Hostels Association 'provides cheap temporary accommodation for young Scots'; and the British Ministry of Defence 'protects Britain against armed attack', or words to that effect. All very simple. Simplicity is essential. I would query any description of either the beneficiaries or the benefit that demands more than half a dozen simple everyday words. This is quite contrary to the public conception of everything to do with 'corporate objectives'; everyone expects this subject to be complex, profound, philosophical.

Why? Because the whole subject area of corporate objectives has been hijacked by academics and strategic planners whose professional coinage is complex intellectual challenge; if it is simple, they are bored with it and so they wrap ordinary everyday words up in sanctimonious oleaginous circumlocutions to make it all sound more learned, complex and impressive (the current craze for mission statements, vision statements and statements of values is typical (see page 115). One reason for all this evasion is that managers do not want their organizations to be judged, nor to be *capable* of being judged, by any simple criterion of success. 'This is a university, John. You must understand it is a very complex and demanding organization.'

But does one have to be so brilliant to determine what say, the Boy Scouts is for, or Alcoholics Anonymous, or a university? When somebody founds an organization do they have some vastly intellectual, complex aim in mind? Surely it will be simplicity itself? To relieve famine, save the whale, provide refuge for battered women or whatever. Determined with great clarity, and, often, with passion; capable of full and comprehensive description in a few simple words. And so if an organization tells me that all this may have been true at one time but is no longer so ('we live in a modern, sophisticated world'), then I am tempted to wonder whether the organization has become encrusted with bureaucracy or perverted by the personal ambitions of its managers.

Unintelligible nonsense

And just look at the pages of legalistic drivel that makes up the memoranda and articles of association of most of our NPOs:

In furtherance of the said objects, but not further or otherwise, the Company shall have the power: (a) to

cause to be written, and printed or otherwise
reproduced and circulated, gratuitously or otherwise,
periodicals, magazines, books, ...

and so on for 14 pages (extracts from a memorandum approved by the Charities Commission in 1991—no, not *1791*). I hope you understood it, because I did not.

So, let us get our feet back on the ground. What about prisons—what exactly are they trying to do for whom? Are they to punish, to prevent recurrence, to rehabilitate or to protect society? What exactly are the Girl Guides trying to do for their girls? What exactly is the Ministry of Agriculture, Fisheries and Food doing for consumers? What is the Church of England doing for its members? What do we mean when we ask a school to educate our children?

Would it do to describe what the BMA does, for example, as services to doctors? And Southtown Council as providing services to the people of Southtown? And the AA—services to motorists? Is this word 'services' too broad and undefined? Perhaps we should demand a closer specification; after all, we would not accept 'services to children' as an adequate description of a school, and 'services to future generations' would be absurdly general for the National Trust. (One way to match benefit and beneficiary with unusual accuracy is to do what one of my client organizations attempted to do; they defined the benefit as 'services' and the beneficiaries as 'those who receive our services'. Full marks for ingenuity!)

Rules for defining the benefit

So what exactly are the criteria that any organization should meet when defining the benefit element in its corporate objectives? I should like to suggest the following five rules.

1 The intended beneficiaries must first be defined as described above—that is, just one, homogeneous group of people must be designated before the benefit can even be considered.

2 The benefit being offered must also be homogeneous and capable of being defined in just a few words. It must, in other words, be simple.

3 It must be capable of being targeted and of empirical verification— essentially, then, it must be quantifiable.

4 It must be of perceived significance to the beneficiaries.

5 Finally, it must not be something of which society disapproves.

I hope there is no need to dwell further on the first of these— obviously one cannot begin to determine the benefit until one has identified who the beneficiaries are. The more homogeneous they are the more diverse the benefits may be without incurring trade-off disputes between them, for if they are homogeneous they will, by definition, be of like mind.

Thus, in the case of the Church of England, the more it attempts to welcome those other faiths that have recently appeared in Britain—Muslims, Hindus and so on—the more it will have to water down its (arguably) already diluted beliefs and the less effective will it become in the minds of its established intended beneficiaries.

Simple benefits

The second criterion above, simplicity, further underpins the basic theme of the beneficiary doctrine, that organizations must clearly and accurately identify their corporate objectives. If a benefit is complex, or can only be described in the prolix language of the lawyer or the civil servant, then it is most unlikely to have been correctly identified—people do not found organizations for complicated reasons, they form them for blunt, simple ones such as to relieve famine, make war, earn money. Here again, therefore, I need to emphasize that organizations trying to deliver more than one simple, homogeneous benefit will be at a severe disadvantage.

Consider, for instance, the newly established Scottish Enterprise. Its beneficiaries are obviously Scots, an admirably homogeneous set of intended beneficiaries. But the 'prime objectives' of this body are to 'further economic development in Scotland *and to improve the environment*' (my italics). It seems to me quite insane to set up an organization with two such radically different aims. What if, in 10 years time, all the unsightly coal-tips and slums have been duly cleared away but the Scottish economy has patently collapsed? Is Scottish Enterprise to be congratulated on half the job well done? Or vice versa, if the economy is booming but the environment is in ruins; is that the more laudable performance? This lunacy provokes the question, why not invite this wonderfully versatile organization to undertake another half-dozen duties such as reorganizing the teaching of reel-dancing and the maintenance of mountain footpaths?

So perverse do I consider this agency's 'corporate objective' to be that I am prepared to believe that 'the environment' was added deliberately to make evaluation impossible; the one thing politicians hate is having their performance evaluated. Here, in other words, is a typical, calculated, wilful, premeditated spoiler. The chief executive who took the job had no objections to this definition either, one presumes (I wonder how they calculate his performance bonuses). You may say, 'But without mention of the environment Scottish Enterprise might expand the economy without regard for the environment'. But the environment, and all other untoward consequences of growth, such as inflation, are obviously proscribed, if not by common sense, then certainly under the no harm principle (page 188). (And anyhow, it says *improve* the environment').

More metaphysics

The government has also just launched 82 local TECs (Training and Enterprise Councils). What they are for is clear: it is to 'unlock potential and build a more prosperous future'—it would be hard not to feel a sense of entrepreneurial exhilaration at such a vision. In addition to their main task, training, they are going to 'accelerate the regeneration of local economies to meet the competitive challenge of the 1990s' and 'help businesses start up, expand ... '. Gosh, how marvellous! Yet how will you know if your TEC is working better than mine? How will I know if mine is working at all?

Alas, we cannot; it is just another pathetically puerile political ploy to persuade us that our government is doing something wonderfully vigorous on our behalf. Training *and* enterprise? Maybe you can measure training—indeed, unusually for a government NPO, these TECs have actually been given targets—to increase the number of young people with National Vocational Qualifications (NVQs)—but how do you measure enterprise? One answer the TECs give is 'the failure rate among the businesses they sponsor', another is 'inward private investment into our region'. But what are we to conclude if, in your area, NVQs rise by 25 per cent and the failure rate rises by 30 per cent—is that better than the score in my area—15 per cent and 50 per cent? How should we trade off NVQs against failed businesses—or inward investment? You cannot. So what will happen? None of the 82 chief executives will ever be sacked, none of the TECs will ever be wound up.

It must be perfectly plain that Scottish Enterprise should drop all reference to the environment in its objectives, and that the TECs should become simply training agencies. If Scotland requires an environment agency, fine, let it have one (I thought it already had several), and if our regions want enterprise agencies, fine, let them have these too. But let them all be separate, specialist, organizations whose performance we might have some chance of monitoring.

Double-barrelled NPOs

But there are dozens of double-barrelled NPOs like this; The Civil Aviation Authority (CAA) regulates civil air activity but it also *operates* the civil air traffic controllers. How are we supposed to judge this organization—or any of these government hybrids which both provide or operate a service *and* regulate it?

It is no great surprise that, of all the United Nations agencies, it was

UNESCO that the USA, Britain and others withdrew from a few years ago in the belief that its aims had become perverted. Why UNESCO? Because it was (and still is) trying to deliver three benefits (educational, scientific and cultural), each hopelessly ill-defined, each entirely different, to the developing nations of the world. The World Health Organization (WHO), on the other hand, has been, so far as one may judge, relatively successful because it strives to deliver just one verifiable benefit—the control of disease; as far as one can tell the diseases it targets are, generally, in decline or coming under control. It is perfectly obvious that UNESCO should be split into three.

The Press Council was given seven duties (seven!) including 'to preserve the established freedom of the British Press' and 'to maintain the character of the British Press ... in accordance with the highest professional and commercial standards' and 'to consider complaints about the conduct of the Press ...' (By the way, here the Press Council apparently had to defend the freedom *of* the press and the citizen *against* the press. Is that something one organization is even theoretically capable of doing?) And then there are *four more* duties in its articles which I shall not spell out for fear of making you dizzy. My point is simple; here is an organization—one of weighty public importance, which solemnly presided over the British press for 50 years—trying to complete seven impossible tasks before breakfast. Thank goodness it was abolished in 1990.

So, to summarize rules 2 and 3: the benefits, like the beneficiaries themselves, should be homogeneous and simple. They must be quantifiable and verifiable so that we can set targets for our socially significant organizations and see if they have hit them.

Perceived value

The fourth rule is far more important than it sounds. It appears merely to say, 'do not set up an organization unless it is going to do something really useful'. It might be supposed that no one would, and that any organization with merely trivial ambitions would quietly die. But I suspect this error is very common; consider an organization formed quite recently to warn adolescents of the danger of Aids. Now surely, 'reducing the incidence of Aids among teenagers' would be so much more significant than 'informing teenagers of the dangers of Aids' that, to me, it calls into question the validity of the latter. Teenagers know all about safe sex; what I care about here is not what they know but whether they avoid getting Aids.

Again, some would argue that 'keeping them in' is what a prison is for. But it seems to me that to employ 30 000 people to keep another 50 000 people behind bars, as we do in Britain, without rendering them, or society, any other visible service (some would say a gross disservice), is a benefit of such puny insignificance compared to, say, 're-directing them so they do not come back', that I cannot but challenge the validity of the former.

Or, again, what exactly is the effect on disabled people of a week on a sailing ship? Where is the evidence that it changes the following five years (or five weeks, even) of their lives? There are dozens of well-meaning organizations providing this sort of service, and, while it must be wonderful for these people (and their beleaguered carers), to enjoy a short holiday it would be still more wonderful if it could be shown to do them any good.

But this fourth rule is much more profound than merely warning of the obvious; we all know that the more attractive, desirable, essential and compelling the benefit is (to the beneficiaries) the more successful the organization will be. But I am going to say later that *unless* the benefit provided is both verifiable and compelling the organization should be re-formed or closed down. Why such a brutal conclusion? Because, below a certain threshold of usefulness, organizations will be simply wasting society's resources. Just as thousands of companies go bust every year because they fail to earn a satisfactory return on shareholders' capital, so, I believe, thousands of NPOs should be granted euthanasia for lack of evidence that they are doing any real, significant good. Suggesting the closure of an NPO is considered sacrilege, akin to murder, especially if it is 'caring', but the volume and variety of menacing defects in our society is so vast and the number of people who desperately need help so pressing, that we surely should not be addressing any calls that do not justify priority.

Half of them are useless

My belief is that about half of all our NPOs are not worth having; as will be seen later (page 131), as soon as we start actually measuring performance we are in for a few shocks. We should not be surprised if half our NPOs are useless; after all, at any one time 10 per cent of companies are unprofitable. The difference is that the companies are very well aware of it and are frantically trying to put it right. Meanwhile NPOs do not even know they are bust. This rule 4 then, could knock out a large number of organizations.

Finally I suggested in rule 5 that the benefit must be something of which society does not disapprove. I am, in fact, not sure that this criterion is strictly valid. Society disapproves of a gang of burglars; but what we abhor here is not the aim of this organization (which, we might be persuaded, is 'to generate capital gains for its members') but its methods—burglary. Nor do we object to an organization devoted to overthrowing a government (many of us take great pleasure in doing that ourselves every five years). What we object to is the anarchist and terrorist who attempts to do this by force— means, again, not aims. So I suspect that in no case does society disapprove of the aims of any organization. If that is so then this rule lapses and the sole legitimate concern of society is how an organization behaves and the means it employs to achieve its aims (see Chapter 14), rather than what those aims may be.

Summary

Any organization wishing to identify how well it is getting on needs to clarify the answers to five questions, the first two of which require an accurate verbal definition of the intended beneficiaries—only one group or set of homogeneous people is allowed by the beneficiary doctrine—and of the intended benefit where, again, only one homogeneous benefit is permitted.

Many NPOs try to persuade us that they can satisfy more than one beneficiary with more than one benefit; this claim is a deliberate spoiler, however, as is the stakeholder theory itself which systematically promotes the cause of multi-beneficiary aims.

The benefits offered should be of compelling concern to the beneficiaries; where this is not the case the organization may be using resources of society which could be better employed elsewhere.

The prime conclusion in this chapter is this: any organization seeking to satisfy more than one homogeneous beneficiary with more than one simple benefit will be unable to say how well it is performing and will, in the context of the beneficiary doctrine, be invalid.

CHAPTER FIVE

Performance indicators

In the previous chapter I rehearsed the first two questions of the purpose sequence in which an organization is expected to define, in the simplest possible words, who its intended beneficiaries are and the benefit they expect from it. This was the 'What are you doing for whom?' question.

Now we have to move on to quantify this corporate purpose and to set targets that can be monitored and verified in the real world. This is the 'and how well are you doing it?' query, which, put more formally, becomes the three questions of the target sequence:

3 How do you measure this benefit *with figures*?

4 What level of performance do the beneficiaries consider satisfactory, and, even more important, what level would they say is unsatisfactory?

5 What level of performance did you actually deliver to them over the past 5 to 10 years?

I wish I could dispose of these relatively simple issues in one chapter. Alas, so profound and widespread are the misconceptions over quantification and performance indicators (PIs), which feature so prominently in question 3, that I must spend this chapter disentangling them. Only later can I tackle question 4 on setting targets.

Words will not do

If quantification is such a formidable hurdle perhaps we ought first to verify that it is really necessary. It has already been made clear that a tenet at the very heart of the beneficiary doctrine is that, if we want our organizations to be seen to fulfil the needs of their beneficiaries as effectively as companies do theirs, then we must measure their performance as effectively as companies do. Since we obviously care even more about our children's education, or whether crime is being tackled effectively, or our humanities preserved, than about how much profit ICI has made this year, we must learn to measure these things as competently as ICI measures its profits.

But surely, you may protest, we do not actually need to measure *with figures*, can we not use good old common sense, peer judgement, qualitative assessment, expert appraisals, enquiries by the media, opinion surveys, government commissions, academic observation? In any case, however desirable it may be to quantify their outputs, most NPOs state quite categorically that, in their particular case, it is simply not possible to measure their performance and the plain fact is that, even after many decades of trying, most have failed to make any significant progress in this direction at all. (I recall vividly being told quite categorically by the chief executive in one of our major west country cities that it was not possible to measure the performance of his organization, and by the chief executive of Barnardo's that the performance of his organization cannot be quantified.)

Universal bias

Surely, you will argue, knowledgeable observers and critics in universities, in comparable organizations, in government and the media should be able to ascertain, without having to use figures, how well any given organization is performing? But the trouble with experts is that they are always so enthusiastically engrossed in their subject; everyone, without exception, has some inner reason for warping the available evidence: the press does it to generate news; the government to justify intervention; universities to extract research funds, and on and on endlessly.

The extent to which experts' opinions are prejudiced, not to say downright distorted, is not generally understood. Partiality is not exceptional, it is routine, systemic, habitual. Study a research paper on the effect of smoking on human health and you can tell at a glance whether the author (who is supposed to be an objective, unbiased scientist, remember) was sponsored by the tobacco lobby or an anti-smoking pressure group. So strong is the motive behind these passions that, even though the authors know that revealing their prejudice damages their case, they cannot control themselves.

Ask a judge how our legal system could be improved and he or she will recommend more authority for judges; ask a barrister, and it will be barristers; a solicitor, solicitors. If you form a committee to study improvements to the law, whom do you select, those with, or without, a knowledge of the law? How objective will their recommendations then be? In any case, remember what we are trying to do: to raise the standard of judging the corporate performance of NPOs to the level seen in companies (shareholders can tell by a glance at the profits how well their companies have performed). To me the need to quantify is axiomatic, especially for the long periods over which we need to judge large, socially significant organizations.

It is sometimes argued that we do not need to evaluate their performance at all; we can safely leave most organizations in the hands of their dedicated, professional staff; we can rely on their devotion and commitment to deliver the best possible results. 'Trust us'. But can we? What about the Church of England? The devotion of its clergy to their calling is palpable yet that organization has been in manifest decline for decades. And what if the NHS was managed and controlled by devoted doctors and nurses; would they not simply consume, for the most appealing of motives, the entire wealth of the nation? And the police; does anyone seriously believe we should leave the police to police themselves?

Measurement and the modern world

There are many reasons why non-numerical methods of corporate assessment are no longer adequate in the modern world.

The fact that many NPOs still do not measure their performance places them at an increasing disadvantage compared to companies—indeed, this is the defect mainly responsible for the degraded position of NPOs in modern society. Quantification may not have mattered decades ago, when managers could not deliver results with the precision they can today. To be able to define an organization's aims with numerical accuracy has become a massive competitive advantage in the modern world. (And, adds the beneficiary doctrine, if their corporate objectives cannot be quantified, it probably means they have not been properly defined in the first place.)

We can rank companies in a performance league table where it is possible to compare not only like with like but with unlike as well—not just ICI with other British chemical companies but with, for example, an American computer company or a Japanese bank. We cannot do that with NPOs; we cannot even compare the performance of Northtown Adult College with Southtown Adult College, let alone with Northtown Waste Disposal Authority and certainly not with Alcoholics Anonymous of Tokyo. So, while we know how to channel investment into the best companies, by simply noting their place in a global profitability league table, we do not know how to direct society's resources into the best NPOs because we do not know which they are—an incredibly severe penalty for even the wealthiest of nations. Heaven knows how much of our valuable social assets are simply being squandered.

Words are far less definitive and stable than figures and their meanings shift and slide unnoticed over the years. Because we are here mainly interested in larger organizations, those of some social significance, this is exactly the time frame over which they have to be evaluated. To safeguard our archetypal norms we need to use definitions of performance that are so stable and sturdy that they cannot be degraded over long periods of time in spite of the natural tendency for standards of quality to slip—'bad drives out good'. This means they have to be quantified.

Because we do not measure the performance of some of our most influential organizations we do not know when they have lost their way and it is years before we wake up to find they have become outdated and ineffective. But in today's fast-moving world we need to know continuously how they are performing, indeed we need to know *before* things go wrong! How do you perform that miracle? By forecasting. Companies do it all the time because they know that historic data come too late for effective management action in today's rapidly changing world (see the remarkable gap analysis technique in Chapter 17). How do you forecast? With figures.

'If you cannot measure, you cannot manage' is not an empty slogan; in the modern world it is a truism. Virtually none of the modern methods of management may be used without quantification: in particular, strategic planning and control and project appraisal, the two most significant techniques for top management (as I shall illustrate later) certainly cannot. Thus the past five decades of development in management technology, which now enables companies to perform dramatic feats of organizational control, are out of reach of many NPOs. It is not a question of whether NPOs are well or badly managed; some are not managed *at all* in the modern sense of that word.

If we want to judge the quality of a management team then we must measure the performance of their organization. How else are we supposed to do it? What else is management for? And if the managers themselves wish to experience the warm glow of achievement when the performance of their organization is verifiably seen to improve then they have to measure it to see if it has. Moreover, if they also wish to rebut all the jibes of incompetence that the popular press and the government perennially hurl at managers in NPOs, they had better find some meaningful figures to fling back in self-defence. If we are to offer these managers performance incentives then we have to know what 'performance' means; to reward it we have to measure it.

Most people who become managers respond to being set targets— indeed, I would question the suitability of any modern management candidate who did not do so with evident enthusiasm. An organization which is able to set its managers quantified targets can tap this preoccupation (obsession, almost) and link it with attractive incentives; organizations which cannot exploit these avenues are at a massive disadvantage in our modern, materialist, environment. But note this: while it is easy, and increasingly common, to measure *operations* and *activities* within organizations it remains difficult (most NPOs say impossible) and unusual to measure the performance of corporate wholes, and that means that although middle and junior managers can enjoy meaningful performance bonuses, top managers, those responsible for corporate wholes, cannot.

Everything else we do is being increasingly subject to quantification. IQ tests, after a lifetime of ridicule, are now used, routinely and highly effectively, all around the world. Even your average C2 shopper buys duvets by their heat retention quotients. It is notable that when a branch of science surges forward it is almost always because someone has discovered how to quantify its phenomena. And so on; wherever there is progress, there is quantification. It is doubtful whether the one may be seen at all without the other. And how many games and sports do you play where the score is not central to your enjoyment?

Moreover, the data that underly quantification can today be garnered and correlated by electronic devices that were undreamed of a couple of decades ago.

Fear of the facts

The case for quantification seems quite overwhelming. So why do managers of NPOs continue to claim that it is not possible 'in our case' to measure their performance. (Note that they do not say that it is not *practical* to do so, or that it is *expensive* to do so; no, it is not *possible*—they are quite definite about that.) I refer the reader, once again, to Chapter 8 in which I describe the spoilers which account for this curious, almost universal, phenomenon. To put it briefly here: managers of NPOs fear that, if they ever were to admit that it is possible to measure their performance, someone will come along and measure it and they will be found wanting or even—fearful thought—their organization may be seen to be useless to its beneficiaries and completely without value to society (or even worse: see 'negative-sum organizations' on page 191). I claim that many NPOs are indeed in this category and that managers' anxieties on this score are fully justified. And that, on the contrary, it will also be found, once they dare to measure their performance, that some organizations, and some of the operations within them, are immensely effective and should be massively expanded.

Am I really suggesting that we should actually quantify the results of such wonderfully concerned organizations as the Samaritans or the Salvation Army? Is that not horribly soulless? Would it not transform all our caring institutions into the playthings of accountants? Well, my attitude is that if they wish to be taken seriously in the modern world then NPOs must quantify their results in the same professional manner that companies measure theirs. The world is full of troubles; we desperately need organizations that can demonstrate that they can solve them for us and can be seen to be doing so. We do not need ones that cannot.

Am I suggesting that everything can be quantified and even valued in terms of pounds, shillings and pence—freedom, the air we breathe, art, love, life itself? I do not know. I doubt it. Anyhow, I would not presume to discuss the quantification of everything on earth, only of the output of human organizations.

Beware the intangibles

There is one very real danger in attempting to quantify corporate performance (apart from its undoubted inherent difficulty, as we shall shortly see), and that is the risk of overlooking the 'non-quantifiables'—those indefinable and intangible aspects of the benefits that many organizations provide to their beneficiaries, some of which are central to their aims. What about the various social skills that children should also learn at school, but which no exam can evaluate, for instance? What about the way a company treats its employees? What about the arts, the environment, morality, spirituality? How are we going to measure these humanities? But if we fail to include such things we will fail severely.

When the World Wildlife Fund (WWF) decided to adopt 'raise funds for wildlife' as their 'corporate objective' they increased their income in Britain from £0.6m in 1977 to £12m in 1990—a magnificent achievement, greeted by a chorus of congratulation (and which provides yet more proof, if any is needed, of the electrifying power of setting a single, quantified objective). But alas, raising funds is just half the battle for wildlife; actually saving endangered species is the other half—by far the more significant one (indeed in my view *it is the only one*). Raising money is no more than the means to an end, the end being the saving of wildlife. (I note that there has been some public criticism (in 1990) of the WWF for their lack of progress in actually saving wildlife, in particular some of the more notable endangered species in *The Red Data Book*.)

I find it unnerving that such an eminent organization should confuse purpose with strategy, aims with means, quite so conspicuously, and throughout an entire decade (although, having drawn attention to the frequency of this error on page 42, perhaps I should not be too surprised to witness it yet again). Moreover, this example displays one of the causes of this phenomenon; it is often easier to quantify means than aims, as will be fully described below, and, in their desire to adopt a quantified target, managers often promote means above aims precisely to be able to say they have quantified the 'aims'.

So we must bear this particular danger fully in mind when we get down to the task of designing performance indicators. The last thing we must do is to emulate the WWF and chose an indicator that measures the bath water but not the baby. (It is pleasing to note that the WWF adopted a new strategy in 1990 in which conservation takes pride of place.)

Let me remind you where we are: having convinced ourselves that we do need to quantify the aims of organizations, we are about to search for a suitable methodology. Inevitably we reach out for 'performance indicators'. What are they?

Performance indicators

There are two distinct types of performance indicators.

Take first the performance indictators (PIs) known to every manager in the world. These measure such factors as efficiency, volume, costs, response times, service levels, failure rates and so forth, of departments, units and sections of organizations and of equipment, people and managers. Tons per day, beds per patient, defects per thousand, cost per mile, student/staff ratios, occupancy rates, waiting time per customer, capital adequacy—these are all PIs. PIs measure what managers need to know for planning and controlling the efficient operation of that part of an organization for which they are responsible.

While many PIs are ratios (where the output is expressed as a percentage or fraction of relevant inputs), some are simple numbers like 'turnover' or 'membership' and are often compared with the same number in a different time period. Hundreds and thousands of PIs are being used at any given moment in a large organization. Notice that PIs are designed for use *by managers*.

Then there is the corporate performance indicator or CPI. This measures the *overall corporate performance* of an organization. A CPI allows senior executives to plan and control their organization as a corporate whole. The archetypal CPI is, of course, 'profit', which measures the performance of a company as a corporate whole (notice that 'profit' measures the company as a whole, not its parts). Most companies do not know how profitable most of their parts are—indeed, the word 'profit' is meaningless for many sub units of a company; most companies have no idea whether their boiler house, for example, or their dispatch department is profitable or not. To judge such parts, sections or sub-units, a company would not normally attempt to use profits, they would use a battery of PIs designed and selected for these special operations: carbon dioxide in the exit gasses of the boiler, trucks loaded per hour, and other abstruse notions. PIs for parts, CPIs for wholes.

All-embracing profits

But profit not only measures a company's *overall* corporate performance it embraces both the quantifiable *and* the non-quantifiable elements, for if a company does not meet the needs of its customers, or mistreats its employees, say, or offends the local community, then its profits will reflect these unquantifiable defects very quickly. Can anyone doubt that the reason Marks and Spencer is so profitable is that it behaves itself with such unusual and attractive decorum towards its employees, customers and local community? Profits tell you when you have got everything right, it is a reward for doing what society wants you to do. Of course, like everything

65

else, people of ill-will can distort the profit figure, but, on the whole, it tells us what we want to know about a company's overall performance.

So this remarkable CPI measures everything in just one single figure— even all these intangibles and unquantifiables. This is entirely contrary to the generally accepted views on the use of single performance indicators. A booklet on *Performance Indicators in Further Education* by a leading educational staff college is utterly typical. It clearly states that one single indicator will 'of necessity' reveal only one dimension of performance and that if we want to measure overall performance we will have to employ a number of indicators. Patently not true.

A handful of targets

Or take any government White Paper on setting corporate objectives to the nationalized industries (the best known was CMD 7131 of 1978), which invites them to set half a dozen PIs by which to measure their overall performance. Or see where, right up to 1991, the same advice is still being given to the 'autonomous agencies' which the government is setting up: they are advised to use 'a handful of robust and meaningful top level output targets' (Fraser, 1991).

Why do governments insist on these multiple targets? There are two reasons: one is that they have not understood the distinction between a PI and a CPI (of which more later); the other is that if you set several targets there is a good chance of one of them being hit, and that is the one the politicians can selectively emphasize in their press conferences. This is not just a cynical joke. The culture in many NPOs makes it crucially important that executive performance should *not* be capable of being unequivocally measured, and that they should be provided with an escape route from personal responsibility. A set of multiple targets allows this game of pick-the-winner to be played; if unemployment is up, never mind, with any luck the finance minister can point with pride to inflation moving down.

And how many 'handfuls' are we going to need fully to reflect trends in the health of a nation, for example? This very day, as I write, the government has announced a substantial reduction in waiting lists for operations in the NHS. Meanwhile (but not announced), deaths from lung cancer are up again.

There is another problem. The criteria for judging a town might include street litter, unemployment, housing, and so on—a very sensible-looking handful. But what about the quality of architecture which you cannot even measure? If you cannot measure it, you cannot include it in the handful. So, while any set of indicators is almost certainly preferable to no measurement at all, no 'handful' is ever adequate; nor can it ever include items that cannot be quantified—a massive defect, one we swore we would not accept.

Another feature clouding the measurement of the performance of organization is that all modern organizations are complex. A bus service, for example, has to be comfortable, punctual, safe, clean, quiet, available to the disabled, must observe traffic regulations, employment directives, and so on and so on almost to infinity. Yet none of these desiderata, constraints, controls, restrictions, all of which certainly have to be measured and monitored, is what the bus service is *for*, which is, I presume, to get people from A to B. This is what this book is about—measuring *corporate* objectives, not measuring everything that may be of interest to society.

A turning point

I believe a revolutionary concept is unfolding here. We have PIs, which are used by operational managers to measure parts of organizations. We have CPIs which measure the performance of corporate wholes for use by top managers. But 'profit' also measures something else: it informs the shareholders how much return they will receive on their capital. The shifts in emphasis that I am noting here, from (1) measuring the performance of parts of an organization, of its operations and activities for middle managers, to (2) measuring the entire organization so that the top managers can plan and control it as a corporate whole, and from there to take the further leap to (3) measuring the *output of benefit to the beneficiaries*, is absolutely revolutionary. We will see later how it turns the world of traditional management upside down.

These distinctions are pivotal in breaking away from the old methods of judging organizations to the new, quantitative, beneficiaries-centred one—as opposed to management-centred ones—that is the hallmark of the beneficiary doctrine. Later, I even want to devise a CPI that will allow us to evaluate whether each *individual* beneficiary has received a fair share of benefit!

Look at the annual reports of any NPO. What you will see is a bewildering mass of PIs. What you will not see is a CPI. Thus the annual report of the children's charity Barnardo's (one of the most professional NPOs in Britain) is full of the number of children it helped the previous year—but that is a PI; only the managers are interested in this. The children (the beneficiaries) do not care a fig how many other children have been helped. The report gives no inkling of how much good they did any or all these children—that would be a CPI, measuring what the *children* want, what Barnardo's is *for*, and it is entirely missing. Look at the Automobile Association's report: it is full of figures, the number of members, the number of rescue vehicles, the number of members assisted at the roadside—all PIs, and all about what it does, not what it is for, what the managers are keen to hear, not what the members want. Who cares how many rescue vans the AA employs as long as they get to *me* quickly?

Study the Home Office report on prisons: page after page of PIs, the number of the various category of prisoner, costs, suicides, educational facilities; not a word about whether prison did them any good. Why all these PIs? Because these describe the organization's activities and operations, and this is what the managers are interested in, and it is the managers who write the reports. Concerning what the beneficiaries want: *silence*. In complete and total contrast, company reports show profits—and that *is* what the beneficiaries want to know. That is what companies are for.

PIs and CPIs

Let me repeat this ascending sequence. PIs measure the efficiencies of parts for middle managers; they are published in their thousands. CPIs measure the performance of the corporate whole for top managers *and* they measure the benefit to beneficiaries; but these are seldom remarked in NPOs. I want organizations to become obsessed with CPIs, to go to the ends of the earth to measure what they are doing for their intended beneficiaries. What they are for, not what they do.

In spite of the fact that 'profit' is quite plainly a single indicator, and equally plainly measures, the corporate performance of a company to a degree of accuracy that satisfies most people most of the time, all the textbooks state categorically that an organization's corporate performance can only be measured by the use of half a dozen indicators. I noted a particular example of this belief in Chapter 1 where I mentioned that Northtown College was judged by its local education authority by means of no less than nine indicators—but this view is common throughout the literature as I have just noted.

Two related misconceptions seem widespread: that you can fashion a CPI by adding together a number of PIs, and that you can judge the performance of a corporate body by means of a battery of PIs.

But you cannot construct a CPI by adding up a number of PIs. It is perfectly clear that you cannot do this with companies: add sales per region to tons produced per day to the gearing ratio and you just get gibberish. They just do not add up. It is apples and plums. And you cannot measure a town by adding the crime rate to the traffic flows at rush-hour to the 'street-litter index' and dividing by the square root of the area of parks and open spaces. Furthermore, this procedure will certainly omit many of the non-quantifiables: what about, say, the accessibility of the arts of the citizens of this town? If this cannot be measured, and I do not think it can, then it cannot be included in the index for the town. We resolved above not to adopt any means of measuring performance that excludes these essential intangibles.

Neither collectively nor singly

Not only can you not add these PIs together to form an index, but you cannot use them separately, as a battery, either. Suppose Northtown's score is 20,

30, 40, 50 (on a scale of 100) for swimming pools, traffic flows, crime rate and open spaces respectively, and suppose Southtown scores 50, 40, 30, 20. Which is the best town? You do not know because you cannot weight these items. It is apples and plums again. By the way, I forgot to tell you that Northtown's unemployment rate is 3 per cent and Southtown's is 11 per cent—how do you include that? No amount of juggling with any number of PIs will tell us *about the town*; what we need is a CPI for the town as a whole, not PIs for facets and aspects of it.

The NHS uses 400 PIs to measure the performance of each of its hospitals. But not even 400 PIs can tell us how any one hospital, as a corporate whole, is performing; all they can do (and this is what they were originally designed to do) is to tell managers about parts or sections of the hospital, such as how many kidney operations were performed this year compared with last, or how many beds per nurse there were last week. It will not tell them how effective their hospital is compared with another hospital (especially if it provides a different mix of services), nor with itself in a previous period, unless the mix has remained the same, which, in this changing world, it is unlikely to do.

These PIs may be vital for the sectional managers—indeed they *will* be vital to them—but to the top managers of the hospital itself they say nothing unless we can weight them, and we cannot do that with nurses and kidneys any more than with apples and plums. Notice, too, that to the beneficiaries—patients in this case—all these PIs relating to nurses and kidneys are devoid of any meaning or value whatever; yet that is exactly what we are looking for—a measure of performance that means something to *them*; a CPI, not a mass of PIs that just 'blind them with science'.

1 + 128 = 27!

Diverse fatuous attempts to use batteries or handfuls of PIs as a CPI continue daily all across the world. I have just seen a typical 'league table' which claims to rank 200 of Europe's top companies according to their 'efficiency'. But instead of being content with one indicator the authors have to be clever and use three, namely, margin (profit as a percentage of turnover), return on capital (profit as a percentage of capital) and added-value per employee as calculated from their latest annual reports. The company with the highest score in each of these three categories scores one, the second scores two and so on; add these three rankings together and the company with the lowest total comes top of the league. So here is another typical attempt to form a CPI by adding up a number of PIs. In this example margin, return and added-value are all given equal value (an equation devised by a financial idiot, in my view, but that is another, rather technical, story springing from the fact that return on capital is, surely, of vastly greater weight than the other two measures).

You can judge what nonsense these calculations generate when you note that the company which comes 27th overall came *128th* for margin and *1st* for return on capital! How anyone could have an ounce of confidence in a scoring system that yields such a discrepancy is beyond me. Adding apples and plums has always generated gibberish and not even P-E International, one of the world's best known management consulting firms, who devised this chimera, can alter this comprehensively established fact of life. (And all this ignores the other moronic aspect of this league table: that it invites us to judge these huge global companies on one year's performance!) Professor Altman's Z-scores, Professor Reinhart Schmidt's RSW, and all similar devices which rely on summing PIs, however ingenious and however valuable as indicators of partial knowledge they may be, are entirely useless as *CPIs*.

A similar battery is used by Paul Cheshire [1990] to rank Europe's cities where he uses four criteria: income per head; unemployment; hotel bedrooms; and migration. The first three measure the standard of living in the cities, which is fine. But how relevant is migration? What if it is deliberate policy to move people out of major city centres as it has been in Britain where, over the past five decades, the population of inner London has fallen by one-third? Sure enough, London comes 74th out of the 117 cities in his list. I simply marvel at the gall some experts have in proposing such monstrosities (and see page 157, this time for similar balderdash from the United Nations).

Not the sum of its parts

So, part of the problem we have in this chapter is that people have just not understood the distinction I am now making between the functions of PIs and CPIs. The literature is full of repeated attempts to persuade a battery of PIs to behave like a CPI. All are doomed to be a waste of everybody's time. We need to measure the performance of an organization as a corporate whole, not as a sum of its parts.

And here is the contrary myth. It is said that a CPI will break down into PIs. Profit, for instance, may be used as a CPI for a company and can then be 'allocated' as a PI for each subsidiary or profit centre. This is so in the case of profit (although, as noted above for boiler houses and dispatch departments, it becomes increasingly meaningless as more and more notional 'overheads' have to be 'allocated' as one moves down the operational hierarchy). But just as you cannot sum PIs to generate a CPI so most CPIs *cannot* be broken down and devolved. Earnings per share (EpS) cannot, for example, nor can 'market capitalization' or 'share price' or 'shareholder value', all of which are even more effective CPIs for companies than are profits, as we will learn in Chapter 7. It is worth emphasizing this: the most significant CPI for companies, EpS, *cannot* be broken down into PIs, and no permutation of operational PIs can be reconstituted into EpS.

One reason that the sum of a set of PIs does not equal the CPI is because the sum of the parts of an organization are not equal to the whole (as I keep saying, what an organization *does* is not what it is *for*). Thus the overall, national, effect of an organization that operates in, say, 10 regions is not the sum of the work of those 10 units; it might be less than this (if head office is just a useless cost, which, let us face it, some head offices are), or it might be far more than the sum of the parts if head office exerts a substantial extra influence of its own on, say, central government policy. By the same token the aims of a subsidiary are not always the same as those of its parent organization; thus while all the subsidiaries of a profitmaking company are also profitmaking, it may also contain a number of cost centres which makes the simple summation of PIs into CPIs impossible. Many charities own some profitmaking subsidiaries alongside their spending departments, which makes it impossible to add the parts for them too.

Efficiency

While it must be right for managers to be obsessed with the efficiency of the operations in their charge and with the PIs that measure it, we are here interested neither in managers nor in efficiency. In many cases we do not know how efficient any given organization may be (is the Salvation Army efficient? The British Museum? I do not even know what it means). No doubt we could calculate whether their individual operations or activities are efficient; but how can we tell if the organization itself is? Often it does not even matter.

PIs have been used by managers to plan and control their operations for decades, centuries even. Because of this they have always been readily available in even the most non-numerate NPOs. But using a figure just because it is available is like the person who drops a coin in the dark but looks for it under the nearest lamp-post. Using the wrong figure, just because it happens to be available, is an act of desperation; 'lamp-post data' is useless. Unfortunately it is also self-perpetuating; if you start using new figures (however much more relevant they may be) you promptly lose both the historical continuity of the old series and comparability with those organizations still using the old ones—two fearful practical penalties. And so another part of our problem is that the relevant data by which to judge corporate performance are not normally available in NPOs and, as we will see later, the cost of obtaining such data is substantial.

One type of lamp-post figure is called a 'proxy'; these are figures which, while not measuring exactly what the organization is aiming to do, are believed to approximate to this and at the same time are either available or are readily measured. Exam results are used to judge schools and colleges; but do exam results truly reflect how students get on in life after school? The

71

one is much easier to measure than the other but 'proxy-drift' is a very real defect over the long time periods we are discussing here. I do not want to rely on proxies; they are just not good enough for the beneficiary doctrine. I want to measure the real thing. The trouble with the real thing, though, is that it may take many years to reveal itself, and in such cases proxies are legitimate if, but only if, they have proven predictive accuracy. Most do not.

Summary

The belief that organizations must be given a number of targets (which parallels the belief that they are multi-purpose) is both false and damaging. Performance indicators (PIs) cannot be employed as corporate performance indicators (CPIs) because the whole is never the sum of the parts. A special tool is required to measure the whole.

Of course, all this assumes that measurement of corporate performance is necessary; the view that it is not—and, anyhow, that it cannot be done—is just another spoiler. It can be done, indeed it must be, but it is difficult and expensive, and great care must be taken with the design of the CPI, not least to ensure that all the intangibles are included in its sweep.

What we are interested in in this book is not efficiency, not value for money or any of the other factors that managers need to measure, but in the yield of benefits to the beneficiaries—quite different and distinct, certainly meriting its own technology.

CHAPTER SIX

The target sequence

In the previous chapter I began to establish that, just as multi-purpose organizations are unacceptable today, so multiple performance indicators are impractical as *corporate* performance indicators.

In this chapter I shall first show that single CPIs are not only a viable concept but also essential. Then I shall review further requirements of these indicators and finally we will find what we have been waiting so long for—a device for setting targets for organizations as corporate wholes.

The single CPI

Just as the beneficiary doctrine demands that no organization should ever attempt to serve more than one beneficiary, so it requires the use of just one CPI to measure corporate performance. Remember again: I want to lift NPOs to the standards companies use and, as will be seen in detail in Chapter 7, they use just one overall measure. It is this fact that largely accounts for the reputation that companies have as the most effective form of human organization in the modern world.

But what about those who say 'most organizations are not simple; it is naïve to expect a single unequivocal measure to reflect the performance of the City of Birmingham, say, or the Church of England'. I reply that companies are complex too—some far more so than some NPOs—and profits work very well for them, regardless of their complexity. I would add, 'I am sure your organization is very complex; but are you sure its *aims* are? Frankly, if you think your NPO has multifarious aims I wonder if it has lost its way.'

There is one thing a single CPI cannot do: it cannot faithfully reflect the views of more than one beneficiary. Take Southtown College again. It serves (1) school-leavers who need to pass exams to obtain skilled jobs, and (2) mature students, and adults who merely wish to learn for their own personal, usually non-vocational, satisfaction ('leisure learning'). How do we combine these two very different benefits to these two very different beneficiaries? Do we ask each of them whether they were 'satisfied' and maybe add up all the yeses and subtract the noes? Surely not.

In any case, because it is subjective, the indicator would be distorted by such trivia as whether the students liked the teachers. Or they may just give the answer they think the interviewer wants—a phenomenon so common with opinion surveys that many are rendered useless (you can tell at once whether a survey on salaries, say, has been commissioned by the left-wing Low Pay Unit or the right-wing Institute of Directors). Besides, the whole idea is to lift the CPI technology as applied to NPOs to the same level as for companies, and no one judges the performance of a company by going round asking the shareholders if they are satisfied; we do not need to because we, they, everyone, can see from the profit figures how well they have done compared with alternative investments. It is objective, unarguable, impartial, unbiased.

Two into one will not go

It is logically impossible to devise a single CPI that reflects the benefits to two different beneficiaries precisely because they are different. And this reveals an important point: so long as an organization has not quantified its performance it can get away with pretending that it can satisfy two disparate beneficiaries (such as some of those I noted on page 49). As soon as it attempts to quantify, behold! the deception is revealed. As I said before, if the target sequence cannot be completed it almost certainly means that the corporate purpose has not been correctly identified. The act of quantification will disclose all such defects, in this case that having two beneficiaries is illegitimate.

If we cannot use one CPI to amalgamate the views of two different beneficiaries what about using two CPIs, one for each? OK, let us try it. Assume that Southtown College scores 50 for the adults (on a scale of 100 for satisfactions or whatever other criterion you like to choose) and 70 for the youngsters. Imagine that the nearby Northtown College scores 70 and 50 respectively. Which is best? Or suppose Eastville College scores 30 and 80 this year and 40 and 70 last year—has it improved? The reason you do not know is that there is no way to trade off the adults' score against the youngsters'. Clearly the latter are more important—their whole future careers depend on what they learn at this college—but how much more? Twice? A hundredfold?

No, using two CPIs actually *precludes* comparison of one organization with any of its competitors or comparators—an essential thing to do in the modern world—and it even prevents comparison with itself at a different period of time. I see the use of two CPIs, like the attempt to satisfy two different beneficiaries, as just another spoiler. The single, homogeneous beneficiary is a necessary condition for establishing a single-figure CPI. If an organization believes it needs more than one CPI, then it has, quite simply, got its corporate objectives wrong. Just as investors need to decide whether to expand this company or that one, and can do so by comparing their profit figures, so society needs to know which of its organizations to expand and which to contract. To do that we require a single CPI.

The single CPI and management

But there is another equally cogent reason for selecting just one CPI. A single CPI is essential also for the proper management of any organization. This is because organizations prosper or decline by decision-steps: ICI grows by undertaking projects such as building a new factory in Estonia, introducing a new high-density plastic in Australia, closing down its offices in Uganda. All organizations do this: the Samaritans grow by opening or closing new branches and new services, and so on, universally. Project appraisal, then, is a crucial element in the management of organizations: adopt a few large misguided projects and your organization will decline, get them right and it will flourish. But a project is not just a major once-for-all decision that hits the headlines; every decision, however small and routine, is a project in the sense that it is a new or renewed activity. The current performance of every organization *is* the cumulative sum of all its manager's past decisions, large or small.

Now a single CPI allows projects to be appraised, that is, it allows the managers to choose rationally between alternative decisions. Let us do it. Imagine two projects being considered by ICI which both cost £100m; one (A) shows a profit of £20m, the other (B) £15m. Which do you choose? Not very difficult was it! (I did, of course, spare you the usual complexities of these exercises, such as risk analysis, hurdle rates, discounting, technological obsolescence, sensitivity analysis, market forecasting and so on.) So, a single-criterion decision is easy, at least in principle, you just compare the single figure on the bottom line.

Now try the same projects with *two* criteria; imagine you are told that, in addition to profits, ICI must also take account of the effect of these projects on local unemployment. Assume that Project A provides employment for 100 people while B employs 110. *Now* which do you choose? You have no idea, you are lost—unless you can somehow equate the employment of those 10 extra people with ICI's profits. I do not know how to do this. Of course, there is an equation; ICI might say to itself, 'if we employ an extra 10 people this will so delight the local community that it will be the £5m profit we lose on Project B—so we will adopt Project B'. But this just proves the point I was making because what we have now done is to whittle the two criteria, ICI's profits and local employment, down to just one: ICI's profit (and the trade-off was entirely arbitrary, was it not?).

Study a manager in a company; every decision taken is prefaced by the question, 'which would improve our profits most—decision A or decision B?' Every decision (provided it is ethical, see Chapter 14) is tested against this single criterion. This urgent simplicity is not available to most NPOs and that is why project appraisal—the evaluation of management decisions large or small—in NPOs is so controversial and why they so often have to be taken on non-rational grounds (I nearly said irrational).

I turn now to yet more reasons for employing a single CPI. (And if all this is not enough, you will see in the next chapter how two CPIs are inevitably mathematically incompatible and are unusable for this reason as well as all the ones reviewed here.)

Further requirements of the CPI

What do you think of a company which made a profit last year of $8m? You have no idea. You need to know at least one other figure before you can even begin to form an opinion. So let me tell you that its profit the year before was $10m—profits have dropped 20 per cent. Now what do you think? But you still do not know because, as it happens, all the other companies in the same sector of business dropped 30 per cent in the same period—so, contrary to your first impression, its performance was actually not too bad, surely?

A single performance statistic, then, on its own, is useless; even comparing one period with another for the same organization may be misleading; for a full revelation you must compare with other, similar organizations over several periods; we cannot judge Glasgow as a city unless we compare it with Edinburgh; London with Paris, Detroit with Los Angeles—and not just today; we need a film over several years, not a snapshot. And the more widely comparable the better. As noted above it is possible to compare every imaginable type of company—a British chemical company with an American computer company and a Japanese bank—an extraordinarily convincing thing to be able to do.

When we have developed the practice of using CPIs more fully we shall be able to compare a wide selection of NPOs too. First we will be able to compare like with like, then, later, with unlike. To do this we shall have to devise progressively more and more general measures so that, ultimately, all NPOs become comparable with all others and with companies as well. Clearly this means moving towards financial measures of benefit to the beneficiaries. (Many liberals, on hearing the proposal to use money as a measure of value immediately protest that money is no more than a symbol of profits and greed. I find this view utterly infuriating for it deprives us of the only universal unit of value society has yet been able to contrive. But we know why these embittered people hold this view, do we not? It is another spoiler; they will do anything to stop us measuring the performance of their organization.)

Comparability

Comparability is important for another reason. Many NPO managers claim that one reason their performance cannot be judged is that they have so little control over their environment. Thus the police explain that their activities are only one out of many factors that make up a movement in the crime statistics; hospitals contribute only partially to health in their community; schools vie with parents, neighbours, television, for their effect on children. But compare Manchester's crime with Liverpool's, Glasgow's health with Edinburgh's, and this argument is demolished because all these police forces, hospitals, whatever, experience the same lack of control over the very same (or closely comparable) exogenous variables. If crime is rising in London, no conclusions can be drawn; but if crime is rising faster in London than in Manchester, Birmingham, Edinburgh, Paris, Rome, Washington and Tokyo, well, one would need to ask some piercing questions of the London police. So, comparability is one further requirement in a CPI.

Another is validity over considerable periods of time. Most of the organizations we have in mind in this book are of such dimensions that they cannot be judged over periods of less than a few years or even decades. This means that any CPIs we devise must be capable of being corrected for the effects of inflation. It is wholly dishonest to claim 'profits are up by 8 per cent this year' when inflation is at 10 per cent. Profits are *not* up in this situation; they are *down*. It is no better than a lie to claim they are up. We are going to have to be able to quote performance figures in real terms, therefore. And CPIs must also allow for the effect of time on values (see 'discounting' in the next chapter).

Creative accounting

And, of course, a CPI must not be susceptible to manipulation. In fact managers of most organizations can, for a time, easily falsify their records: ask any accountant how simple it is for a company to employ creative accounting; it is very, very easy. However, it is *not* so easy to maintain a significant deception for more than a year or two. This is one reason why no one should ever expect to judge any organization's performance in less than a few years; you have to wait that long to see if the figures have been massaged. One of the reasons companies always appear to go bust *suddenly* is that, to conceal the coming disaster, the management will have been fiddling the profit figures for several years; eventually they reach the point where they can distort them no further and the dam of deceit bursts 'suddenly'. In truth no company *ever* goes bust suddenly. Every company that has ever gone bust, however proud and honourable, has fiddled its figures in the previous few years. (Even such an exceptionally prestigious company as Rolls Royce was not above capitalizing their research costs before collapsing in 1971 (Argenti, 1976).)

But notice this: because no CPI is ever completely accurate we need to check whether a company's earnings per share (EpS), say, has really moved as the company claims. How would an auditor or financial analyst do that? By examining a whole host of those financial ratios which go to make up EpS, such as profits, tax, interest on loans, depreciation, the number of shares in issue. But note the distinction here between flag-poles and guy-ropes; what we have is one flag-pole (EpS) supported by half a dozen guy-ropes (profits, tax, etc.) — we do not have half a dozen flag-poles. You cannot judge a company by the movement of any one of the above indicators, nor by any permutation of them, except EpS.

It is said 'you can prove anything with statistics'. Actually you cannot. You can prove anything by quoting second-level PIs as if they were top-level CPIs — some are bound to be up some of the time — but a properly designed CPI is unequivocal over any reasonable time-span.

We should, therefore, put our efforts into devising one effective indicator, rather than waste our time with a meaningless battery.

Strategy neutral

Yet another feature of the CPI is that it must be 'strategy neutral'. This means that a CPI must not, of itself, lead to the taking of any specific management action. Set a company the corporate aim 'increase market share' and this at once requires the management to increase market share — what else can they do? But suppose the logic of the company's strategic situation argues for *reducing* its market share, as is quite often the case (imagine a UK company deciding to move into continental Europe — its share of the UK market would, indeed should, decline), there would be a tussle between the top corporate aim and the strategy the managers may properly wish to pursue.

The corporate aim 'increase profits' is, on the other hand, strategy neutral; it demands the adoption of no specific strategy — indeed, it positively challenges the management to search for exciting new ways to increase profits. The first aim (market share) was in fact a *PI* and so led inexorably to a specific management action (PIs are for managers, remember); this second aim (profit) is a CPI and left the managers a free hand to devise whatever strategies best increase profits (one of which, of course, might well turn out to be to increase market share!). To set a corporate aim which pre-empts managers' choice may be a silly thing to do, yet it is extremely common (it is fair to say that *most* organizations do it).

Again, if you announce that you will judge a city by its population growth the management will act promptly to increase its population even if that ruins the quality of life in the city for its current inhabitants which, surely, is the real top aim, not growth of population. Again, if you pontificate that 'this charity exists to run residential homes for disturbed children', then that is what the management must do, even though running homes is only what the organization does, it is not what it is for. What it is for is to help these children and, had that statement not pre-empted them, the managers might have devised better ways, perhaps non-residential, to do this. The number of occasions where a PI has been promoted to the top slot, which I wish to reserve for CPIs, is legion; the damage this does is immense.

Tied up in knots

And the litany does not end there, for there is another problem related to strategic management and multiple targets. Suppose you set your company a return on capital target of 10 per cent—that is fine, it does not constrain the management in any way, they can confidently pursue any bright idea that looks like hitting it. But now you tell them that you also want turnover to rise by 15 per cent per annum. At once that pre-empts any strategies which lead to growth of less than 15 per cent—even if the managers have devised a superb new product which is expected to grow at only 10 per cent, but which will (because it costs less to produce, say) double return on capital to 20 per cent. Next you add yet another target: 'margins must not fall below 12 per cent', you tell them. And now you have ruled out another huge raft of products and strategies which will not fit your criteria but which might have given you an even better return than you asked for.

If you go on like that you will have set such a comprehensive package of targets to the management that they will be completely hog-tied and, frankly, you might as well do their job for them. Now, we are looking for a CPI that is strategy neutral; not only do double targets have strategic consequences, sometimes highly unexpected and undesirable ones, just imagine the strategic effects of setting multiple targets as some textbooks recommend and as Northtown College was told to (nine of them!). They tie the organization up in tight strategic knots; all the management is allowed to do is to maintain the company in its frozen strait-jacket of predetermined, arbitrarily selected, ratios. Not a good idea in a world of rapid change!

Finally, the CPI must be unequivocal—that is, when this figure improves this must unequivocally signify that the intended beneficiaries have received more benefit. Do you recall, for example, the student/staff ratio used by Northtown College in Chapter 1? We saw there that this indicator could move *up* although the students were being *less* well served, and vice versa. This ratio was not unequivocal, then, and is useless for measuring the delivery of benefit. Patients per bed is similarly useless as a measure of a hospital's performance to its beneficiaries; indeed, patients are often better served by non-residential treatment (day surgery for instance), which involves no beds at all! Very few CPIs are unequivocal;

the search to find just the one that is right for each organization is long and hard.

Summary of the CPI criteria

To answer question 3 in the target sequence, 'How do you measure this *with figures?*', each organization needs to devise a CPI which displays all these features:

1 It must measure the extent of the benefit delivered by the organization to the intended beneficiaries as a class or, better still, individually. It should be entirely distinct from all PIs which measure departmental, sectional and personal performance and efficiencies. A CPI measures what the intended beneficiaries get, while PIs measure what managers do. The CPI is the indicator at the very top; it is as logically different from a PI as a flag-pole to its guys.

2 Only one CPI is ever required. If more than one is being used that simply means the corporate purpose has not been correctly identified and this will render modern management inoperable. It is never possible to trade off one CPI against another in the same organization, so using two CPIs is ruled out for this reason, too. Moreover, two CPIs are often mathematically incompatible.

3 No set, or battery or index composed of PIs can be used as a CPI. No sum of any PIs can be used as a CPI. Conversely, a CPI will not always break down into a set of PIs.

4 It must make comparison possible with other similar, or even dissimilar, organizations. Its use over long periods of time is normal. It must be unequivocal. It must be strategy neutral. It must not be capable of manipulation. It must embrace the non-quantifiables.

This is a complex and difficult specification. But at last we have defined the tool by which targets may be set for organizations as corporate wholes.

Setting targets

In Chapter 4 we learnt how to identify the intended beneficiaries and how to define what we are trying to do for them; we now know what the CPI, by which to measure the volume of this benefit, is going to look like. Now we come to the step in the purpose sequence where we set the targets for the organization. This is question 4: 'What level of performance do the beneficiaries consider satisfactory, and, even more important, what level would they say is unsatisfactory?'.

People suffer from at least three delusions about targets. The first is that they do not set their aims far enough ahead. I hope it is clear throughout this book that I am talking about the most fundamental and longest range of all possible targets—the performance of an organization *as a corporate whole*. This is the target which reflects the way it is attaining its very *raison d'être* so it is certain that, for any socially significant organization (and for any which take themselves seriously) a horizon of less than several years would be quite inadequate. We are talking of organizations which may already be a century old and expect to live for decades or centuries more; anything less than five years is a barely significant time-span in which to appraise their performance.

In passing: by what manner of madness did the UK government set the top targets to British Rail—a huge organization even by world standards—one year at a time? Only in 1989 did they hand them three-year targets! The level of understanding displayed in this target-setting area really is abysmal, especially among governments. It is said that some of the more successful Japanese companies, with global domination in mind, set their aims decades ahead. (We are becoming used to these huge time-spans: some environmentalists are now asking for CO_2 targets into the twenty-fourth century.)

And remember this: the shorter the span we use the more likely we are to be setting standards of operational performance rather than corporate performance; if you are interested in *that* then you are reading the wrong book—you need one on management, not on governance. Long-term CPIs, please, not fly-by-night, ephemeral, PIs.

A target is what you want

Secondly, when anyone suggests that a five-year target be set, people throw up their hands in horror and declare, 'I cannot see that far ahead'. But I am not asking for a forecast, I am asking for a target. A target is what you want, a forecast is what you expect. So I am not asking, 'How well do you expect your organization to perform over the next five years?', I am sure you do not know that. I am asking, 'How well would you *like it to* perform over the next five years?'. Targets and forecasts are quite different. (This distinction between targets and forecasts is disregarded in business plans and budgets—one of their major defects.)

When President Kennedy invited NASA to 'put a man on the moon and bring him safely back within the decade' no one had the slightest idea how this was to be achieved. The very purpose of setting an ambitious target like this is to challenge the management to new and daring thought and deed. More than that, this is the very nub and centre of what management is—management *is* 'achieving targets'. To set a target that everyone knows can be achieved (that is, one that is equal to the forecast) is an insult to any manager worth his or her salary.

But be careful, for here is the third trap! In ordinary life, in ordinary down-to-earth, everyday, organizations, you have to be very careful indeed when setting targets at highly ambitious levels. It is not only the very obvious concomitants of overweening ambition—ruthlessness and dishonesty—that we need to guard against, it is also that if you set them too high you run the risk of being seen, perhaps very publicly, of missing your aim, with extremely regrettable effects on morale. One such target, set in all serious-ness for a small company (called Atlantic Acceptance (Argenti, 1976)) many years ago always sticks in my memory: 'Overtake General Motors!'. Of course, they went bust a couple of years later—a well-deserved and pre-dictable nemesis for their hubris. Did not Khrushchev set Russia the goal of overtaking the American standard of living with the boast, 'we will bury you'?

So, if it is dangerous to set ambitious targets, should we set unambitious ones? That is not a very attractive idea, is it? Over the past 20 years I have developed a technique which has met with almost universal approval. It involves setting targets at two levels, not one.

Tmin

First, in order to get its feet firmly on the ground, every organization should ask itself what level of performance over, say, the next five years, would be unacceptably poor. I call this 'Tmin'—the 'minimum acceptable target'—a level below which the intended beneficiaries would consider dismissing the chief executive and perhaps even start discussing the disposal or closure of the organization.

This, clearly, is a level of performance that everyone agrees is to be avoided. Notice that Tmin is not failure: it is somewhat prior to that, it is a warning of failure to come if that level is maintained for another few years. It is the point at which the intended beneficiaries should begin to express serious dissatisfaction with the long-term performance of their organization; where the senior managers themselves begin to feel embarrassed by their lack of achievement; where it dawns on everyone that drastic corrective action must be taken—action far beyond the routine run of strategy formula-tion. It is where it becomes clear that things are going badly wrong, where anxiety begins to be felt for its long-term viability. Tmin represents the performance of a poorly managed organization. It is 'significantly below average' compared with suitable comparators.

The concept of Tmin is extremely powerful. I believe that, if some of our national organizations had, explicitly and publicly, established their Tmins a few decades ago, it would have alerted them to the need to make some drastic change of strategic direction. I am thinking of such abysmal trage-dies as the performance of the British economy in the seventies, of the Church of England in the past few decades, of our inner cities, of our prisons (indeed the entire British system of criminal justice). Each of these, in my view, disappeared below any imaginable Tmin many years ago, but, because no Tmin had actually been determined, let alone published, the management were able to pretend that nothing was seriously amiss and that no painful action was required. Had a company performed to these atro-cious levels, board-level mayhem would have occurred long before—years before, even decades before—such parlous depths had been plumbed.

Would it not have been a simple matter to have set a target for the Equal Opportunities Commission, for example, in terms of women's pay catching up with men's? Is it really so hard to think of a suitable target for the High Court? Do the people of Northtown really not know how bad the crime rate has to become in their town before they sack their chief constable?

I believe there is a natural Tmin for every organization that has ever existed and, provided they face up to reality, everyone concerned knows perfectly well what it is. Moreover, they know this *now*; it is never necessary to wait until performance has sunk to Tmin and then start expressing concern at how bad things have become. Indeed, we know on the day the organization is founded what level of performance would be unacceptably poor. What we do not do is to state this openly. We should have the guts to do so.

Tsat

Having placed this essential 'floor' under the performance of an organi-zation it is then desirable to set the second of the two targets, the one I call 'Tsat'—the level of performance which the intended beneficiaries would consider satisfactory, the level at which they might make further awards or bonuses to the management, or consider a major expansion in the range of activities or duties of the organization. It is the performance of a well-managed organization. It is significantly above average.

To ask for targets to be set at two levels may be thought to be excessive. But in fact, and this is another feature of this subject area that seems to have been ignored, no individual ever has a single target. All targets are just selected bands on a continuous range of ambitions that all of us feel for ourselves, our family or our organizations. Think about your own ambitions; you will not have set yourself a single aim for any of your important dreams. For your job, for example, you will have said, 'I hope to earn $100 000 per annum by the time I am 40—and would it not be awful if I was still only earning $30 000 by the time I retired?', or whatever.

Two targets. A bracket with a lower and an upper boundary. Whenever you look forward to anything you know instinctively what are your hopes *and* fears—your Tsat and Tmin. To employ a single figure in any target-setting exercise is an outrage against all that we know about human desires, aspirations and ambitions in the real world.

Tmin and Tsat represent points significantly above and significantly below average; no one ever aims to be average. These two are by far the most important locations in a range of possible outcomes. Others might be 'Tfan' (fantastic, challenging, amazing) and 'Tmax' (maximum, uppermost, top limit). I would like to warn against setting Tfan; organizations which actually achieve a fantastic performance (or 'excellence', come to that) are, by definition, extremely rare. My guess is that these levels of achievement are only obtained by organizations headed by those extraordinary human beings who provide vision and leadership far beyond the norm. I very much doubt if Tfan is attainable by mere teams of mortals under a 'first among equals' chief executive of the sort for whom this book is mainly written. Alas, ordinary mortals who attempt Tfan all too often go up like a rocket and down like the stick.

Moreover, let us not forget one of the central themes of the beneficiary doctrine: that while all organizations should constantly strive for a better performance, this should never be at the expense of other people. The more ambitious we are the more likely are we (as individuals and as organizations) to transgress the norms of decent behaviour. And note this too, most books on management urge managers to strive for massive improvements in performance—'The Thrusting Manager' and 'Selling Your Grandmother' —all that self-important claptrap. But what matters to the more responsible organization is not brilliant success, but a sober, long-term regular, reliable, *satisfactory* performance, one that is comfortably above average. This is *far* more valuable to its beneficiaries than the shooting star which then burns out to the utter, bitter, despair of all concerned.

It is a central theme in this book, then, that we must not thoughtlessly importune organizations to go for Tfan (remember who won the race in the fable of the tortoise and the hare?). On the other hand, those few which are capable of achieving it, without infringing decent ethical standards, should certainly not be dissuaded from it.

Performance envelope

Turning to Tmax, it is sometimes appropriate to identify the point where a strong performance might actually represent a threat to the organization— such as when, in a socialist society, a too-profitable bank might be sequestered, or when, in any society, an organization exploits a monopoly position. Or, as in the seventies, certain British trade unions were so 'successful' that they threatened the stability of the nation itself and had to be brought down (an event from which, I suspect, they will never recover). Occasionally, then, one needs to identify Tmax in order to avoid it.

Apart from the simple imperative of realism, there is a second, technical reason for setting two targets. I have suggested that we do not look kindly on organizations, especially those with heavy social responsibilities, which let us down. So what every such organization requires is a set of strategies which not only takes them to success, but which also protects them from disgrace: a two-dimensional set of strategies. I would suggest that, for the socially significant organizations for which this book is intended, avoiding disgrace is arguably more essential than achieving success, and that a disgrace-avoiding strategy is an essential shot in their locker.

Setting Tmin and Tsat shows an organization's management what is the 'performance envelope' within which their strategies must deliver. Typically in this absurdly neglected area, most organizations still set themselves one single, wildly ambitious target, and then wonder why they miss it, some-times disastrously.

Dynamic growth

As will be seen when we set targets for companies and for NPOs in the next few chapters, targets should also be dynamic—they should call for higher standards of performance every year. One of the distinguishing marks of companies is the way they mount deliberate, long-term, quantified attacks on productivity in which they aim to improve output per resource sys-tematically each year by a specified amount (so routine is this concept that it is often known by the initials 'PI' for profit improvement). Few NPOs do this. Some even claim that it is not possible to improve productivity 'because we are a service organization'. But medicine is a service industry and look at the miracles of productivity that have arisen there in recent years (keyhole surgery, for example).

I believe that most organizations will see 'annual growth of benefit to beneficiaries' as the primary criterion of success (note well: growth of *benefit*, not *physical* growth, see page 172). Moreover, Tmin and Tsat growth targets almost set themselves: Tmin is a rate of growth that is barely perceptible; in other words, an organization which yields benefits that are not perceptibly higher this year than last, and the year before that, might well be deemed to be falling below Tmin.

Now, because the performance of most organizations varies greatly over the years, and even during each year, the rate of growth that Tmin repre-sents must be at least sufficient to be observed through these normal vicissitudes; one must be able to detect the 'signal' through the 'noise'. Performance must be sufficiently evident for the beneficiaries to perceive a statistically significant trend-line within a reasonable period of time, typi-cally two or three years. If they cannot tell if there has been a significant improvement in their benefits over such a period then, I suggest, if you cannot see it, it is not there, and one may conclude that the organization is performing so poorly that the chief executive should at least be given an official warning.

Tsat, on the other hand, will often be associated with a performance that is 'significantly above the average comparator', and the notion of 'being in the upper quartile' is frequently mentioned. Sometimes the words 'at a sustainable rate over a period of many years' is employed to qualify any given growth target.

Static and dynamic targets

Notice, then, that targets may be set in two formats (and I shall later describe a third):

1 An organization may compare itself with its comparators or competitors using a CPI that is recognized among its peers as relevant (health indicators among hospitals, say, or exam results between schools) and in this context Tmin would be 'below the average of its comparators' while Tsat might be 'in the upper quartile'. So one might have, 'We aim to achieve a mortality rate of 10 per cent compared with the national average of 12'. But this approach has two limitations. This is a static criterion: it does not call for an annual improvement in performance. And it can only be used to compare one organization with another of the same type (hospitals with hospitals, schools with schools).

2 An organization can set a more dynamic target in terms of growth, or improvement, of the benefit it delivers to its intended beneficiaries. Thus Northtown Health Authority might set itself the task of 'continuously reducing mortality by x per cent each year'. In this format Tmin would be a rate that is barely perceptible, while a satisfactory rate, Tsat, would be one recognized by comparators as better than average or in the upper quartile. Again, however, one can only compare similar organizations; again, it is not possible, using these specialist indicators, to compare all types of organization as one can with companies—although you can compare their rate of improvement, which may be useful.

As a rule companies are enthusiastic supporters of the 'better every year' target, while NPOs tend to set the less aggressive static targets, partly because a dynamic one can only be monitored if the performance of one's own and comparable organizations is known for the past few years— something that most NPOs do not at present know because they do not have the relevant statistics. Setting targets for future performance can only follow the measuring of historic corporate performance and, even then, several years' records will be required to provide a stable basis for assessment.

Just a word about targets for project organizations: those which are formed to achieve a particular effect and, having attained it (or having become convinced that they cannot), then disband. Clearly 'growth of benefit' targets would not be appropriate here; instead, they will relate to the time-frame within which some specific aim is to be achieved or the extent to which it is attained. Thus, 'raise $50 000 by 1 July' might be Tmin for an appeals organization, while 'raise $100 000 by 1 May' is its Tsat. 'Win the election by a bare majority' would be Tmin, perhaps, for an election campaign committee, while 'win the election by 5000 votes' would be its Tsat.

While 'put a man on the moon ... ' would be a most appropriate and exciting example of a target for a project organization, it was actually handed to a permanent one (NASA) with, at first, amazing results but, please note, as soon as it was achieved the effect was thoroughly demotivating and disorientating. Unless one can devise a whole sequence of exciting steps to aim at, date/event targets are less relevant for permanent organizations. 'Better every year' targets for permanent organizations, date/event targets for project ones, seems a helpful rule.

Why bother with targets?

Why do we need to set targets at all? Because they tell us the scale of what we have to do. If a company is earning $100m profits this year its management knows that every year they will have to devise new products, or new projects, or cut costs, or *something*, to deliver first another $10m next year, say, then an extra $10m the year after, then $10m, and so on. An organization without a target is like someone strolling along the beach idly picking up pebbles—any pebble will do. An organization with a target is like a collector who knows exactly what to look for, recognizes when it is found and, very important surely, can even select the best places to look.

Moreover, setting performance targets can act as a surrogate to the 'free market' considered so essential by modern economists that they even devise artificial 'internal markets' to simulate the real thing. How might targets help here? Well, just as athletes can pace themselves against the clock—there does not have to be another competitor on the track—so professional managers can pace themselves against a properly set target. There does not have to be a competitor or a market, real or contrived. Now would not that be useful for monopoly situations?

Finally, I suspect that the old adage 'all objectives are subjective' is not correct. I am not convinced that there is no rational level at which to set targets for an organization, that the only grounds are purely personal preferences and opinions. I suspect that all organizations do have an innate Tmin, and perhaps a Tsat, that reflects very accurately indeed what that particular organization should be striving to achieve. Once target setting becomes widespread, I believe each type of organization will discover that norms for both Tmin and for Tsat will emerge (see page 103 where that occurs). Be that as it may, giving organizations a long-term target electrifies them; neglect this and they droop and doze.

Summary

This chapter contains the most controversial and, in practice, the most difficult, demand of the beneficiary doctrine: that every organization should employ a single, quantified, CPI.

How strange. Everyone else tries to set several targets at one level: I recommend setting one target at several levels, two to be precise, Tmin and Tsat, defined as follows:

1 **Tmin**: A level of performance below which the beneficiaries would consider dismissing the chief executive and perhaps, if it persists, disposing of, or closing down the organization. A performance below the average of comparators. A rate of real growth that is barely perceptible over a period of years. A performance that embarrasses the senior managers themselves. A performance that demands an exceptionally abrupt and brutal change in strategic direction.

2 **Tsat**: A level of performance at which the beneficiaries would express their satisfaction, would consider additional rewards to the management and might discuss a further expansion or diversification. A performance among the top quartile of comparators. A rate of real, sustainable, perceptible growth over a period of years.

I noted that Tfan, while thoroughly laudable and enviable when achieved without infringing the norms of decency, is not a sensible aim for socially responsible organizations: to achieve Tsat, and avoid Tmin, is all that is required to raise the general level of our national life very remarkably.

The consequences of being able to set sensible corporate targets to organizations will be immense. Setting a target, even at quite a reasonable level of ambition, electrifies managers—the modern manager is nothing if not a target-hitting warrior—and the impact on corporate effectiveness, even on the most arrogant of monopolies, will astound us all.

CHAPTER SEVEN

The purpose sequence for companies

In this chapter I propose to use the 'purpose sequence', described in the previous four chapters, to identify the corporate purpose for companies and to develop a set of targets for them. The reason for starting with companies before moving on to NPOs is that target setting is much more highly developed in the private sector; indeed, as I have explained, I believe that virtually the *sole* reason that companies appear to be so much more effective than most NPOs is that companies know how to set targets, not just for individual managers and departments, which NPOs are beginning to understand very well, but for their beneficiaries.

There may be a multitude of other differences between companies and NPOs but none of these, I believe, comes near this key distinction: that, over the past few decades, companies have learnt how to reflect single-mindedness in their corporate targets. It would be sensible, first, to study how they do this, and then aim to apply these methods to NPOs. I must not give the impression that all companies know how to do this, or that all of them actually do it, for they do not. I believe that those which do, even when this is rather informal, are more consistently successful than those that do not.

The corporate purpose for companies

I believe the corporate purpose of all companies is, 'to make a satisfactory return on the owners' capital', or words to that effect. This brief sentence clearly identifies the first two elements required by the purpose sequence:

● The intended beneficiaries are the owners (the shareholders)
● The intended benefit is a satisfactory return on their investment

Take a very simple example. John Finch might select this corporate purpose statement for his small family business:

Corporate purpose for John Finch Limited

The intended beneficiaries John and Mary Finch
The intended benefit Satisfactory return on our capital

In other words, the Finches will be content if the management (in this simple case it may be just John and his wife Mary) achieves a satisfactory return on their capital. Exactly how much this should be will, of course, be the subject of discussion below when we come to the target sequence.

Now, because John and Mary Finch are the sole beneficiaries they can vary any of these statements whenever they like; they are the sole arbiters. They could, if they wish, add their daughter to the list of beneficiaries, and then an extra benefit might be '... and a job for Jane in the company'. Or they could state, 'the company is to remain independent'. Or they could mandate 10 per cent of its profits to their favourite charity.

This is another example of the principle noted in Chapter 4 that the more homogeneous the beneficiaries are the more widely may the benefit be drawn without incurring trade-off disputes among them. But note this: while they may drop any of these other subsidiary aims, the one aim they will never abandon is that of making a long-term satisfactory profit. If they ever did that, John Finch Limited would cease to be a company.

Quoted companies

So that is the complete, and very simple, answer to this company's corporate purpose. Now let us move to the other end of the scale. Imagine a major publicly quoted company with millions of shareholders. It will no doubt express its purpose as follows:

Corporate purpose for Mallard Universal plc

The intended beneficiaries	All current shareholders
The intended benefit	Satisfactory return on their capital

In my view there is very little more to be said about a public company's corporate purpose— return on shareholder's capital is 'it'—period! I very much doubt if a quoted company can ever legitimately add any of the personal aims that private companies may select such as 'remain independent' or 'employ members of our family'. If they did so (and many do) the beneficiaries could quite lawfully complain that the resources of their organization were being perverted.

This is the appropriate moment to note that it is the governing directors, who represent the shareholders (see Chapter 16), who should be moving through the purpose sequence for their company, of course, not the managers.

Not just profits?

All that remains to do, having stated the purpose of both these companies in a couple of simple sentences, is to quantify them and to set targets, which I shall describe below.

I must pause long enough to note that not everyone agrees that 'satisfactory return on shareholders' capital' is the correct definition of corporate purpose for companies, nor that it is their sole *raison d'être*; many people, certainly most company chairmen in their public pronouncements, claim that companies work for their employees, their customers, indeed for the whole community, not just for their shareholders, but I reject this stakeholder theory in Chapter 13.

Others claim that aiming 'to increase market share' is the true aim of a company, as Japanese businesses are said to do. But Japanese companies are also said to aim for world domination and deliberately to set out to destroy their foreign competitors, and I cannot see these aims as being vastly more desirable and ethical than making profits for shareholders. In any case, for whose benefit are such triumphs of megalomania to be achieved? *Cui bono*? And if profit is not their aim how come Japanese shareholders received about 9 per cent on their capital over the past 30 years while American shareholders only had 7 per cent?

So now we must get on with questions 3 and 4 of the target sequence catechism: 'How do you measure this *with figures*?' and 'What level of performance do the beneficiaries consider satisfactory, and, even more important, what level would they say is unsatisfactory?'. (Question 5, 'What level of performance did you actually deliver to them over the past 5 or 10 years?' will be tackled in Chapter 16.)

I have commented before on the belief that selecting performance indicators for companies is uncomplicated—managers in NPOs constantly refer with envy to the ease with which this can apparently be done. But in fact there are severe technical difficulties here. The reason that companies are able to measure their performance with so much greater facility than NPOs is not that it is inherently or technically any easier, but that they have been searching for the correct solution to this conundrum for decades while, in general, NPOs have barely started.

Performance indicators for companies

To demonstrate the depth and severity of this struggle to find their ideal measure I propose to review the history of CPIs for companies over the past four or five decades because it contains the clues we need to solve many of the problems for NPOs that we are going to meet in the next four chapters.

Many decades ago most companies used volume, turnover or margin as their routine corporate indicators. Some of these are still in use as CPIs in some companies; right up to 1989, for instance, the government set 'margin' as the overall *corporate* target for the Post Office (they now use 'return on capital employed' (ROCE), a measure most major companies have also long since discarded. Gradually, however, most professionally run companies learnt to make the very detailed and complex calculations that allowed them to use the far more appropriate 'profit' as the CPI; in this they were greatly assisted by the assiduous efforts of the accounting profession to develop standard definitions and, of course, by the appearance of the computer.

The signal advantage of profit over volume, turnover, margin and any other similar second-level PI, is that it is unequivocal—when it rises the shareholders are pleased and vice versa—which is not the case with any of those PIs; when, for example, turnover rises the *managers* are pleased (especially the sales managers) but more turnover does not always mean more profit. For example, IBM is currently (1992) America's fourth largest company by turnover, 267th by return to shareholders.

Now, when managers switch from using these PIs to using profits in their decision-making calculations, they quickly discover that many of the decisions they had previously made have to be heavily revised and even reversed. It is not an exaggeration to say that their world is turned upside-down; products which had sold like hot cakes, and, judged by turnover were rated highly by the managers, are found to be actually making losses; whole departments are found to be redundant, or, on the contrary, products and departments which had been decried are found to be high-earning stars. (Naturally, give an organization the right corporate objective having previously given it the wrong one and you should expect some fireworks. And, of course, this shock therapy continues today—ask the managers of any recently privatized state corporation what effect it has had on their decision-making!) Even now many sales staff are still motivated by incentives linked to volume rather than to profit (or 'contribution').

Incompatible targets

Then the accounting profession began to standardize definitions not only of profit, but also of 'capital employed' thus making it possible to measure profitability or return on capital employed (ROCE). For a while, then, ROCE was gleefully adopted as the top company indicator before four snags emerged.

Firstly, because it does not measure growth, with which companies were becoming obsessed, ROCE had to be supplemented by a 'profits growth' target—two targets in harness with the consequent mathematical riddles that twin aims always generate. Imagine a governing board sets the company two targets: 10 per cent ROCE and 5 per cent per annum growth of profits. Now do the sums. Suppose the company employs £100m capital. Let its ROCE be 10 per cent so its profits will be £10m. Now imagine that tax takes £3m and dividends are set at £4m, the profit retained will be £3m, and consequently, next year the company's profits will grow by 3 per cent. No matter how loudly the chairman thumps the boardroom table, 10 per cent ROCE is mathematically compatible only with 3 per cent growth, not with 5 per cent. Of course he or she can halve the dividend—but was that the original intention when the target was set? I doubt it.

Further trouble with twins

Another problem occurs with double targets: you do not know which combination of results is best. Take two companies, the profits of one are growing at 10 per cent and its ROCE is 15 per cent, the other company is growing at 15 per cent and its ROCE is 10 per cent. Which is best? You have no idea, have you? We have seen it all before in the previous chapter in a different context; two CPIs do not work, cannot work. It has to be one. And did you notice my 'deliberate mistake'? Fifteen per cent growth is mathematically incompatible with 10 per cent ROCE, as we saw above.

I said that there were four problems with ROCE: the first was that you have to use it in conjunction with another target; the second is that it measures return on capital *employed*, an accountant's concept based on notional 'book values' which are not at all the same as *shareholders'* capital, that is, what their shares are worth in real coin of the realm. It is even possible for ROCE and ROSC (return on shareholders' capital), to move in opposite directions (in a property revaluation, for example, or a merger). Which is preferable, do you think? ROCE which measures book values or ROSC which measures shareholder value? It has to be ROSC—yet for *decades* companies used ROCE! Many, especially family businesses, still do (and subsidiaries have to, of course, which leads to the 'conglomerate accounting syndrome' as I call it, where group headquarters cannot compare the ROCEs of its various different subsidiaries simply because they are different. A 20 per cent ROCE for a hotel subsidiary may not compare with a 20 per cent ROCE for an engineering one, for example, a problem that also pesters NPOs as we shall see).

Earnings per share (EpS)

Third, 'profits' fails to take any account of tax, interest on loans and mergers—three critical features of company performance whose influence was becoming increasingly significant and which any modern management should unquestionably be judged upon. Now, a CPI with that number of defects has obviously outlived its usefulness, and about a decade ago attention began to shift to 'growth of earnings per share' (EpS) as the key indicator.

This meets many of the criteria for a CPI listed on page 80, in particular: (a) that it should be dynamic (growth of EpS calls for higher earnings every year); (b) that it should measure the benefit that *each beneficiary* receives (earnings *per share*, notice); (*c*) it is (almost) strategy neutral; (*d*) it is unequivocal; (*e*) it is readily comparable across the entire world for every type of company; (*f*) it is very difficult for managers to window-dress it for more than a couple of years running; (*g*) it may be used with discounting techniques (see below) which ROCE cannot; (*h*) it embraces all non-quantifiables; and (*i*) it correctly reflects the effects of take-over bids from the shareholders' point of view, not the managers'.

Growth of EpS is, moreover, a major force in determining the price of a company's shares (through the price earnings ratio). Plainly, EpS is a winner in the CPI stakes; no wonder that it is now in almost universal use by professional companies.

However, we are not there yet. What shareholders want even more than growth of EpS is growth in the value of their shares (which ROCE also does not measure—its fourth defect). Unfortunately, this is difficult to measure, and even more to predict, because although growth of EpS is the factor that most affects the value of a company's shares it is not the only one: which 'sector' of the market the company is deemed to be in is another; its cash flow; its exposure to risks; the 'quality' of its earnings; its 'break-up value'; the strength of its balance sheet; these are all important. Above all, violent stock-market gyrations can wipe a third of the value off the shares in a single day.

Progressively sophisticated

The very latest view is that perhaps share prices can, after all, be reliably measured by quoting share prices relative to a relevant stock-market index (or the relevant sector index). Or how about the 'free cash flow' method; or the rent method, where you deduct a notional rent on the company's assets before striking the 'profit' figure; or the economic value-added approach . . . .

I hope the above is quite sufficient to ensure that no one is left in any doubt whatever that the criterion of 'profits' is not foolproof. Contrary to the firm beliefs of almost every NPO manager I have ever met, by modern standards 'profits' is almost useless as a company CPI. I hope it is also clear that reaching even the present rough consensus on a more cogent CPI—growth of EpS—is still not the end of the voyage of discovery and that, even though this odyssey has already lasted for several decades, new and more sophisticated devices for measuring company performance are always being tried and tested. But at least companies know what it is they wish to measure; their battle now is to hone the method. By contrast, most NPOs do not yet know what they want to measure; most of them believe that, even if they knew what it was, it *cannot* be measured. There is a significant difference in belief here, is there not? Companies say, we know what we want to measure; we will try to do it better. NPOs say we do not know what we want to measure and anyhow it cannot be.

From PIs to CPIs

It is interesting that companies used PIs first, then graduated to the CPIs that managers found most useful (profit and ROCE, for instance) and then, finally and after many decades, to the CPIs that the *shareholders* wanted (EpS and ROSC). In all these cases, too, the indicators have become progressively more embracing: profits, the primal CPI, ignores tax and bank interest; earnings, another measure we briefly flirted with, includes these but misstates mergers; EpS includes these but ignores stock-market crashes; and, finally, ROSC includes everything, but is, of course, extremely difficult to calculate. In my view the path will be much the same for NPOs over the next two decades; they will soon move beyond PIs to find manager-based CPIs which will increasingly take account of more and more factors in an organization's performance until, at last, they reach a comprehensive CPI that measures everything including the intangibles. I shudder to think how long it will take, especially if, because of all those spoilers, they never start.

On this route are many pitfalls. I shall present a prize to any reader who can unravel the aims of the British Airports Authority (BAA) just before it was privatized a few years ago: 'to achieve on average a minimum rate of return on average net assets of 3 per cent plus one-fifth of the annual percentage growth in terminal passengers on a cumulative basis in each successive year'. Presumably some brilliant civil servant with an IQ of 300 solemnly sat down and devised this chimera; it was presented to the BAA management and they accepted it, nodding their heads sagely, in full agreement with its intrinsic wisdom, not daring to exclaim that they had not the faintest idea what it meant. The fancy that corporate objectives need to be incredibly sophisticated and convoluted is widespread.

(Did you notice that this example is the fourth entirely lunatic target set by a British government: the British Airports Authority, the Post Office (page 91), CMD 7131 (page 66) and British Rail (page 81). Oh dear! And another thing, the government demands a lower return on all its operations than does the private sector (did you notice the 3 per cent return for BAA?) thus offering a more sympathetic definition of 'success' to their own activities and guaranteeing priority allocation of society's hard-earned capital for their profligate schemes.)

Growth of EpS

And so the current standard CPI for the modern company is growth of EpS; it is applicable to every size and type, virtually without exception. Note that this CPI measures growth of EpS and not growth of *anything* else—it is not growth of sales turnover, growth of employee numbers, growth of market share, or number of products or floor area or, indeed, growth of anything physical at all. On the contrary, it is perfectly possible—and surely desirable (especially in view of the anxiety some people feel for the ability of this planet to sustain headlong physical growth)—for all of these actually to *decline* while EpS keeps rising. The key to this trick is, of course, productivity—one of the most powerful of all the corporate strategies open to managers to achieve more EpS.

The EpS of one of Britain's most successful companies, Sainsbury's, has grown by 15.6 per cent per annum in the past decade (in real terms), while turnover has only risen by 10.4 per cent—excellent news for everyone concerned for it suggests a quite remarkable attention to productivity. But let us not go overboard; Sainsbury's physical size *has* increased—indeed physical growth remains a key strategy for most companies. Some gurus claim that 'better not bigger' is a more attractive slogan for companies today. This is true: instead of producing more jet engines Rolls Royce should produce better engines—more power from each but cheaper, with less noise and less pollution. That is fine. But I imagine Rolls Royce would still very much like to produce *more* engines as well as better ones. Growth is still the Holy Grail to companies.

Let me repeat that EpS is a measure of the benefit that *each* individual beneficiary receives from a company—it is earnings *per share*. When we turn to NPOs in the next chapter we should try to emulate this remarkably personalized feature which so powerfully underscores the importance of delivering benefit to the *individual* beneficiaries of organizations—a philosophy right at the heart of the beneficiary doctrine; hence its name.

Moreover, although most company managers are obsessed by growth, the one thing they do not aim to do is to increase the number of shareholders. They aim to increase the earnings for each *existing* shareholder. (In stark contrast see what NPO managers do in Chapters 9 to 12.)

Three versions of PI

So momentous do I consider the difference between a CPI that tells top managers what they need to know, and one that tells the beneficiaries what they want to know, that I am, at the risk of confusing everyone by my terminology, going to call the former CPIs and the latter BPIs—beneficiaries' performance indicators. Both measure the overall, *corporate*, performance of organizations but the one tells the top managers what they need to know to plan and control the organization strategically, as a corporate whole, while the other tells the beneficiaries what the organization is doing *for them*. I hope it has now emerged with great clarity that ROCE is a CPI; ROSC is a BPI. Profits is a CPI; EpS is a BPI.

And I must return briefly to PIs. These are indicators which, you will recall, measure performance, especially efficiencies and so on for departments, functions, equipment, people—all the things that middle managers are interested in but which we, in this book, are not. I am going to rechristen them MPIs—managers' performance indicators.

To summarize these three terms:

Managers' performance indicators (MPI)

Used by managers to plan and control parts, sections, departments of organizations, and to measure activities and efficiencies of the people, equipment, operations, which they manage. For example, tons per day, sales per region, value for money, length of queue, complaints per customer, etc. MPIs tell managers how things are going in their part of an organization, but they cannot be summed, added together, or indexed to form a CPI or BPI.

Corporate performance indicators (CPI)

Used by top executives to plan and control their organization strategically as a corporate whole. For instance, profits, earnings, return on capital employed (ROCE), etc. The CPI tells top managers how things are going in their organization as a corporate body.

Beneficiaries' performance indicators (BPI)

Also measure the overall corporate performance of an organization but instead of measuring its operational efficiency as CPIs do, these measure the volume of benefit received by the intended beneficiaries. Note that, crucially, it should measure not only the aggregate benefit generated by an organisation as a whole but the benefit that each individual beneficiary receives (precisely what the beneficiary doctrine requires). BPIs are often of little use to top managers for planning and controlling the operations of their organization. Examples of BPIs are: earnings per share (EpS), share price and return on shareholders' capital (ROSC).

I now need to discuss the obsession that business managers have with 'growth', because I am going to suggest later that managers of NPOs should also be obsessed by something similar.

Growth

'If a business is not growing it is dying' is a typical modern cliché. In fact, although most managers and shareholders believe that growth *should* be the prime aim for businesses there really is no logical reason for its primacy.

After all, when you invest in fixed interest stocks, such as government bonds or 'gilts', you get no growth at all; if the coupon says 10 per cent and you buy £100 of it then all you get is a payment of £10 every year. It does not increase at all, and some of these ('long-dated gilts') run for 30 years, as flat as a pancake, or even (the 'undated') for ever! And why not? If you are happy with 10 per cent return why not take it as a constant 10, 10, 10 ...?

Essential or not, growth does seem to be a very satisfying ambition to the professional manager; as the company grows so does the manager's salary and status. Growth eases a number of management problems, such as career opportunities for employees, increased economies of size, greater 'clout' in the market-place, and so on. Shareholders, too, like the ever-escalating dividend and share values. Environmentalists do not like it, of course, and we must note here, emphatically, the massive distinction between growth of physical things like cars and chemicals or tons of steel, and growth of non-things like insurance, art, sport (and profits) which do not, so far as I know, damage the ozone layer.

Aarrog (average annual real rate of growth)

If long-term growth is to be such an important element in the setting of targets for companies, and perhaps NPOs as well, I need to describe two technical aspects of long-term target setting. I first need to introduce 'Aarrog', my shorthand for 'average annual real rate of growth'. I shall take care that all figures in this book are in real terms—that is, at 'constant prices'; all my growth rates are in 'beat inflation by' terms. 'Rate of growth' means compound, exponential growth, in per cent per annum, over a number of years, so Aarrog measures the average annual real rate of growth. You cannot calculate a meaningful Aarrog trend over less than a few years because, of course, profits, indeed most 'benefits', fluctuate from year to year. Everyone knows how widely these indicators vary over short periods of time (a year or two, say) yet, absurdly, we go on judging organizations by their annual results.

So the concept of average annual real rate of growth is a valuable tool in the evaluation of corporate performance, because it allows us to compare rates of growth over long periods during which there might have been differing rates of inflation. The second piece of technology is rather more complex.

DCF (discounted cash flow)

Over short periods of time the value of money is approximately constant; if I offered you a gift of $100 you would not mind whether I handed it to you today or tomorrow or even next week. But if the choice was today or in five years' time, that is very different! The difference is not just to do with not trusting me (you will just have to) nor is it to do with money losing its value due to inflation (this could have been part of it, but, as I have just said, I want to leave inflation out of all our discussions; let us stick to 'real terms'). No, it is related to the 'time value of money'; in short, the sooner you get your $100

TABLE 7.1
Which was the best investment?

	Company A	Company B
Cost of shares ($) bought in year 0	$100	$100
Dividend in year 1	$10	$50
Dividend in year 2	$15	$40
Dividend in year 3	$20	$30
Dividend in year 4	$25	$20
Value of shares when sold in year 5	$130	$40

the sooner you can employ it. Thus, if you invested it at 10 per cent, that $100 today would be worth $161 in five years' time—so you would have had a raw deal if you had opted to wait five years for the $100! This calculation also tells you that if you had been offered $100 today or $161 in five years' time, then, assuming you could invest at 10 per cent, you would find it impossible to choose between the offers.

Now, because we are concerned with long periods of time in this book, the time value of money is going to be an important feature in the evaluation of corporate performance and in target setting. For example, if you invested $100 in these two companies, which would have given the best return by year 5, company A which is slowly growing, or B which is in decline and looks like going bust in year 7 or 8? (See Table 7.1.)

The answer is: assuming interest rates were 10 per cent, and you invested all the dividends you received from each company, then you are better off with company B! Why? Because you would have been earning 10 per cent compound interest on company B's generous $50 dividend in year 1 for five years (and on $40 for four years, and so on); meanwhile all you got from company A for those five years was a rather miserable trickle of dividends. It is true that you received a handsome $130 from selling the shares in A five years later—but you have lost five years' interest on that sum at 10 per cent.

A bird in the hand

So, it turns out, the 'net present value' (its value to you in year 0) of the future stream of cash from A is worth $134 in year 0 values, while B's is worth $140. (Check this calculation by assuming you have $134 in year 0. You should be able to reproduce the pattern of cash flow from company A by investing that $134 at 10 per cent. To reproduce B's performance you would need $140.)

It is interesting that the company in decline gave a better return or had a 'higher net worth' in year 0 than the growing one: as I said above, growth is not an essential ingredient for an acceptable rate of return. But the real importance of DCF (the discounted cash flow method) is that it settles once and for all the age-old conundrums of the short-term versus long-term. Not just between dividends now and capital gains later, or between growth and decline as we have just seen, but also such questions as: Which $100m project should an organization choose? One that gives a return of $20m a year for the next 10 years or one that yields nothing for 14 years and then a single, huge, windfall of $500m? (The answer, surprisingly, is the former which gives 15 per cent return while the latter yields only 12 per cent.)

DCF turns income into capital and vice versa, so the age-old riddles of 'rent or buy', or 'high salary versus job security' and 'now or later' can also be unequivocally settled. Notice that 'now' is often better than 'later' because the value of money fades away in the later years, as illustrated by the fact that, although A's shares were worth three times those of B, by the time you got them their 'value' had withered. There is another reason why DCF is so useful: the figures that lie furthest ahead have the least impact; when you make long-range forecasts, as we are going to do later, the most inaccurate figures are the ones that are furthest ahead and, in present values, they matter least.

Now we know why a bird in the hand is worth two in the bush!

ROSC (return on shareholders' capital)

The DCF concept also allows us to develop the ultimate device for measuring company performance—ROSC (return on shareholders' capital). The essential principle of ROSC was illustrated in Table 7.1, where a shareholder buys shares and as a result experiences a stream of revenue or capital payments over time. This stream of cash can be equated, using DCF, with any alternative use of the shareholder's money, including investing it in any alternative savings instrument. Or, more generally, using DCF, anything that can be valued can be equated with anything else that can be valued regardless of when any relevant transactions occur. So this allows one to take account of all sorts of unusual one-off, occasional, transactions (rights issues, convertibles, warrants, etc.) Moreover, as the example showed, it does not assume that growth is an essential component of performance (or rather, it can handle growth, no-growth and decline). But it also allows us to take account of stock-market gyrations.

Now, one of the claimed advantages of growth of EpS as an indicator is that it specifically excludes these gyrations, thus allowing us to judge management performance for those things within their control but absolving them from any stock-market jolts over which they have no control. But these events do actually occur in the real world; stock-market crashes and surges occur every few years and, surely, it is just as necessary for company managers to take note of these as it is for them to weave oil crises, strikes, recessions and other discontinuities into their strategic plans. Indeed, one might argue that a major *disadvantage* of using EpS is that it encourages managers *not* to devise strategies to protect their company's share price in a stock-market downturn.

A global criterion

People often ask 'What is so fundamental about return on *capital*? Why not return on employees' pay, or return on sales, or per hectare of land—or, come to that, added-value per employee, or any other "overall" indicator?' The answer is that capital is the ultimate scarce resource; everything else—land, employees, raw materials—can be converted into capital; if you have capital more of all these others may be obtained; without it nothing can. With almost no exceptions everything that we humans love or hate can be bought and sold—disgraceful, immoral, repulsive though this may be, it is true.

But there is something else. Just as the speed of light is constant throughout the known universe at 299 792km per second, so the cost of (risk-free) capital throughout the world is around 4 per cent, and has been for several decades. To judge the viability of any project anywhere in the world you compare its expected return to this cost of capital (or a related 'hurdle rate'): if it is prudently above it, you go ahead, if not you do not. But it is not just projects, you can judge whole organizations. If the overall return on capital of a company is above the cost of capital it should be expanded until the return trends towards its cost; if below, it should be cut back to its core business; if still below, it should be closed down. Nothing like this immensely valuable universal bench-mark, complete with its unequivocal on/off switch for deciding the fate of projects and whole organizations, is available anywhere else. It is this phenomenon that underlies and forms the basis for all management decisions in all companies everywhere: the bedrock of capitalism.

Fair shares for all

Were companies to employ this ROSC concept a further advantage would accrue. As large companies are all too aware, shareholders differ. 'Widows and orphans' want dividends, pension funds want capital gains, market operators dash in and out of companies in search of a fast buck. Using ROSC it is possible to devise every kind of financial instrument which, while all generating identical returns, deliver a combination of dividends and capital gains tailor-made to meet the needs of each individual type of share-holder. Thus ROSC is a splendid umpire, ensuring that the return on a company's junk bond (a share with a huge cash dividend), say, is fair

YOUR ORGANIZATION: WHAT IS IT FOR?

compared to its scrip dividends (no cash at all). ROSC deserves more attention from shareholders, and it will prove most useful later on when we come to NPOs, where fairness in the distribution of benefits is often even more important than it is to shareholders.

And, finally, ROSC uses *cash*; the figures you use in the DCF calculations are not some mythical 'book value' as dreamed up by the accountants in ROCE, but good hard coin of the realm as when the shareholder writes a cheque to buy the shares, receives dividends through the letter box, and so on. The one figure no one can fiddle is cash.

Just to illustrate the wide comparability of ROSC: the real return on American equities has averaged around 7 per cent over the past 70 years; Sainsbury's ROSC was about 18 per cent over the past 10 years (if you had bought £1000 shares in 1981 you would have received a total of £572 in dividends during the decade and your shares could have been sold for £7300 in 1991). ICI's ROSC for that decade has hovered in the region of 9 per cent. Etc., etc. Using ROSC, every company's performance can be compared to every other in the world over any time period.

ROSC, then, in my opinion, is streets ahead of EpS. The fact is, though, virtually everyone still uses EpS.

Examine past performance

Let me review where we are. We have identified growth of EpS as the most popular BPI for companies today. We have noted that company managements are obsessed with 'growth', possibly with good reason. All that remains, therefore, is to set the two targets developed on pages 82–83 (Tmin and Tsat) using growth of EpS as the chosen BPI.

There is one small task to be performed before doing this. A company has to make sure that they are starting the target-setting exercise from a normal base—we do not want to build future aims on present performance and economic circumstances if these are in any way exceptional. And we must remember that all targets are set relative to comparators and that a single year's comparison is never adequate; one needs to see several years' results to even out the inevitable annual fluctuations and to take account of the obvious fact that, for socially significant companies, no judgement of their performance as a corporate whole, made on the basis of only a year or two, could possibly be valid—a point to be borne equally strongly in mind when we come to NPOs.

And so before setting its targets a company should study its past and present performance compared with its competitors. To do this it needs to decide how many years' history it wishes to examine; I consider that anything less than five years is inadequate. Table 7.2 presents a typical five-year company record of EpS with a couple of competitors' performance as a comparison (all in real terms).

TABLE 7.2

*Five-year record for Sparrow & Co Ltd and competitors
(EpS in pence adjusted for inflation)*

Year	−5	−4	−3	−2	−1	0
Sparrow & Co Ltd: EpS	7.1	7.9	8.1	8.3	9.1	10.8
annual growth per cent	−	11.3	2.5	2.5	9.6	18.7
Wren Ltd: EpS	18.1	20.1	22.3	22.3	26.4	26.8
annual growth per cent	−	11.0	10.9	0.0	18.4	1.5
Corncrake plc: EpS	68.2	69.1	71.1	73.7	81.1	88.7
annual growth per cent	−	1.3	2.9	3.6	10.0	9.4

Sparrow's governing directors should try to summarize their conclusions about this past performance of their company, perhaps as follows:

Sparrow's past performance

Eps record: Good. Our EpS has increased by over 50 per cent in the past five years (averaging 8.8 per cent per annum) while our competitors have risen by 48 per cent and 30 per cent.

Year 0: We had a good year, better than competitors. All our other financial indicators, ROCE, gearing, dividend cover, etc., are normal and have not shown any significant anomalies for some years.

Having established that their present position forms a neutral, stable, base, they are now ready to set their targets for the coming five-year period.

Setting the targets

In other words the company must now decide what figures they would like to see for growth of EpS over the next five years at the two levels we discussed earlier: Tmin and Tsat.

Tmin, you will recall, would be a rate of growth that is barely perceptible. Thus if a company's EpS was growing at 1 or 2 per cent per annum we would have to scrutinize it for several years running before we could conclude whether it was being actively managed or had gone to sleep. As a rule then, in normal economic circumstances, many companies consider that 3 per cent Aarrog over a five-year period is just about the lowest one could contemplate without the shareholders becoming restless and thinking seriously of dismissing the chief executive.

A further justification for the 3 per cent figure is that, over the past several decades, the economies of the developed nations (OECD) have grown at an average of about 3 per cent per annum and, obviously, any company that has not grown at this rate has achieved a performance that is below average. Now, no company can possibly aim at a performance significantly below average, hence this 'magic figure' of 3 per cent. The justification for 3 per cent is thus twofold; it is 'just perceptible growth' and it is 'just not below average for OECD'.

Turning now to Tsat, recall that this represents a performance for which the management ought to be congratulated and perhaps additionally remunerated. It is a level of achievement at which the organization may be seen as a success and where it feels it could move ahead into the future with considerable confidence, perhaps even expanding its activities into new areas. Of course, it depends how fast one's competitors are growing, but many shareholders and managers would have been satisfied if their EpS had grown at 7 per cent per annum Aarrog (up to the 1991/92 recession).

A few managements consider 10 per cent Aarrog is a more appropriate level for Tsat in normal economic conditions, and very young or very fortunate companies would expect to achieve 15 per cent (doubling every five years) or even more. Sainsbury's has achieved 15.6 per cent over the past *10* years, the rate never falling below 11 per cent nor rising above 23 per cent—a *tour de force* of management and control that few could equal and which, therefore, is well above Tsat for most ordinary mortals.

Very occasionally a company achieves 30 or 40 per cent growth for a few years, but these often end by collapsing or burning out. I am personally very nervous of managers who insist on setting themselves Tfan targets. If they apply due diligence to devising strategies to get them to Tsat they are likely to over-achieve it by a handsome margin, while striving for Tfan can lead to excessively dangerous—and unethical—strategies. Of course, if a company habitually operates at a Tfan level then it should strive to maintain this; my concern here is for ordinary companies aiming too high. We would do well to note that the connection between over-expansion and collapse is remorseless; we have known for 2000 years that nemesis follows hubris relentlessly. The pain this natural law causes to those involved and to many innocent bystanders is intense.

Displaying the figures

Sparrow & Co Ltd might set their two targets as indicated in Table 7.3. These targets might be represented on a graph as illustrated in Figure 7.1.

I have been present on many occasions when the directors of a wide variety of companies have discussed this topic and I have reached three conclusions about this target-setting exercise: the first is that most

TABLE 7.3

Five-year targets for Sparrow & Co Ltd
(EpS in pence per share)

Year	0	1	2	3	4	5
Tmin (3 per cent p.a.)	10.8	11.1	11.5	11.8	12.2	12.5
Tsat (10 per cent p.a.)	10.8	11.9	13.1	14.4	15.8	17.4

F I G U R E **7.1** *Five-year targets for Sparrow & Co Ltd*
(EpS in pence per share)

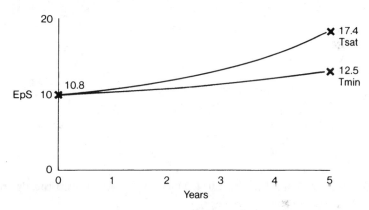

companies have not yet attempted it; the second is that when they do it always arouses intense interest and invariably inspires a marked sense of cohesion among the top executive team who suddenly find themselves all rooting for the same goal; and the third is that it has a quite startling and dramatic effect upon the next few years' profits.

Changing the targets

Does it really make sense to set targets like this? Surely it is just not possible to foresee the course of the next few years with sufficient accuracy to endow these figures with any credibility? I believe that asking this question betrays a misunderstanding of what I am suggesting. I am not asking for a *forecast*; I am asking for a *target*. I am asking, 'Assuming nothing wholly unexpected happens in the world, what level of performance do you *want* from your company?' That seems to me an entirely legitimate question, one that is also perfectly practical and, as I say, you only have to see the effect it has on companies to know that it is one of the most important questions you will ever ask!

But what if something unexpected does happen? Why, then we will have to change the targets! (That is why part of the governing director's job is to monitor long-term performance; see Chapter 16.) But please note, these target figures may *only* be varied if shareholder expectations in general change. The meaning of the word 'satisfactory' would no longer be '10 per cent growth per annum' if a company's competitors are growing at 15 per cent due to a lengthy world boom, and, vice versa, in a prolonged slump even 3 per cent growth could become 'satisfactory'. It is *not* legitimate to adjust targets just because your particular company, or your particular industry or nation, is under-performing. Six per cent is *not* satisfactory if everyone else you compare yourself with is growing at 8 per cent. It is if everyone else is growing at 4 per cent.

What a governing board must never think of doing, then, is to change the target simply because the management cannot achieve it. What they should do under those circumstances is to demand the management find a new strategy or, if they cannot do that, then they must find a new management.

The role of the governing directors

It is the board of governing directors who are to shoulder the responsibility for selecting these targets and monitoring progress towards them; these are two of their three key duties (the other relates to conduct—see Chapter 16). It is *not* the job of the managers to set *corporate* targets, although, as I have noted several times before, it is, at present, invariably—and irrationally— they who do so.

Once the governing directors have made their decision, they should hand these long-term targets down to the top management. The management would, presumably, see it as their first duty to underpin the organization's minimum performance—they must *not*, under any circumstances, allow performance to sink to the level defined as Tmin. They would therefore seek a set of strategies which, as best one can in an uncertain world, protects their organization from this unacceptable performance. Next they should search for strategies which underpin a satisfactory performance. The set of strategies they devise, then, would need to be two-dimensional; it must give the company a good chance of hitting Tsat while at the same time protecting it from Tmin. If they have been given a Tfan, they should devise further, presumably progressively more risky, strategies to take them to that level (I discuss management and strategy formulation very briefly in Chapter 17).

I wish to stress that Tmin is more important than Tsat. No governing director could tolerate an organization performing at a level that brings despair to the beneficiaries, disgrace to the governors, and dismissal for the chief executive. So important do I consider Tmin that it should always be set before Tsat.

Finally, let this be clear—and it is obviously not clear to some of them—the function of a manager is to achieve goals. In recent decades managers have both set the goals and rewarded themselves when they achieve them (and even when they have not). In my view this is a most dangerous practice and we have been lucky to get away with it so lightly— surely we all understand the dangers of being judge and jury in one's own case. I want governing directors to set the goals and management to achieve them—and if they do, then, no doubt, they will be handsomely rewarded.

A progression of performance indicators

A number of lessons are emerging from this and the preceding chapters. There seems to be an ascending scale of corporate objectives all the way from the crude and barely acceptable up to the ultimate in validity.

1 *Qualitative*. At its lowest useful level a corporate objective may be expressed verbally. For instance, 'We aim to be a highly profitable company' or 'to help children'. The problem is that words are very difficult to monitor; it becomes a matter of personal opinion as to whether or not the aim is being achieved.

2 *Quantified*. Figures are far more precise than words; employing them allows the definition and monitoring of corporate objectives to be made much more accurately: 'We aim to make 10 per cent return on capital' or 'We hope to get 10 per cent of blind children into jobs'. But, because each type of organization is different, their corporate objectives will be expressed in different units and, although this allows us to compare like with like it does not make it possible to compare the performance of one type of organization with another type. You can compare companies with companies but not with children's charities.

3 *Money*. Using money it is possible to compare the output or performance of many different types of organization. Thus 'turnover' would enable one to compare the growth of any organization who can value its output in money terms with any other—you *can* compare $6 worth of apples with $6 worth of plums. But not all organizations can value their output and, even if they could, a children's charity that has spent $10m on their children is not 'equal' in any meaningful sense with a company that has sold $10m of widgets.

4 *Growth*. Here you can compare any organization with any other. It may very well be useful to know that 'total student hours', for example, in school A has grown faster than in school B. Or EpS for companies.

5 *Return on capital*. This is the ultimate criterion because it would allow us to compare all organizations with all others and to evaluate the investment of

society's resources in any project in any organization. To have achieved 10 per cent return by helping blind children *is* comparable with a cement company earning 10 per cent—society would be equally happy to invest in either of these while it would be less happy to invest in either a company or a charity which earned only 9 per cent. And it would not be happy at all if the ROSC of any organization fell below the world's cost of capital, namely around 4 per cent.

There is this ascending scale of usefulness in these types of target, then. Companies have reached somewhere between 'money' and 'return'. Most NPOs are stuck on 'qualitative'.

Summary

Building on the assumption that 'satisfactory return on shareholders' capital' is the fundamental purpose of a company, we have to devise a reliable means of measuring this return. Companies have moved, painfully, through a succession of indicators—turnover, margin, profits, ROCE, EpS and ROSC—each one more difficult and expensive to calculate but more all-embracing, ending up with a measure which, very significantly, reflects the shareholders' desires, not the managers'.

The progression from MPI to CPI and then to BPI is seen as another turning point in the book, matching the earlier decision to limit the beneficiaries to one, homogeneous group.

If growth is an important aim for companies (and it obviously is) then, if we wish to measure performance in these sophisticated terms, certain highly technical issues have to be faced—accounting for inflation and the time value of money, for example.

Finally, two 'magic figures' emerged—3 per cent growth for Tmin and 10 per cent for Tsat.

CHAPTER EIGHT

The spoilers

I have already mentioned this phenomenon several times: the use by managers of deliberately defective definitions of their corporate purpose in order to evade both the evaluation of past performance and the imposition of meaningful targets upon their organizations. Company managers do indulge in this practice (several of the spoilers listed below relate specifically to them), although the chief culprits are NPOs (especially those supervised by those most delicate creatures, the politicians). Now that we are about to move on to the use of the purpose sequence for NPOs in the next few chapters it is time to list these spoilers so that we can be sure of avoiding them.

The sense of hostility among managers in NPOs towards being set quantified targets is strong and widely held. One study (Smith and Tomlinson, 1989), reported that teachers objected to their pupils being tested on the grounds that it would have 'a deadening and negative effect' on the children—a transparently and typically defensive reaction. Many, perhaps most, managers in NPOs claim that it is not possible 'in our particular case' to measure their corporate performance. The rest, while not explicitly claiming this, nevertheless do not, in fact, measure it.

A spoiler, then, is a deliberate ploy designed to obfuscate an organization's aims and to prevent the judgement of its performance.

Survival

I have already mentioned this canard. It is said that the prime purpose of all organizations is survival. I would respectfully suggest, however, that no organization in the history of civilization has ever been formed in order to survive. Organizations are founded to do something useful for someone, like make a profit, feed the starving or help broken-down motorists.

You could argue that an organization would not survive if it failed to achieve its aims and therefore its first aim was to survive. I see that as just a trivial tautology which distracts attention from the fact that some organizations have already endured far too long for anyone's good. Of course, a company, or an NPO, that is in trouble will struggle to survive for another year or so in the hope that it can then turn the corner. But this is a short-term minnow of an objective; it is hardly what we mean by 'the corporate purpose'.

And what about project organizations which are deliberately formed to tackle a specific task and then be unceremoniously disbanded? What is wrong with forming a firm to make a quick buck and then go out of business? A company which cost you $1000 to set up, earns you $500 and then is liquidated for $800 the following year gives you a *far* better return on capital than the interminable ICI ever will!

No, 'survival' is nonsense; all it does is distract attention from the true aim. The idea that survival could be the purpose of any organization is due to a silly mix-up with the word 'organism', as I said in Chapter 3; the survival of their species does appear to be the aim of all organisms but organisms are not organizations; we *know* what they are for because we create them for our purpose.

I cannot help noticing that 'survival' suits managers very well indeed—no wonder it is repeated parrot-fashion by all the gurus in the management literature. We have swallowed it so thoroughly that closing down an organization, however ineffectual it has become, is deemed akin to murder.

Maximize

The problem with such objectives as, 'We aim to maximize benefits' or, 'to optimize return on capital' or, 'Our objective is to minimize costs' or, '... as much as possible', or '... the best' or '... excellence', is that you cannot verify whether you have achieved it. A major burden of this book is to argue that if you cannot tell whether or not you have achieved your objective there is no point whatever in setting it.

All the textbooks say that companies aim to maximize their profits, but I am not sure they do; most of them have a highly specific ambition in mind; to hit $10m profit for the first time, to overtake their largest competitor by year five, to be the biggest (all these are highly verifiable, please notice, unlike 'maximize' but, notice also, most of these aims are management ambitions and this is definitely not what we are looking for in this book).

I believe the words 'maximize', 'as much as possible', 'minimize' are all spoilers, designed to make it impossible to check performance, and should never pass the lips of a professional manager in any organization; all aims should be expressed in verifiable, quantified, targets so you know when you have hit them. 'Excellence' is out, too, for the same reason (and see below for two more).

And another thing: the word 'maximize' sounds so aggressive. I suspect it leads to the relentless pursuit of profit (or any other aim—it is not only single-minded companies that behave like demons, remember) at the expense of decent behaviour, and so is entirely contrary to the beneficiary doctrine's central themes. It also leads to the boom and slump results which are so damaging to society.

Lamp-post targets

Because managers have ruled the roost for so long most of the figures that are available to most organizations are MPIs, not BPIs, and, because these are the ones in daily use to gauge operational performance, they are the ones that continue to be collected, analysed, promulgated, often in enormous volumes. Because they are so freely available they are pressed into service to measure corporate performance in spite of the fact that this is a role they cannot play—they are mere lamp-post figures, used because they are available, not because they are valid.

I have explained that most MPIs cannot be summed to form BPIs and that they cannot be used to set *corporate* targets, yet most organizations use them for this; so you get service levels, defects per thousand, added-value per employee, all used as top performance indicators—all admirable targets for managers and employees throughout the rest of the organization but absolutely irrelevant at the corporate level and of minimal interest to the intended beneficiaries.

Value for money, efficiency and excellence

It costs £15 000 a year to keep a criminal in a British jail. Now which would you prefer: that the prison service tried to cut this to £14 000 by 'improving efficiency' or that they spend £16 000 to encourage fewer prisoners to reoffend? What does 'efficiency' mean here: cost per prisoner, or cost per crime? Until someone decides this no action to improve efficiency of the prisons can be taken and, needless to say, it has not been decided. How efficient are the Samaritans, the National Gallery, the Rotary Club? We are constantly being told how important efficiency is, that value for money is essential, but I do not even know what it means here.

In recent years companies have learnt that what a lot of us want today is better service even if it is at a higher cost. You only have to dine at an expensive restaurant, or enjoy any luxury in this sybaritic world, to know that some companies are not efficient at all—they are positively and even disgracefully wasteful! What companies are especially good at is not 'efficiency' but being responsive to the needs of the customer. Sometimes, it is true, we do want efficiency, but increasingly, it is something else.

People in marketing use the slogan, 'do it cheaper, do it better or do it different'. To aim at 'efficiency' automatically steers managers to this first strategy and away from the latter two, precisely the ones that are in the ascendant. Alas, what we have here is the use of an MPI (efficiency) instead of a BPI and, as usual, setting an MPI in place of a BPI forces managers to adopt a specific strategy, usually one completely at variance with what we want. Sure enough, give them an efficiency target and off the managers dutifully go and vigorously cut costs whether we, the beneficiaries, want a cheaper, down-market product or not.

The Audit Commission does much good work in calculating efficiencies in government NPOs yet, alas, by pressing this particular strategic choice upon the managers so forcefully in preference to 'doing it better' or 'doing it different', it undermines much of its value.

It is interesting that just as aiming for efficiency tends to take an organization automatically down to the cheaper mass-market end of its market, so 'striving for excellence' takes them willy-nilly up-market. To position an organization in its market-place—always a critically important strategy—by simply mouthing slogans does not seem to me very professional. In any case (by definition) half of society's organizations are not so much 'striving for excellence' as 'struggling for average'.

Multi-purpose organizations and multiple targets

I have explained these spoilers at length, so this entry is here as a reminder only. If an organization tries to serve more than one beneficiary this renders the evaluation of performance impossible. Any organization which sets itself more than one 'top' target has simply not thought it out. You can no more drive an organization in two directions at once than you can a bus.

And here is a variation; imagine a charity which helps 20 000 children every year. Now imagine one that helps 2000. Which is the most important organization and which of their two chief executives would be paid the most? Obviously the first. But now we discover that their expenditure budgets are the same—$20m per annum—so one spends about $1000 on each child, the other $10 000. Now who would be paid the most? Same again—the former. But my bet is that this charity would be completely unable to measure the effect they have on these children from that miserly $1000, while the second one would have quite an impact—a measurable one—on their lives. So the lesson is: if you want to avoid having a verifiable impact, and thus avoid being measured, go for low-service levels to many clients rather than the other way round. Of course, it is the exact opposite of what the beneficiaries want, but who cares about them?

The stakeholder theory

This doctrine holds that the people who come into contact with an organization—employees, customers, suppliers, the local community and so on—are all intended beneficiaries, and that organizations are, therefore, essentially multi-purpose. I describe this ideology in Chapter 13 and will only say here that I see it as a prime cause of corporate perversion and of the dismal performance of many of our leading organizations. It also precludes the measurement of performance.

Purpose and strategy

I discussed this error at length on page 39 where I noted the three entirely different meanings of the words 'corporate objective'. Because of this logical mix-up, many organizations are saddled with strategies instead of corporate objectives at the top, means instead of aims, MPIs not BPIs. Why does it matter? Because when managers select a strategy as a corporate objective they are inviting us to judge their corporate performance by reference to something that is within their immediate control; 'increase turnover' for instance, is an MPI and is infinitely easier to achieve than a true corporate objective such as 'increase EpS' (a BPI).

Why do so many organizations allow a strategy to be selected as well as, or instead of a purpose? Because they are management-orientated, not beneficiary-orientated. Strategies are for managers; aims are for beneficiaries; but it is the managers who devise and publish mission statements and corporate objectives.

'We are different, we cannot be measured'

There is undoubtedly a cachet in being able to claim that one's own organization is different. Everyone likes to believe in their own exclusivity, their uniqueness; even perfectly standard widget companies insist that their company, or their widgets, are unique.

But no organization is an island, all of them have competitors—indeed there is no way of judging the performance of any organization on its own, it can only be assessed by comparing it with other similar organizations. So this claim of singularity has to be rejected, otherwise every management would be able to escape evaluation—and that is exactly the motive behind the protestation, 'We are so remarkable, unusual, peculiar, rare, unique even, that there is no way to evaluate our performance'.

I believe the reason many NPOs cannot be measured is that they *deliberately* design their operations to preclude evaluation. I have expatiated at length over double-beneficiary and multi-purpose organizations who, I am convinced, have deliberately selected more than one beneficiary in the full knowledge that this precludes the evaluation of their performance. Other ploys are legion. I know one local town government (100 000 population) who claim they cannot be compared with other superficially identical towns of exactly the same size all around them in the Midlands because they have an unusually large rural area. The idea of hiving off the figures for this area and comparing the residual town area with similar towns had occurred to them, but, alas, this raises the problem of the accuracy of the definition of the town/rural boundaries. In fact, by no stretch of the imagination could the rural area account for more than a tiny part of their overall figures, and this reference to accuracy was a deliberate red herring.

No, the demand for accuracy is yet another subterfuge to obscure, cloak and conceal the true picture from our prying eyes; I am asking for accuracy no better than companies achieve, which, as we saw earlier, is in fact very poor. It is good enough to judge the performance of a company over a period of years, however.

'We cannot be measured because we are a teaching hospital'. Nonsense! You just estimate the additional relevant costs and revenues and slice them off the total thus rendering comparability with 'normal' hospitals entirely practical.

And I am sure the police retain so many non-crime-related activities simply to preclude measurement of their crime performance. Children's charities, too, offer several very different services, each of which can be measured, but which cannot be summed to yield a *corporate* performance figure. Universities cling to their two functions—teaching and research—not because the two are linked in any essential way, but because it precludes evaluation. Indeed, all organizations with more than one beneficiary and with diverse benefits are playing just this game with us. No one in their right mind would form an organization to perform many diverse functions; the only explanation of such an extraordinary, deliberately perverse decision is that it frustrates measurement. That is why it is such a favourite ploy for politicians (as I mentioned on page 55, the British government has, within the past two years, set up two enormous double-purpose organizations to add to its already outrageous collection).

A senior civil servant quite openly admitted to me that, even if a single aim could be defined for the city he was now running, he would not accept it. 'It's boring to have a single aim', he said. I have no doubt whatever that this attitude is widespread in NPOs, chiefly because most of the best brains gravitate into this arena rather than into 'trade', and those with high IQs love flirting with complexity.

'We are a non-profitmaking organization'

The full expression, usually stated with an air of righteous indignation and a slightly raised nose, is: 'We are not a profitmaking organization; *we* provide a service to the community.'

The implication is that profitmaking organizations do *not* provide a service to the community, or, if they do, they 'only' do so to make a profit. I am aware that some of the things done in the name of profit are utterly repulsive and repugnant, yet to condemn everything that any company does on the grounds that it is done for profit goes beyond all reason. We hear it constantly. Those who make these statements seem to believe that the non-profitmaking service they provide is in some way more wholesome than the equivalent provided by a company. Do these enthusiasts seek out government-run shops and offices because they find the service there so much better than Marks and Spencer? And I think they forget that a company makes a profit *because* it provides the customers with what they want—not in spite of it or in addition to it but because of it.

Variations on this theme include; 'Ah, but we are not like profitmaking organizations—we have moral responsibilities.' And, 'Ah, but we do not have a single overall corporate objective; we serve the whole community.' Or, of a privatized prison, 'Making a profit out of punishment'. As for 'Ah, but we work for society', that is what *all* organizations do, in the sense that as soon as they recruit their first employee, rent their first office, deliver their first product, they have (unwittingly, often) served society. The only organizations which do not serve society are illegal ones like a gang of burglars. All these are variations on the 'Keep away. Do not attempt to measure our performance' syndrome.

Finally, money. Liberals hate the idea of using money, cash, salary, financial indicators. It is dirty, the vehicle of greed, the chariot of capitalist running-dogs. But money is the only universal indicator of value that humanity has yet invented. To be dissuaded from using it—as many NPOs are—is a tragedy of massive proportions. I doubt if any liberal misconception has done more to hold back the progress of society than this bigoted view. But it is clear why so many NPOs hate using performance indicators based on money; it is the most powerful and universal of them all.

Mission, mandates, vision and values

A veritable craze for these statements had broken out in recent years. For example, Barnardo's published an entire corpus of purpose, values, aims and mission statements (see page 125); the Sydney Opera House has a charter, a mission, a philosophy; many large companies publish mission, values and vision statements; some NPOs talk about mandates, missions, goals and objectives.

I confess I find myself wholly confused by all these terms, and I would consider such statements to be of trivial importance compared with the subject of this book were it not for the following acute dangers:

1 *They pre-empt the purpose sequence*
If top executives issue these statements (sometimes referred to as 'leader's vision') as the starting point for all further discussions they would pre-empt my purpose sequence and, sure enough, most mission statements do not even mention the intended beneficiaries. For example, 'By 1995 we will become the pre-eminent group selling financial and related services to the UK mass market'. *Cui bono?* Klemm, Sanderson and Luffman (1991) say quite categorically that the key purpose of such statements is to stamp the manager's authority on the organization. Exactly what I want to avoid. I want to stamp the beneficiaries' needs on it. I classify these statements as spoilers because I suspect many are deliberate attempts to conceal the true purpose of their organization and to pervert it to the aims of the managers.

2 *They pre-empt the planning process*
But not only do such statements pre-empt my purpose sequence, they also pre-empt any form of rational strategic discussions such as the corporate planning process described on page 233. Notice how the example above commits this company to (1) becoming 'pre-eminent', (2) remaining in financial services, (3) remaining a UK provider, (4) remaining down-market. What about all the alternative strategies they might have pursued—move into a niche, get into Europe, introduce a premium service, move into information technology? Where were all these discussed? Of course, if these statements were the neat, pithy summaries at the end of careful, rational strategic exercises in which all these alternatives were thrashed out, then that is fine. Alas, this is not their normal genesis.

3 *Bland and vacuous*
Many of these statements are of the bland 'God and motherhood' variety which gave such a bad name to corporate planning some decades ago on account of their banal slushy sentimentality and oleaginous unobtainability. I cannot think that 'We will encourage good, strong management' (Sydney Opera House) adds much to human knowledge (they are not likely to encourage rotten, weak management); and how about 'A community of excellence' which describes the US army base at Tooele where chemical weapons are said to be stored? Management by slogan does not seem to me a very advanced form of activity.

I question whether any mission statements have more than a very temporary marginal motivating impact on employees, clients, customers, shareholders or the public, probably less than that of a well-conceived logo. I concede that some, such as Barnardo's 'Challenge disadvantage', are good strong rallying cries, but did Barnardo's slogan really inspire its employees and volunteers for more than 10 minutes; were they not already very well aware what they were doing and already highly committed to their task? What matters, I believe, is whether an organization knows its purpose, its conduct and its strategies and actually puts them into operation in the real world; if it can also neatly summarize these in fine words, well, OK, that is a bonus.

And, as you would by now expect me to say, if a mission statement cannot be quantified it is useless. Most cannot.

Summary

Having seen, in the previous chapter, how companies may move through the purpose sequence we are in a much better position to take NPOs through it in the next few chapters. Whether we shall reach nirvana depends to some extent on whether we can avoid all these spoilers.

The panoply includes 'maximize', 'survival', all lamp-post figures and proxies, 'efficiency', 'value for money', multi-purpose organizations, the stakeholder theory, the confusion between purpose and strategies or aims and means and finally, the idea that NPOs are different and cannot be measured.

Quite an impressive corpus of ingenious managerial evasion!

CHAPTER NINE

The purpose sequence for NPOs

$\mathbf{I}$n Chapter 7 I demonstrated how the governing directors of a company might move through the purpose sequence to identify first, its intended beneficiaries, then the benefit, followed by its BPI and, finally, a suitable Tmin and Tsat. The reason we found all the answers relatively easy is probably because a huge intellectual effort has been devoted to this conundrum by companies over the past several decades.

I now wish to attempt the same exercise for NPOs, knowing before we even start that it is going to be much more difficult partly because of the widely accepted belief that the quantification of corporate objectives for NPOs is 'not possible'. At least we have the advantage of having seen how companies do it and having in our armoury the various concepts of MPIs, CPIs and BPIs.

Over the next four chapters I intend to move through the purpose sequence for a number of well-known British NPOs in turn alphabetically. I shall first relate their objectives and targets as defined by their articles of association, or as supplied to me by their management, and I shall then attempt to apply my purpose sequence. As will be seen this leads me into some severe difficulties as well as a few successes; but at least we learn a little more as we discuss each organization and eventually we reach some interesting conclusions.

Let me make clear what I am *not* trying to do here. I am not hoping to provide each of these well-known NPOs with a final definitive solution to the definition of their corporate objectives along with suitable targets. Not only would that be arrogant, it would also take about 40 years, if the history of the development of BPIs for companies described in Chapter 7 is any guide. No, what I want to do is to discuss their aims as they presently define them, test these according to the principles of the beneficiary doctrine, avoid any spoilers and see if any other definitions fit the doctrine better. I am more interested in learning some general lessons for setting objectives for all NPOs than achieving precise conclusions for any particular one of my guinea-pigs; that precision will have to be supplied by the organizations themselves.

NPOs and companies

Before starting this quest it might be helpful to remind ourselves of the key differences between companies and NPOs. The most obvious distinction is that companies know what their corporate objectives are and dare to set corporate targets for themselves, while most NPOs lack any analogue of profit, or 'bottom line', and maintain that they cannot set corporate targets even if they wanted to. This is the distinction that crops up, time after time, in discussions with senior managers and in the literature; this absence of a challenging target lies at the root of many of the other differences outlined below.

To mention a couple of random but entirely typical examples of this deficiency, Hatten (1982) explains that NPOs cannot devise their corporate strategies by reference to an overall corporate objective *'because there isn't one'* (my italics); they develop their strategies, he says, by taking their existing strategy and improving it (how you know what 'improved' means without a corporate objective to test it by, he does not explain). Another example: Wilson and Butler (1986) say that the key influence in developing strategy in NPOs is not the task (corporate objective) but interdependence with other organizations (defence of their domain against incursion from others being, these authors say, an important aspect).

Of course, for me, any strategy not directed to achieving a corporate objective is pure nonsense, an oxymoron, a contradiction in terms, a travesty. It is not possible to devise a strategy, nor to evaluate one, except by reference to the aims it is intended to achieve. If you do not know what you are building any brick will do. Be that as it may, what these authors suggest is that NPOs either do not have corporate objectives or the strategies they develop are not related to them. Worse, strategies are devised to defend managers' territory rather than to benefit the beneficiaries.

Strategic constraints

Another difference often recounted includes the belief that NPOs are more restricted than are companies, either by their charters or by government regulation, as to the choice of strategy they may adopt. It is pointed out, for instance, that NPOs may not diversify. But in fact there is nothing whatever to prevent a charity providing a service 'for blind ex-servicemen' re-forming to widen this service to 'for the blind'—a very substantial diversification, surely. (And, in fact, few companies do actually diversify more abruptly than this, and they seldom, as many NPO managers seem to imagine, leap from, say, fish-farming to manufacturing helicopters overnight.)

While accepting that there are more constraints on NPOs, that still leaves enormous scope for strategic ingenuity. The number of ways in which, say, an animal welfare charity might go about its aims must be legion: it would

119

include everything from actually treating distressed animals themselves in their own clinics, to gently applying pressure on public opinion, to vigorously prosecuting cruelty offenders, right up to persuading the international community to set up a global instrument of strategy such as CITES (which regulates world trade in endangered species), for example. The range of these various options is simply vast; infinity minus one, would be my guess, compared to infinity for companies.

Government intervention

Another distinction is that governments habitually interfere, often casually, ignorantly and arbitrarily, with the detailed management of those NPOs that they sponsor and control (British Rail, for example, will invest about £1bn a year, but has to get government approval for any project over £5m!). But those who draw special attention to this item can never, it seems to me, have worked for a subsidiary company when 'head office' is on the war-path. A further distinction is that many NPOs are given statutory duties. But companies have to meet stringent legislation, too; NPOs also have certain legal protections which companies do not enjoy, and they certainly occupy a less hostile taxation environment than companies.

Managers in NPOs also point out that, because government is such a key, and unpredictable, influence upon them (government is sometimes supplier and customer, as well as sponsor), they cannot forecast their future. However, companies cannot forecast theirs either—many companies also supply just one customer (quite often it is also the government), have one supplier, rely on one shareholder, and so forth, so I am not at all certain that this commonly noted distinction is valid.

Cultures taut and relaxed

Finally, there are the undoubted cultural differences. NPOs are more tolerant towards their employees, are far less competitive and combative, and behave better than companies do in society. It is said that there are fewer autocrats in NPOs than in companies; it may be so, but Lord Reith stamped his values on the BBC so effectively that they have lasted until today, and I doubt if he was the sole autocrat in the history of NPOs. What may be more significant is that companies always designate one named person to be responsible for each major project or activity, while NPOs bury responsibility in huge faceless committees whenever they can; the design of the management hierarchy in a company is explicitly intended to pinpoint, highlight and broadcast personal authority, while in NPOs its purpose is to hide, obfuscate and disguise it. NPOs employ evasive titles such as 'deputy' and 'joint' and are still trying to operate gothic 'matrix' structures long after most companies have abandoned them.

Employees in NPOs are said to be more fulfilled by the worthwhile jobs they do, even though they are often less well paid. But I am not sure of that either; while working with children is plainly more rewarding than working with widgets, not everyone in NPOs works with children. Scientific and technical work is much the same whether you work for ICI or Northtown Council. Cleaning a school is very like cleaning an office; typing a memo, driving a van, nursing a patient—all much the same whether one is doing it for a profitmaker or an NPO. This is a rather marginal argument, I would think, even though it does run through much of Peter Drucker's writings (Drucker, 1990 for instance).

To summarize: my impression is that although many of these distinctions between companies and NPOs are valid, the only one that makes any significant difference is the one that this book is all about—corporate objectives. The two types of organization are otherwise not so different that we need separate rules for each; they are both 'organizations' within the meaning of the word.

I shall now move through a small number of guinea-pig organizations to see if I can make any better sense of their corporate objectives than they have.

The Automobile Association (AA)

Founded in 1905, the AA claims to be an 'innovative membership-based service organization' for motorists. Policy is determined by a committee of 22 members; the director general reports to the committee and is responsible for the 13 000 employees. The organization, a charity, is split into a number of semi-autonomous 'companies' each providing specialist services.

The AA's Corporate Purpose

Here there is complete clarity regarding the intended beneficiaries, even though, as with so many of the organizations discussed in this chapter, no formal statement of the corporate objective appears in the annual reports and the word 'motorist' barely appears anywhere.

As to the benefits: the AA provides 'services' to its members. I hinted before that I was dubious of 'services to' as a component in the definition of a corporate objective (it would not do to describe a school as 'services to children', for example), but for now we may formally recite the purpose as follows:

Corporate purpose for the Automobile Association

The intended beneficiaries	British motorists
The intended benefit	Services

We now need to select a suitable BPI to measure the AA's performance. In this there is a problem because neither the AA, nor any of the NPOs discussed in these four chapters, even hint of a method of doing this, nor did they admit that they had a BPI, not even when I specifically invited them to reveal it. Several said that their corporate performance could not be quantified.

A CPI for the AA

A glance through the AA's annual report suggests to me that the indicator most conspicuously reported is 'growth of membership'. Membership has grown from 10 000 in 1909 to 7m in 1988—a prominently displayed table tells us so—and this is an Aarrog of 8.6 per cent, an astonishing record over nearly eight decades, one that certainly exceeds most company growth rates over such a period. Over the past two decades, however, membership has grown at only 2.8 per cent (substantially lower than the 3.5 per cent rate of growth of road traffic in Britain) although in the past five years it recovered to 4.6 per cent.

So should 'membership' be adopted as the CPI? One problem with this indicator is that it is possible, certainly for old, established organizations which have built up substantial financial reserves, to suppress subscription rates, at least for a number of years, in order to boost membership; the membership figure can thus be 'dressed' all too easily. But, more importantly, just as company managers need to regulate both the volume and the selling price of their products as an essential part of their marketing strategies, so NPO managers may wish to adjust membership volume and subscription levels for perfectly legitimate strategic marketing reasons.

It is clear, I think, that 'membership' is not a CPI but an MPI; it is just one of the many concerns of the management of the AA, albeit a very important one. We will see below that many NPOs place substantial emphasis on membership growth but I equate this with 'sales volume' for a company—it is just an MPI for managers. Moreover, if adopted as a CPI managers could, by 'going for growth', damage the interests of the existing membership in what is often referred to as 'empire-building'; to increase membership the managers might cut the subscription rates thus jeopardizing the quality of service. Using 'membership' as a corporate target will not do, therefore.

Growth of income as an indicator

Perhaps 'growth of total subscription income' would be better. The AA's subscription income has risen by 5.4 per cent Aarrog in the past five years (thus income has risen faster than membership). That is not bad—remember that one aim in this book is to compare performance of NPOs with other NPOs and with companies. I am suggesting that, if we accept 'growth of subscription income' as the AA's equivalent of 'growth of EpS', we could use this to compare the AA with many different types of organization—for example, comparing this with companies over the past five years, the AA's 5 per cent approaches the 7 per cent that the average company has achieved.

But wait! We have made a serious error here; 'growth of subscription income' is *not* the same as 'growth of EpS'. It is only the same as a company's 'growth of turnover'—it is just another MPI. While its *managers* certainly want to see the AA's subscription income rising—their pay and status presumably depends on this factor—the AA's *members* do not give a hoot about this. What they care about is the services they get. We have fallen into the same trap that *company* managers fall into when they tell us that 'growth of sales turnover' is the appropriate corporate performance measure. In fact, shareholders do not give a fig for the physical size of their company or its turnover (except that a company's stability—and, therefore, its 'shareholder value'—is enhanced above a certain size threshold). What shareholders care about is 'growth of earnings per share', remember; as far as they are concerned the company itself can shrink physically every year, its number of employees can decline, its products be rationalized to one, its factories closed, its turnover and market share can dwindle—so long as the dividend that comes through the letterbox, and the value of their shares, goes on rising year after year.

A BPI for the AA

We forgot the basic tenet of the beneficiary doctrine: that it is 'growth of benefits to intended beneficiaries' that we should be measuring, not growth of anything physical. This rather alters things for the AA because we presumably ought to look for the figure that shows how well the *beneficiaries* have been served; a BPI, not a CPI. But what figure? Where is it in the annual report? I can only assume that 'services per member' is the appropriate unit but I cannot find it calculated anywhere. I presume we should take expenditure on services and divide by the number of members to get a 'services per member' figure as a parallel to 'earnings per share'. The details are: in 1983, 5·6m members shared a total expenditure on services of £150m (in 1988 pounds)—that is, £26.80 each; in 1988, 7·0m members shared £204m—that is, £29.10 per head. In real terms this works out at only 1.6 per cent Aarrog (i.e., the AA spent 1.6 per cent more each year on each member)—a very poor performance compared with many companies' growth of EpS, well below Tmin.

Is this really an appropriate BPI? It tells a quite different story to membership or subscription income. But this is common; profit (the company manager's measure, or CPI) often tells a different story to EpS (the shareholders' measure, or BPI) as noted on page 93 and, in my view, the management of the AA have been monitoring the wrong figure. They must do what companies have learnt to do: use 'growth of benefit to beneficiaries' rather than growth of the size of their organization.

But wait a minute; merely measuring what the AA spends on services tells us nothing about the volume and quality of benefit the members actually receive. For all we know the AA might be wasting millions. They may indeed have spent £204m but the members might only have received services worth £102m. (I noticed from the annual accounts, for instance, that they spent £14m on sales promotion, that is, 6.6 per cent of their total annual expenditure, to attract new members—but that is not likely to enhance the services to *existing* members who presumably are the *intended* beneficiaries.) Perhaps we should take 'direct costs' only. Direct costs are those specifically incurred in providing the services to motorists and exclude all other costs such as management, property, advertising, postage and head office. And we should certainly exclude any 'surpluses'—funds put to reserves for the future which, again, will not benefit the *existing* members. Thus the proposed BPI now becomes 'growth of direct costs of services per member'. It is impossible to calculate what the past Aarrog is for this from the reports.

Targets for the AA

Turning now to the targets; these will, we may assume, be the same as for companies: 3 per cent for Tmin and 7 to 10 per cent for Tsat. With current performance well below Tmin this represents a major challenge. However, I suspect that the management of the AA have been evaluating all their projects against the ambition of growth of the AA—the wrong criterion, surely. If they adopt the proposed BPI ('growth of direct spending on services per member') I have no doubt that, using this as the gauge for all their decisions, they will greatly improve performance for their members and, consequently, the number of members.

We have learnt a number of new guide-lines from this organization. First, that 'growth of membership', which is used as an almost universal indicator of success by managers in NPOs, is entirely irrelevant even as a CPI. 'Growth of income' is much more relevant. It is interesting that membership figures are not only given great prominence in annual reports, they are often displayed for many years into the past—for decades in the case of the AA. Meanwhile 'income' is relegated to the back pages and *never* shown for more than two years—a wholly ridiculous period in which to be invited to judge the performance of organizations as important as these. Plainly most NPOs have their priorities back to front here; income is far more significant than the number of members.

And having said all that, both growth of membership *and* of income is ruled out by the beneficiary doctrine because they are mere CPIs, and, as will be seen in a moment, are not even useful proxies for the true BPI; and, as I noted on page 96, the one thing company managers never try to do, in their obsessive search for 'growth', is to increase the number of shareholders.

The best BPI I could devise here was 'growth of direct spending on services per member', a sort of 'EpB' (expenditure per beneficiary) to mimic EpS. I am very conscious that this does not measure the benefit they actually receive but, because of the wide spread of services offered it would be virtually impossible to make this calculation.

We end in failure

Frankly, we have failed to find a valid BPI for the AA. All we have done is to suggest a move onwards from the equivalent to a company's 'sales volume' (membership) through 'turnover' (income) to a sort of 'EpS' (expenditure on services per beneficiary). We have failed to reach a genuine EpS or a ROSC. I am left wondering whether 'services', employed by innumerable NPOs to describe what they do, can ever be an adequate description of an organization's aims. First, the word itself is too wide to admit to quantification, and second, since most NPOs pride themselves on the breadth of the services they offer they must run into the conglomerate accounting syndrome mentioned on page 93. 'Services', it appears, are non-quantifiable.

Barnardo's

Barnardo's is a 'Christian child-care association whose purpose is to express the love of God by serving children, young people, their families and the community'. That is their purpose statement.

They also have a values statement which mentions 'adopting attitudes that are accepting and caring', 'working in partnership, 'drawing on volunteers'. They have an aims statement which includes 'providing selected services', 'changing children's circumstances', 'improving quality of life', 'raising awareness of needs', 'exploring new ways of helping' and, importantly, to 'speak out on behalf of young people and families'. There is a mission statement too: 'working together to challenge disadvantage and create opportunity'.

Barnardo's is governed by a council of 30 members; the chief executive ('senior director') takes charge of the work of the 4000 staff and 26 000 voluntary helpers.

Barnardo's purpose

You will recall that the first question in the purpose sequence is to identify the intended beneficiaries of an organization. I have explained that one reason I dislike the stakeholder theory is that, by listing a large number of incidental beneficiaries, it distracts one's attention from the organization's true beneficiaries, and here I found it hard to sort out exactly who Barnardo's intended beneficiaries were from all these purpose statements, values, aims and mission statements which, while all pointing in a similar direction, are not all saying quite the same thing. And there is more in the annual report: ' ... helps young people with special needs ... or whose parents need support' and so on.

The problem here is that although everyone knows that the beneficiaries of this extremely well-known organization are unequivocally 'children and young people' these statements keep referring to other persons such as parents, families and the community. Are all these people really beneficiaries of this organization? Surely Barnardo's would only take a case in which children were involved—for example, they would not help childless parents, however deserving (unless they were themselves 'young people'). Children, then, not parents.

More than that: surely Barnardo's would take considerable care to ensure that the parents themselves did *not* benefit from their intervention unless this would benefit their children. In most cases I imagine that if the children are helped then, inevitably, the children's families and the community also benefit but, surely, they are incidental beneficiaries; even if they did not benefit by one iota, Barnardo's would still help those children. It is inconceivable that Barnardo's would say to a child, 'We are not going to help you because the community will not benefit from you being helped'.

Children only

To help the children is sufficient. I am surprised to see all these other interest groups in the purpose statement; it is children that they aim to help; any project that did that would be considered regardless of the effect on these other people, while any that helped anyone else without helping children would be decisively rejected. *Not* parents, *not* families, *not* the community. I would have thought Barnardo's does quite enough good work with children not to have to claim to act for everyone in sight as well.

The next question in the purpose sequence, you will recall, is to ask what is Barnardo's doing for these children? They provide five 'selected services' including residential homes, adoption services, family support, day care and youth services. But that is what Barnardo's *does*. Even that elegant mission statement merely describes what it does. But what is it *for*? I assume it is to help these disadvantaged children enjoy better lives. Then why not say so somewhere?

I presume we can now make this reasonably unequivocal summary:

Corporate purpose for Barnardo's

The intended beneficiaries	Disadvantaged children and young people
The intended benefit	To help them lead better lives

Barnardo's CPI

Now for the CPI. The two most prominent figures in the annual reports are 'the number of children helped' and the 'annual spend on services'. The number helped is displayed in the five different categories of help mentioned above. I would not have thought that the 'total helped' is a meaningful figure, because some services cost several thousand pounds per child, others cost only a few hundred and, as you cannot add apples and plums, any total figure is meaningless. Barnardo's actually does add them and the headlines in the annual reports speak of 'helping 13 750 children' in 1984 and 22 800 in 1989. It cannot mean very much, but the annual growth of total cases is 10.6 per cent—a very rapid rate by any standards.

Turning to the expenditure on services, it is interesting to note that Barnardo's draws very particular attention to the amount actually spent on the children as opposed to the overall income of the organization (the point I raised above with the AA). Barnardo's is proud of the fact that 80 per cent of their income goes directly on children's services and only 20 per cent on management (I am not quite sure why—would it be so disgraceful if they spent another 10 per cent on management if that then improved their services by 20 per cent?). Direct expenditure on services amounted to £22m in 1984 and £41m in 1989, an Aarrog of 7.8 per cent. Again, as with the AA, this represents a performance which many companies would see as Tsat. But, alas, while either of these may be a CPI, neither is the BPI; just because they treated more cases, or just because they spent more, does not mean the children were any better served in 1989 than five years earlier.

Benefits per child, surely?

To measure what the beneficiaries themselves gained we surely need to know what help each, or the average, child received? If so, then, as with the AA, a more appropriate BPI would be the growth of spend on services per child. Taking the £22m spent in 1984 and inflating it to 1989 values brings it up to £28m which, on 13 750 cases, is an average expenditure of £2040 per child. This compares with the £41m spent on 22 800 children in 1989, or £1800 each—it has gone down! It is an Aarrog of *minus* 2.5 per cent. So what happened? Did Barnardo's spend less per case to the detriment of the children? Did they tackle too many cases for their resources? Did the children do just as well in spite of the drop due to improved efficiency or more voluntary work? Was Barnardo's empire-building (going for more clients just as the AA might have been going for more members)? Or was there a change in the mix of services—or merely of accounting practices?

What actually happened was a change in mix; Barnardo's slimmed down their residential services and increased day care and other less expensive activities. While that explains the figures, it raises a far more important question; what effect did this have on the children? Did it result in more help for them, at this lower cost, or were they deprived of an excellent, but expensive service? The answer is: we do not know. That screams out at us; we have not yet found the correct BPI. If we had it would tell us.

Barnardo's BPI

Barnardo's themselves say they cannot quantify their performance. I find this odd because they are rightly regarded as one of the most highly professional charities in Britain (that is why they appear here), and they repeatedly stress that they evaluate their services (they even have a department at head office whose job is to supervise this function). It calls for each project to be evaluated in a particular format, one feature of which is to study the effect of any project on their staff, the parents of the children, other social services, the local community and so on, as well as on the children. While it must be right for their managers to know these effects upon the various stakeholders, my anxiety is that this form of evaluation deflects attention away from the effects on the true beneficiaries—the children. Obviously, if you want to know what happened to five different groups of people in a complex social project this is more diffuse than giving all one's attention to just one, which is what companies do in a project appraisal where all eyes would be on the bottom line—profits.

I am concerned, therefore, that Barnardo's 'project appraisal' format distracts attention from the children to the other stakeholders; I am anxious that a project that scored a notional 20, 30, 40, 50 for children, parents, staff, local community respectively might win against one that scored say, 40, 10, 10, 10. If Barnardo's says, 'No, we would judge the project by the score to the *children*', then what is all that about parents, staff, the community and so on? Either they feature in the evaluation or they do not.

This concentration of attention on results for the children is, however, very fully illustrated in one of Barnardo's own reports (Brownlie, 1988) which (unusually) centres on the before-and-after behaviour of children at one of their Intermediate Treatment Centres (ITC). This ITC takes youngsters who have a record of convictions, guides and educates them on a part-time basis, and then releases them into the community. The report shows that children from this ITC committed (approximately) 20 per cent fewer offences after they left compared with similar youngsters who had attended the government-run equivalent (called Community Homes with Education or CHEs).

Closer to our goal

Oh, so it *is* possible to measure performance in this exceptionally difficult area? Moreover, as a result of doing so the local government in that area no longer sends young offenders to the CHE but to Barnardo's ITC; and certain changes in practice at the ITC have also followed this exercise—thus beautifully illustrating two of the key consequences that flow from being able to quantify performance: it allows comparison with other similar organizations, and it permits strategies to be evaluated. Major, rational, decisions may then follow.

But, alas, we have still not gone very far; we have achieved approximately what a company does when it compares two factory processes (here it is ITC versus CHE), so we still only have an MPI; we have not acquired a CPI, still less a BPI for Barnardo's as a corporate whole; for although we can now compare similar *operational units* in this type of NPO, by how well they improve the records of young offenders, we cannot compare similar organizations as corporate wholes (Barnardo's versus the Children's Society, say), and, because we have not placed any money values on these services, as companies do, we certainly cannot compare dissimilar ones (Barnardo's versus the National Gallery). So what about the next step, to place monetary values on what they do for the youngsters at the ITC so that, at the very least, we can see if the benefits exceed the costs? When I asked if they could do this Barnardo's said they did not have the budget for such an exercise. Barnardo's total annual budget is about £50m! But it *can* be done, as we shall see in the next section.

Measuring schoolchildren

In 1962 Mr David Weikart set up the Perry pre-school programme for three- and four-year-old black disadvantaged children. He randomly selected a number of them from a ghetto in the town of Ypsilanti (Michigan) to attend this school for one or two years, together with an equal number of similar 'pairs' who did not go to this school. He followed their careers for around 15 years by which time, according to a report (Webber, Foster and Weikart, 1978), 67 per cent of the Perry children had completed high school (compared with 49 per cent of the control group); 50 per cent held jobs (32 per cent of the other group); 45 per cent supported themselves (25 per cent); 31 per cent had been arrested for criminal acts (51 per cent); 18 per cent were on public assistance (32 per cent). In other words, the Perry children did about 70 per cent better in later life (my own broad-brush conclusion).

It obviously took a majestic effort to establish these figures over such a time-span. But he then went on to evaluate these improvements in money terms by calculating the savings to the nation of the better school record and social behaviour and (more importantly, as it turns out) the greater earning power of the Perry children compared with the control group. Now, we have to be careful here; while the schooling costs come early, most of the benefits do not appear for many years or decades (the children were four years old when this started), so it is essential to take account of the time value of money. Using DCF (see page 98) he worked out the return at 9 per cent (real) for children who had spent one year at his school and 4 per cent for those who spent two years.

Now the rate of interest ('cost of capital') in America at the relevant time was 4 per cent so, while a one-year stay yielded a very acceptable return on capital (9 per cent approaches the real return on capital that many companies would earn—recall that ICI earned 9 per cent, for example), the two-year programme only just 'broke even', and when the same experiment was tried for non-disadvantaged children there was also a poor return, as there was, too, for disadvantaged girls rather than boys.

Weikart's follow-up is believed to be one of the most prolonged projects in the area of social study ('longitudinal research', as sociologists call it), and one must pay homage to his patience and tenacity (he tells me many of his original three- or four-year-old subjects now have children of that age of their own and, so far as can be seen at present, the favourable differential between the Perry and non-Perry scholars continues into this second generation). (Barnardo's incidentally, is closely associated with similar work in the UK where it is called High/Scope.)

Another turning point

Now I consider that this experiment is of crucial importance to my thesis in this book. It is the fourth turning point. (The insistence on one homogeneous beneficiary was the first; then the concept of a single CPI as distinct from all those MPIs; third, the idea of a BPI for beneficiaries as distinct from the CPI for managers.) Here, now, we have the ability to value benefits in money terms in the real world, as they actually occur to real live people. I see the following major conclusions flowing from Weikart's work:

1 If you really want to measure the effect your organization is having on real people with names and faces in the real world you can do so. You can even devise a method of calculating the return on investment. If you can do this for educating four-year-old disadvantaged children in a ghetto in Michigan you can do it for anything and anyone.

2 The return on some organizations will turn out to be substantial, certainly comparable with returns earned in the private sector. Where this is the case an additional marginal investment of resources would be clearly and

unequivocally indicated—something we can only guess at without the figures.

3 But alas, some returns are poor (note how rapidly the return fell from the one-year to the two-year programme and for non-disadvantaged children, and for girls compared to boys) and, unless the sums are done, no one knows which organizations, and which operations within them, are worth having and which are not. In this case it appears that nearly *half* the children did *not* 'earn' a financially viable benefit from the Perry school project (and I am slightly anxious about some of Weikart's figures which might reduce the return still further).

4 So, for all we know half of all our NPOs, or half of all their activities, would give a return of less than the cost of capital and so are a sheer waste of society's resources; or, on the contrary, we should be shovelling capital into some of them like mad and not investing another penny in ICI. If you do not measure it you have no idea where the cut-off is, and, as I have stated repeatedly, we do not measure it.

Tracking

The cost of monitoring or tracking beneficiaries over the necessary time-spans to determine what the actual, concrete benefits are *to them*, in money terms, will be substantial. However, after some experience the cost of gathering the data will decline rapidly as tracking techniques are developed. For instance, recent research into the records of young offenders recognizes that if early results are favourable (over a period of two or three years, say) then this will probably augur well for many years (Weikart need not have worried after a couple of years; apparently, and, because of the discounting effect, additional figures add little to the calculations after a dozen years or so). The monitoring costs will be further defrayed as more organizations set up tracking systems and share data, as independent specialist tracking organizations appear, as more beneficiaries are invited to track themselves, as more voluntary organizations provide tracking services free, as the principle of engagement (page 193) is applied to tracking, and so on.

The act of beneficiary tracking might itself reveal additional opportunities for service, just as when a company enters a maintenance contract with a customer this both allows the company to monitor the performance of its product in the field and opens the possibility of further sales to that customer.

An overall summary of this section would include these statements: If you are proposing a project, or founding an organization, you *must* say what effect you expect it to have on your individual intended beneficiaries, people with names and faces. You *must* say it with figures. You *must* then check up to see if it had that effect. You *must* calculate the return to the beneficiaries. Otherwise all your efforts are just vanity.

A feature that I shall return to later is that even in the case of these disadvantaged children the salaries they subsequently earned amounted to 60 per cent of the total return on capital, the rest being savings in state support they did not require compared to the help the control group needed throughout their later years.

Implications for the AA

We should now return to the AA and Barnardo's to see if this breakthrough works for them. The two organizations are surprisingly similar in that they claim to provide services to their respective beneficiaries. Both have increased beneficiaries or members rapidly in the past few years, and both have seen a very rapid rise in total expenditure. But both show figures for 'growth of spend per beneficiary' that turns out to be disappointingly low (and in the case of Barnardo's the figure actually declines). It is now clear that this 'spend per beneficiary' was not a valid BPI because it does not tell us what *actually happened* to the beneficiaries. A valid BPI would track what actually happened to them and place cash values on these events as David Weikart did.

Take the AA first. You can picture an AA member's annual subscriptions as a stream of cash flowing out and, to set against this, a stream of savings flowing back from annual discounts on car insurance, say, and intermittently, from not having to pay for breakdown recovery. Let us imagine a member of an AA-type club who pays a subscription of $50 every year and compare the subscriber's experience with a paired non-member, just as Weikart did. Imagine that the member saves $7 a year on insurance premiums, that they both break down at the same place in year 4, and the non-member had to pay a breakdown organization $240 to get home. The cash flows that a member might experience over a five-year period are illustrated in Table 9.1.

TABLE 9.1
Cash flows for a member of an AA-type organization

Year	Subscription to 'AA' ($)	Discount on car insurance ($)	Savings on breakdowns ($)
1	− 50	+ 7	
2	− 50	+ 7	
3	− 50	+ 7	
4	− 50	+ 7	+ 240
5	− 50	+ 7	

Discounting these cash flows, the real return on the member's stream of subscriptions and savings works out at a very reasonable ROSC of 10 per cent; he or she has every right to be happy with the benefits of membership. As noted earlier, a valid BPI allows comparison with other organizations, however dissimilar they may be, and so this member can now decide whether it pays to subscribe to the AA or buy shares in ICI instead (ICI's ROSC was about 9 per cent, if you remember). Although any one member would see wildly differing ROSCs, because it would vary depending on when breakdown recovery was needed, if at all (just as any given share-holder's ROSC varies according to the value of the shares when they were bought and sold), the overall ROSC for the AA as a corporate whole would be easily calculated by aggregating the experience of all the members.

Implications for Barnardo's

What about Barnardo's? Someone pays them £50m per annum to help children. How much are they helped? Answer: at present we do not have any idea. But why not go and evaluate the effect on the children of the services that Barnardo's offer, just as Weikart would have done? If the total 'savings' on improved behaviour, higher earnings and less state interven-tion in the later lives of these children exceeds £50m compared to a non-Barnardo's control group, that gives a positive return, if not, not. So, by aggregating the returns on all their activities we could calculate Barnardo's ROSC as a corporate whole, *and* we could do it for each beneficiary individually an ideal BPI.

Am I suggesting that Barnardo's should routinely track the experience of all 23 000 children every year for the next 10 or 20 years of their lives? Probably not; some NPOs will be able to track each beneficiary indi-vidually, others must rely on statistical sampling. However, Barnardo's maintains detailed case-histories of every child who passes through any of its units, so, in this case, every child's progress could be tracked. What we want to know is simple: did they actually enjoy a better life as a result of Barnardo's services? How much better? In cash terms?

The cost of tracking will be substantial—certainly more than most NPOs currently spend on it. Barnardo's, for example, has produced only one report (such as the one quoted above for the ITC) over the past few years; tracking will certainly require many times that effort. Even tracing the whereabouts of some of their beneficiaries will be costly, and so I would not be surprised if many NPOs found they had to spend 10 per cent of their budgets on tracking—but why not, companies spend something like that on calculating their profits? And note this: what happens to the beneficiaries of an organization is not just another irritating detail the staff might have to bother with if they have a few spare moments; it is as essential as knowing what its profits are to a company. How many companies do you know who cannot say what their profits are? Yet virtually no NPO on the surface of this earth knows their equivalent figure.

Why should Barnardo's continue to pretend that they cannot afford to learn what effect they are having on their children? How are we ever to find out if Barnardo's ITC is not only better than the local government's CHE but is also better than such other alternatives as, say, not taking an offending child out of the family unit but, on the contrary, placing a trained adviser *in* the family for a couple of months? Or arranging fostering? Do we not need to know that?

Summary

I have only managed to discuss two NPOs in this chapter—the AA and Barnardo's—but each has taken us a small step up the learning curve; membership, number of clients, income, expenditure, even my deliberate attempts to manufacture valid indicators such as EpB, are all inappropriate as BPIs.

It was Barnardo's which provided the breakthrough, or rather, their associate, the American High/Scope. While most NPOs, including Barnardo's, claim that it is not possible to measure their performance, David Weikart went ahead and did it—he even calculated the return on capital. That such longitudinal studies are expensive is not in doubt; what is in doubt is whether any modern NPO should be allowed to get away with not doing them. I see beneficiary tracking, evaluating the benefits over a period of time that is sufficient to reach a statistically significant value, as essential, even if the cost of doing so reduces the capacity of some organizations to serve some of their beneficiaries.

What this permits is a statement of the value, in terms of a stream of cash over time, of the benefits the beneficiaries receive which may then be compared with the costs of the organization to obtain a 'return on capital'. It takes everything into account that needs to be included in making a judgement of both the effectiveness and the efficiency of the organization, including even all the relevant intangibles. It would allow virtually all organizations to be compared with all others—and with the world cost of capital. Once relevant data become available it will permit NPOs to measure their performance as effectively as any company with all the implications that this entails.

CHAPTER TEN

A college and the Girl Guides

$\mathbf{W}$e have just seen how two remarkably different organizations—the AA and Barnardo's—might both be able to use the same procedure, a sort of 'return on capital', to measure their performance to their beneficiaries. It was an encouraging start.

Can every service provided by every NPO be quantified? I doubt it. Some charities look after children so severely handicapped that they live out their brief lives immobile, mute, doubly incontinent. I do not imagine the performance of this service can be verifiably measured at all—cost is hardly appropriate, nor is efficiency, nor is the recovery rate, for, sadly, there is none—and we are surely not going to stop caring for them just because we cannot measure the results. But that should not stop us searching for activities where we might be able to improve the way we measure performance.

A college of further education

I will use Northtown College to represent all colleges of tertiary education. This one was founded in 1961 and is one of nearly 500 in Britain and 12 in its county. Its catchment area has a population of 100 000 from which its 2000 students (both youngsters aged 16 to 19 and adults) are drawn via 12 local schools and hundreds of employers. It teaches subjects such as business, engineering, nursing, leisure services through 800 different vocational and non-vocational courses. The student hours total in 1988 was 1 910 000 compared to 1 230 000 10 years earlier (a growth rate of 4.5 per cent per annum).

The college employs 200 graduates, has a budget of £5m and is supervised by the local education authority via a board of governors who are responsible for its general direction, economy, efficiency and effectiveness; they determine the education to be provided and the staff required.

It has been given the following performance indicators or ratios:

Effectiveness:
  Enrolment (students enrolled/target)
  Completions (students completing courses/students enrolled)
  Qualifications (successful students/students enrolled)

Destinations (students going on to higher education or employment/
students enrolled)

Efficiency:
Student/staff ratio
Cost per student
Cost per completing student
Cost per successful student
Overall room utilization

The purpose of a college

A glance at the efficiency indicators shows that they are all MPIs and, while
no doubt of weighty concern to the management, are of little interest to us; it
would be hard to imagine anything more irrelevant than 'room utilization' as
an education indicator. The effectiveness indicators all have major defects:
the enrolment indicator measures the number of students enrolling but says
nothing about the level of education they are aiming at or achieve. The
others do, however, reflect success in teaching—low drop-out rates, high
exam passes, and good employment ratios are indeed what the student
wants and are therefore acceptable proxies.

Unfortunately, as noted before, if the college tries to raise the level of
education the rate of exam passes would fall; vice versa, the college could
improve this ratio by lowering the standard of courses offered and so this
criterion fails my 'unequivocal' test. Good employment ratios are fine, but
does not take account of value—one unemployed nurse is not equal to an
unemployed hairdresser. So these are not good proxies. (Indeed, I would
argue that there are no good proxies. You either measure the ultimate aim of
an organization or you fail to measure its performance in any valid way at all.
Exam passes are not a good guide to success in life after school; health
expenditure is not a good proxy for health, and so on. Moreover exam
results are irrelevant for the non-vocational students.)

I suspect that there is only one way to measure both the efficiency and
effectiveness of a college and that is by noting the salaries the students earn
after attending it compared with before, and setting this improvement
against the cost of education. Whatever motive they may have had in past
decades, youngsters today go to college for no other possible reason than
improving their earnings. Why is this feature missing from the long list of
indicators used by education authorities? Partly because teachers still see it
as too materialistic; they deplore the fact that education is no longer seen as
an end in itself but as a means to a job. Partly because it would be very
expensive to obtain the figures. Both excuses should be rejected firmly as
just more spoilers.

A BPI for the college

What we need to know is this: what did each student earn before attending college (or would have earned if he or she had gone to work straight from school), how much did each student's education cost at the college, and what did he or she earn in the, say, 10 years after leaving? Discount the cash flow and add up the present values.

For example, Tom does not go to college at all (so he is our 'control') and starts work at a salary of £5000 a year. His 'paired sample' (a brother perhaps), Dick, goes to college full-time for one year, which costs £3000 and, on leaving, earns £6000 a year. Their brother, Harry, studies for two years, costing £3000 a year, and then earns £9000.

If bank interest is 4 per cent (real) what is the 'present value' of their educational costs and earnings over the relevant years? In other words: what capital sum would you have to have in year 0 to give Tom an income of £5000 a year for 10 years (Tom's annual cash flow)? What capital would you need if you first had to invest another £3000 in year 1 but then received £6000 for nine years (Dick's annual cash flow), or if you invested £3000 for two years and then received £9000 for eight years (Harry's annual cash flow)? The answers are:

Tom = £42 000
Dick = £42 000
Harry = £52 000

In other words Dick has wasted his money: he spent (or the taxpayer did) £3000 on a year's further education, he lost a year's salary, and never earned enough to justify these costs. Harry's further education, on the other hand, paid off handsomely.

Everything you have ever wanted to know

Great care is required in making these calculations. Take just one issue. As far as Dick himself is concerned the deal was actually highly profitable because, although he lost £5000 of salary while he was at college for the first year, he did not pay for his education—the taxpayer did. So you have to make up your mind in whose name the calculation is being made. Dick himself made a 'profit'; it was 'society' which, having paid the fees and without Dick's contribution to the economy, made a loss. I see the student as the sole intended beneficiary; if the state helps students out financially, that is fine. Indeed, as will be seen in Chapter 14, the principle of engagement requires organizations to persuade all relevant interest groups to help them enhance the benefit they deliver to their intended beneficiaries, and so, if this college can persuade the state, the local community, the students themselves, or their rich relatives, to sponsor them then that is just fine; it is exactly how organizations should behave.

In other words, while society is entitled to make these calculations for itself to calculate what is known as the 'social return' and to decide for itself what attitude it wishes to take towards any given organization, the organization itself is responsible only to its beneficiaries and so should concern itself solely with the 'private rate of return', as it is called, that is, what the *beneficiaries* have gained, including any contribution from outsiders.

These DCF calculations are extremely versatile; you can discover, for example, what sum of money it would be worth spending on Dick's education to raise his salary from £5000 a year over 10 years to, say, £6000. Is it worth the college upgrading a course at a cost of £12 000 a year if it allows 17 extra students to earn an extra £1800 a year? Within how many years do managers who take an MBA recoup the cost in increased salaries? And so on to infinity; every question any one has ever wanted to ask about education may be answered by this method.

My belief is that we would be in for some surprises if we did use it, just as company managers are shocked when they switch from using the wrong indicators, such as turnover, to the right ones such as EpS. Some colleges would find that their most popular course was absurdly ineffective and vice versa; some governments would be amazed at the wastefulness of their most favoured types of educational facility, and vice versa. We might find that some educational schemes give a return far in excess of anything obtained by investing in industry, and that we should indulge ourselves liberally in these; others are a pure liability and a complete waste of society's resources. Are the much-vaunted French and German systems of state education better than ours? Just do the sums. (Are they easy? No. But at least we know which figures we want to see and how accurate they need to be to yield statistically significant conclusions.)

The central role of salaries

Is not this DCF technique an awful fuss? Yes, it is; moreover there is currently no incentive for any college even to attempt to use this approach so long as no others do. To obtain the students' earnings figures a considerable sample of them (and their control group 'pairs') would have to be tracked over many years to obtain the necessary statistical significance. The number of calculations would be considerable.

And yet, do we want to know what effect education is having on our young people or are we happy to use the figures we have got even though we know they are all arrant nonsense and irrelevant (like that blatantly lamppost figure for room utilization)? I am prepared to bet that, decades ago, old Mr Chips knew very well indeed how his students got on in later life, but today we have lost the vital knowledge of what schools are doing for their students. We do not know whether Northtown College is better than Southtown and it is time we did. Why did it take several decades to discover just how awful our educational system had become? Because we were not monitoring results. Why not? Because we could not agree what results we wanted and so the only figures we had were lamp-post ones.

The earning power of the student

The pay (or rather, the remuneration package) that a person earns today reflects everything that educators need to instil in their students: not only the three Rs, but behaviour, initiative, character, citizenship, judgement, ability to work in a team, leadership, appreciation of the arts, ethics. Employers are increasingly reluctant to employ people who lack these qualities; they pay vast sums for a balanced, sensible, rounded, proficient citizen. We keep being told by management gurus such as Peter Drucker that it is knowledge-workers who are in the ascendant today. Knowledge can be tested by exams so if this was true exam results would be a splendid proxy BPI. Alas, Drucker is wrong here, too. What matters today is not mere knowledge—which can be looked up in a computer file—but leadership, character and so on. If our schools and colleges want to know what 'added-value product' means, these are the buttons to press today.

In my view, then, the aim of tertiary education is an unqualified 'to improve the earning power of the student'. So the BPI for any tertiary college or university is the total salary of its annual output of students, minus its costs, versus its comparators; a successful college being one whose students' net aggregate earnings are in the top quartile.

What effect would the use of this BPI have on the tertiary education system? Extensive and wholly beneficial, I believe, for it would direct the designers of courses in these establishments towards those subjects which will earn the student a higher salary; they would ask 'By how much would it increase their earning power if we taught our students this rather than that?'. Students will flock to colleges that teach what they need to know and how they need to behave to get good jobs and will shun those low in published salary-league tables (which should replace exam- and degree-league tables). To enhance their performance figures, colleges will select students according to their ability and their personality to earn high salaries. Excellent—a two-way process; students competing for the best colleges and colleges competing for the best students.

Then there will be a knock-on effect down the line to secondary and primary education through the league table of high-salary tertiaries. There will be a revolution in curricula, teaching methods, financing, everything, to cope with the added-value courses this would call forth. Wonderful—and not before time. Set the right targets for our education system and every-thing will slip into place. It might take a decade or two, but at least it would start happening at last.

Materialism

Recently a Minister of Education published a list of a dozen guide-lines for parents to look for when selecting a school, including, for instance, 'the number of teachers absent for a substantial period'. The reason one has to use such absurd criteria is that the one statistic that really matters—do the children do well in life?—is missing. (I am happy to report, however, that the minister's list did not include 'room utilization'.)

And do I have to say this again? Money is the only *general indicator of value* that we have. That is its importance. Using money as an indicator does not automatically place me in the Club of Greed. I am aware of all the evil that liberal thinkers tell us flows from money; I was under the impression that all these were present in humanity's breast, in full measure, long before money was invented. Liberal and religious thinkers who suppress money as an indicator on so-called ethical grounds have denied society a most valuable intellectual resource.

(Talking of materialism, I am amused to discover (see page 173) that the number of visitors to Lourdes has risen considerably faster over the past five decades than the rate of growth of travel by car in the UK—I can think of few symbols more spiritual than a pilgrimage or an icon more materialistic than a car. So there may be hope for us yet.)

Two sets of students

In conclusion, we have the following completed purpose sequence for Northtown College (and for all tertiary education establishments):

Purpose sequence for Northtown Adult College

The intended beneficiaries	Vocational students
The intended benefit	To enhance their earning power
The BPI	Discounted earnings stream less cost of education and loss of earnings (for each student or, in aggregate, for the college itself)
Targets	Tmin: A return not significantly lower than average similar colleges
	Tsat: A return in the upper quartile of similar colleges

I realize how long it will take to reach the required standard of tracking; as a stop-gap proxy, figures simply showing the proportion of ex-students who are unemployed would be a useful start.

In our drive for a BPI for the youngsters at Northtown College, we have forgotten the non-vocational students. Recall that most adult colleges serve two entirely different categories; youngsters whose livelihoods depend on passing exams and learning new skills, and adults who, largely, attend classes in such delights as embroidery and playing better bridge for their greater enjoyment of life. My suggestion is that these two students are so different that the college should be re-formed into two autonomous organizations—or, better still, three: one to own or manage the facilities and two to make use of them, each with its own, single, homogeneous beneficiaries and its own, single, BPI—see 'Mall management' in Chapter 17. (The BPI for the non-vocational side? Profits? If so, dividends to whom?)

One technique often quoted by academics is the Norrington Table of Oxford University's college performance. You draw up a league table showing degree performance based on a score of 1 for a first, 2 for a second and so on. The college with the best score per student ranks top. That is fine if you are trying to measure academic results (which, as a college principal, Norrington presumably was), but what I want is a league table based on the salaries its ex-students earn in real life. Norrington's Table may rank colleges by a CPI, but it does not come within miles of a BPI. (In any case it is so crude that most colleges revile it endlessly, especially those not near the top! One would think that our leading university would have devised a successor to this monstrosity by now.)

The Girl Guide Association

The Girl Guide Association was formed in 1910 and incorporated by Royal Charter in 1922 to 'help girls and young women to develop emotionally, mentally, physically and spiritually so that they can make a positive contribution to their community and the wider world'.

The organization (now called The Guides) is governed by a council of approximately 60 who serve on a number of general purposes and specialist committees and employ a staff of 180. It is financed largely by subscriptions and operated almost entirely by volunteers.

The purpose of the Girl Guides

The intended beneficiaries are obviously girls (from a typical age of 7 to 18 and beyond). There are no bars to membership other than making 'the Promise'—a simple oath of allegiance. The benefit is much more difficult to express in modern words but I suggest that 'good citizenship' puts it briefly and sums up, I hope, the key words that appear in the Promise: 'loyal, trusted, helpful to others, polite, kind to animals, careful of possessions, self-controlled'.

My version of its aims would read:

Corporate purpose for the Girl Guides

The intended beneficiaries	Girls from 7 to 18 and beyond
The intended benefit	Good citizenship

How are we going to measure how effectively they are doing this? Let us start with all the conventional items: there were 735 000 members in 1989 compared with 890 000 a decade earlier—an Aarrog of *minus* 2 per cent (much of the loss in members being among the older girls).

Subscription income rose in the decade by an Aarrog of 1.4 per cent, achieved by subscriptions per member going up by 3.4 per cent per annum. Expenditure per member rose by a remarkable 7 per cent, achieved partly by increased non-subscription earnings (but all these national figures mean nothing because only a tiny fraction of total income and expenditure goes to the national 'head office', most of it remaining at local level, for which no figures are shown).

Does the decline in membership—it is the first organization we have seen to exhibit this—reflect a failure to deliver the benefit? Is it a warning, especially as it has continued relentlessly over a full decade? It might be, but firstly I have already cast doubt on membership as a CPI and secondly, as noted above, there is the possibility that this organization's management has deliberately adopted the strategy of raising subscriptions or intentionally reducing the number of older girls. But if membership is not the CPI, and certainly not the BPI, what is? How can we measure what the girls actually receive from this organization? For all we know, while fewer may be getting it, each is getting more; the decline of numbers may be good news for them, not bad.

A CPI for the Girl Guides

I hesitate to suggest this but I believe that 'good citizenship' (my shorthand, you remember) could be measured. What do you expect from a good citizen? How will she differ from someone who had not had the benefit of Guiding? A Guide, surely, will be a nicer person, self-assured, trustworthy, kind, competent, and so on—just the sort of person employers are looking for in the modern world! And so I dare to propose 'personal income' as the BPI. Before tackling a few of the technical details let me quote, in defence of this apparently monstrous proposal, the Chief Commissioner's Report for 1989: 'More and more women are working ... employers are searching for the kind of democratic leadership that attracts loyalty through trust ...'. She is, in other words, saying that Guides make good potential managers. I confess I found this confirmation of my guess surprising, but was further comforted when the newly appointed Chief Commissioner wrote in a letter to the *Financial Times* (30 March 1991), 'Former Guides are likely to be the women business leaders of the future'.

Does this mean that the Guides should become an employment training agency? Should they not be teaching word-processing and management? I hope it does not mean anything of the kind; all I am suggesting is that the aim of 'encouraging girls to be good citizens' is not itself empirically verifiable and, unless Guiding has some real, concrete, verifiable, visible, effect on these girls, it is pointless (it breaches rule 4 for benefits set out on page 53: 'The benefit being offered must be of perceived significance to the beneficiaries'). The 'concrete effect' that will appeal to most girls (or their parents who sponsor them) is that it will help them get a better job. As the Commissioner said, most women today work. To most of them work is central to their early adult lives.

My proposed BPI for this organization, then, is 'their members' incomes compared with non-Guides', and the relevant targets will be: Tmin is 'our members' remuneration not to be significantly less than comparable women' and Tsat is '. . . in the upper quartile' or whatever. Unfortunately, as so often with NPOs, there will be no actual data available for the past and little will be available for many years into the future.

Tracking—but not only for Guides

To measure whether they are producing this desirable effect in their members—getting better jobs—I suggest the Guides take a random sample of their girls and track them through the early years of their working lives (typically, I suppose, until motherhood), recording their incomes. At the same time they should take a 'paired sample' (i.e. girls matched by age, background, etc.) of non-Guides from the same school or neighbourhood and track them. Then compare the incomes of the Guides with the non-Guide control group during the relevant period using the standard statistical techniques.

Since this is the third context in which I have mentioned 'beneficiary-tracking' (tracking for short) I should make some further comments on it because I see it as a vital new concept designed to secure the continuing, central, place for beneficiaries within their organizations. Tracking is one of the girders in the steel frame of the beneficiary doctrine edifice.

Tracking is going to be expensive. I would not be surprised if it results in a significant reduction in the overall number of beneficiaries that some organizations can serve. However, the beneficiary doctrine suggests that obtaining concrete proof that an organization has delivered a verified benefit to a few beneficiaries is preferable to delivering an unknown (and possibly non-existent) benefit to many. (Failure to keep proper accounts is a serious offence for a company; shareholders would rightly dismiss the directors responsible for such a crass omission.)

143

Motivation to self-track

One way to track beneficiaries is to gain their enthusiastic cooperation—let they themselves describe what benefit they have actually received. Given the right approach, students would be delighted to take part in such a survey even if it involved revealing their salaries every year for, say, a decade after leaving college. Patients would be happy to describe their medical condition for years after treatment. Criminals would, in confidence to a layperson, disclose their true reoffending record. It is no use attempting to verify a benefit unless the information is willingly, even enthusiastically, provided. Without this motivation, it will be false, or falsified.

And notice what trouble parents take to 'track' their children. At first they observe them continuously, then hourly and later daily; and then, right up to the end of their lives, most parents retain the keenest interest in the continued progress of their then middle-aged offspring. It does not seem to me too much to ask of organizations like the Guides and Barnardo's, who place themselves *in loco parentis*, to demonstrate a commensurate long-term interest in the results of their ministrations. I doubt if it would demand more than an hour or two each year to check up on each ex-beneficiary (and their 'pair'), and I doubt if more than a 10 per cent sample would be required. At a cost of a few pounds per beneficiary, then, it might be possible to verify what effect the Guides, or Barnardo's, for instance, has actually had for the effort and expenditure they devote to each of their children.

The duty to track

I am suggesting that tracking becomes a duty of every organization, that it should be part of the formal or informal contract between every organization and its beneficiaries that they agree to be tracked for as long as necessary to establish a statistically significant estimate of the benefit they have derived from it. So important is tracking that it should be the responsibility of the governing directors not of the management (this does not mean that they personally must track; it means they must be responsible for ensuring that it is executed professionally and that the conclusions are statistically sig-nificant).

Note this philosophy please: the beneficiary doctrine is saying that one crucial task of these governing directors is to monitor the performance of their organization and that this task of governance is every bit as vital as the task of management. To run an organization without knowing whether it is delivering anything worthwhile to its beneficiaries is just not acceptable today. And notice this too: these governing directors are to monitor *results*—what is their organization doing for their beneficiaries? *Not*, as managers do, to monitor operational performance. BPIs, not MPIs.

Completely different to what managers do—and completely different to what so-called 'governors' do today.

I do not want to have to wait until something goes wrong with one of our major organizations and then set up a Royal Commission; I want to know continuously, as it goes wrong, or preferably before (as companies do)—after the event is far too late in the rapidly moving world we live in today. I do not want a cost-benefit analysis, based on theoretical figures which are frequently erroneous. I do not want organizations to rely on some university department launching an inquiry when they happen to have the funding for an occasional doctoral thesis; I do not want a departmental report which takes as long to prepare as the private sector would take to complete effective action. I do not want to have to turn to a watchdog or ombudsman—and certainly not to our disgraceful legal system—*after* something has gone wrong. What I want is a continuous gathering of real-life figures from real live beneficiaries in real time. Tracking is as essential to an organization as verification is to a disarmament treaty; it is useless without it.

Three tentative conclusions

A number of miscellaneous thoughts have arisen in the past two chapters.

The incomes or salary of their beneficiaries is emerging as a central criterion for measuring the performance of NPOs; the college and the Girl Guides here, the AA and Barnardo's earlier. But the definition of an organization is that it exists to benefit people. Put these two thoughts together and it may be that each person's life can be seen as a stream of events all, or nearly all, of which may be evaluated in cash. Some events will be positive—as when a person earns a salary or receives a dividend or a government grant—some negative—as when a person attends a college, suffers an accident, goes to prison. In each of these events an organization is standing by, waiting to serve at that point of a person's life. Thus every organization may be seen as operating upon each human stream of future cash-events in the hope of enhancing it.

The Girl Guides is losing members; but there is no evidence to show that they (or the Church of England, which is also rapidly losing its constituency) are delivering any less benefit to their remaining members than an organization whose membership is growing. That an organization which is providing a satisfactory benefit to its beneficiaries will grow is a reasonable assumption; what may *not* be true is that aiming for growth will result in more benefit for the beneficiaries; on the contrary, the opposite may be the case. The correct strategy seems to be: go for more benefit and this will bring more beneficiaries. Go for more beneficiaries and this could damage the interests of the current ones.

145

It is looking increasingly as though we can quantify the corporate objectives of many NPOs (the next two chapters may well confirm this conclusion). But we will have to consider what to do about those organizations whose performance cannot be measured, and also those whose performance we do measure and deem to be inadequate. Here are some of the strategies we might adopt:

1 Just allow them to continue operating in the full knowledge that they cannot be measured or are not economic. In wealthy developed nations, especially where considerations of humanity apply, this must occasionally be a valid response. A hospice may be a case in point.

2 Inspire their managements to strive harder to find a better way of having the same effect. This is the route most will take. *In extremis*, change the management.

3 Stop doing it. Find some humane excuse for not doing it, as doctors have to when they say no to 70-year-old applicants for kidney transplants. Let us face it, Utopia is not yet. There are billions of things we need to do to make this a better world; let us put our efforts where we can see it does most good.

Summary

I suggested that, in the modern world of work, there could only be one reason for attending tertiary education: to increase one's prospective earnings stream. We should judge our colleges, and what is taught in them, by this criterion alone. We should judge secondary and primary schools by their ability to get their students into high-earning tertiaries.

And the same criterion may be right for the Guides; we need only study the income of ex-Girl Guides to verify their success in inculcating 'good citizenship'.

But, in all these cases, to make the necessary calculations we have to link the DCF technique with thorough beneficiary tracking, an extremely costly activity that will, nevertheless, rapidly become less expensive as tracking techniques develop and as the practice of self-tracking is adopted as routine.

I noted also that most NPOs have taken but few steps down the road I am proposing; most have not even identified their intended beneficiaries, nor defined the benefit (their favourite, 'services', is plainly useless), and any form of quantification is limited to mere MPIs such as membership. There is a long road ahead.

CHAPTER ELEVEN

The prisons. Local and national government

In this chapter I propose to continue to use the purpose sequence to review the corporate objectives of a further number of NPOs.

Her Majesty's Prison Service (HMPS)

Her Majesty's Prison Service, run by the Home Office, employs 30 000 staff to look after approximately 50 000 inmates at a cost of about £1bn per annum (or £300 per prisoner per week). It is managed by a board of 13 senior civil servants, under the Director General.

A mission statement in the annual report declares that the Service: 'Serves the public by keeping in custody those committed by the courts'. This leaves us in no doubt who the intended beneficiary is—it is 'the public'. Whatever the Prison Service does or does not do for the inmates, it does it for the public good and not for them.

Now to the second question in the purpose sequence, 'What benefit do the intended beneficiaries expect?' That is equally plain: it is to 'keep in custody those committed by the courts'.

The Prison Service's Corporate Purpose

Let us formally recite the stated purpose as:

Corporate purpose for HMPS
(First draft)
The intended beneficiaries   The British public
The intended benefit   Keeping prisoners in custody

If we accept this purpose then the CPI is very easily stated: the way to measure the success of HMPS is to count the number of escapes from prisons. The figures for 1989 were much the same as for previous years: 201 from 'closed establishments', 116 from escort and 1155 absconded.

So that is it: we have the beneficiaries, the benefit and the CPI; we could very easily set Tmin and Tsat by reference to the past or to escapes from other prison systems in Europe and could equally easily monitor performance.

147

However, one of my rules for the identification of a true and valid benefit was that it should be of significant value to the intended beneficiaries (page 53), and I seriously question whether 30 000 people engaged in keeping 50 000 other people behind bars is a sufficient reason for the existence of this, or any, organization. The annual report does seem very firm that this is indeed the purpose of HMPS for, in heavy print in a 'task statement', it goes on to say that, 'The task of the Service is to use with maximum efficiency, the staff, money, buildings ... for the following functions: to keep in custody ... ' and so on. Now I have also warned (on page 111) that efficiency is never a sufficient *corporate* objective for any organization and so, on two grounds now, I reject this official statement of the purpose of the Prison Service. A third reason is the use of the word 'maximum', a well-worn spoiler (page 110).

A second corporate objective?

And there is a further complication: the mission statement has a second paragraph, which states: 'Our duty is to look after them with humanity and to help them lead law-abiding and useful lives in custody and after release.'

While the first paragraph was perfectly clear ('Serves the public by keeping in custody those committed by the courts ... '), the second raises two new points: the prisoners are to be treated with humanity—that is fine, it is a simple conduct statement describing how the prisoners are to be treated while inside—but also they are to be helped to lead useful lives. Is this a new aim, a second one, by which we are to judge the Service? Is it more or less important than the first one (keeping them in custody)? It is possible, presumably, to do both—keep them in while helping them to lead useful lives—but we need to know by which criterion we are supposed to judge and if by both how the two are weighted. Suppose that next year fewer escape but more reoffend; are we to be pleased or sorry? We are given no such trade-off criteria nor can I imagine what these might be.

In fact I do not have the slightest hesitation in believing that it is the 'keep them in' aim that predominates, partly because a first paragraph of a mission statement is presumably more important than a second, partly because that 'task statement', in heavy type, refers frequently to that function, and only obliquely to 'useful lives', and partly because it is very evident that the British prison system is quite simply not geared to undertake remedial work, except for a minority of inmates. Notice, incidentally, that none of these statements says anything about being sent to prison *as* a punishment, and certainly not *for* punishment—although most people would consider that conditions in most of our prisons are so far from 'humanity' that punishment is exactly what they are for. But, in any case, what is punishment for if it is not to persuade them not to reoffend? Reoffending, then, comes back into the centre of the argument.

A second attempt

I would like to try an alternative purpose statement which retains 'the public' as the intended beneficiary but adopts not the first but the second paragraph as the key aim, thus:

Corporate purpose for HMPS
(Second draft)

The intended beneficiaries	The British public
The intended benefit	To help prisoners lead law-abiding and useful lives in custody and after release

In other words not 'keep them in' but 'encourage them not to come back'. I suspect this is much closer to what the public believes our prisons should be trying to do for all their inmates, other than the few who are irredeemable. The BPI would now be shown by the record of reoffences (escapes would be included in this figure because escaping is an offence).

While no such figures appear in the annual report for the Prison Service (because, presumably, they do not accept this as a valid indicator) there is reference to reoffenders in a separate Home Office publication called 'Prison Statistics'. This shows reconvictions actually falling over the decade to 1985 by approximately 1 or 2 per cent per annum (depending upon age, type of sentence, and so on). Even though the number of prisoners who reoffend is still well over 50 per cent, this gradual improvement seems to me to be highly creditable; how weird and perverse of the Home Office to include the escape figures in the annual report—figures so low, and measuring a task so trivial—while not even mentioning the data for reconvictions which are surely of far greater social importance and, superficially at any rate, show an encouraging trend.

What they do is not what they are for

The public have the impression, certainly I had, that prison does not work. Yet, if we choose recidivism as the key indicator, this evidence suggests that they do. Alas, apparently it is not so; the idea that prisons might have this effect was enshrined in the old 'Rule 1' of the service relating to rehabilitation, but was abandoned in the 1960s as impractical. Yet I persist. I suspect the reason the Home Office failed in its attempt to get rehabilitation to work all those years ago was due to a lack of money, a lack of commitment from the prison officers and above all a failure to define the corporate objective correctly. And so, in Chapter 18 I attempt a further revision of the corporate objectives for a prison.

Like many other NPOs the Prison Service's annual report is redolent with other statistics of every description: numbers of staff, buildings, facilities (farms, workshops, etc.)—and costs. All these reflect the government's concern, obsession almost, with the efficient use of taxpayer's money. We learn, for example, that the cost of looking after each prisoner has fallen, in real terms, from £16 000 a year to £15 000 over the past five years. Now I have warned before that efficiency and value for money are not valid BPIs but are mere MPIs. What matters to the public is not what each prisoner costs, and certainly not how many cabbages they grow on the prison farms, but whether the prison system is working (what an organization does, remember, is not what it is for). I really do not care whether it costs £16 000 or £15 000 to look after each prisoner (especially when Eton turns out an arguably better product for only £12 000 a year). What I want the prisons to do is not to save money on keeping them in but to spend money to stop them going back. I want some 'added-value', even if it costs more.

When one recalls the dogged determination of the private sector to upgrade and add value to their products (see page 111), and then contemplates the Prison Service's present trifling little aim, one begins to grasp how far NPOs have to go to catch companies!

It is irrelevant to consider a more sophisticated technique for measuring prison performance while we are still unsure who the intended beneficiaries are, or what the benefit is supposed to be, but, just for the record, the ultimate measure is again to use DCF: take the cash spent on each prisoner while inside together with the stream of (legitimate) earnings on release (less any state aid), and calculate the return on these cash flows. I imagine the return would today be heavily negative; the game for society to play is to find some way of dealing with wrongdoers that yields a return on society's capital that exceeds 4 per cent, or whatever the hurdle rate is taken to be.

The Howard League for Penal Reform

Formed in 1866 in memory of John Howard, prison reformer of 1777, the Howard League campaigns for 'a rational reform of the criminal justice and penal systems' and, in particular, for a 'marked reduction in the use of prison within the penal system and for improved conditions in prison'. Prison, they say, is expensive (20 times more costly than probation), demoralizing, inhumane and ineffective—half the prisoners come back within two years.

The League is managed by a council and committees of 40 voluntary members and a staff of three full-time employees and is financed by the members, donations and legacies. It is by far the smallest of the organizations I have chosen here but as its reputation outshines its size I decided to include it as an interesting and relevant companion to the Prison Service.

The purpose of the Howard League

So far in these NPO chapters we have had little difficulty in deciding who the intended beneficiaries were for the various organizations we have discussed, but who are the intended beneficiaries of the Howard League? Obviously it is an extrovert organization, so it is not members, as it was for the AA; but are they criminals or society? The Howard League's literature is full of humanitarian concern for criminals and so I have no doubt that they are the intended beneficiaries. One might think that this would be stated explicitly in their literature but, as with most of the NPOs listed here, it is not; the AA may be right to assume that everyone knows who their beneficiaries are but in this case (and, for example, in the case of the Ministry of Agriculture, Fisheries and Food, see page 46) we could do with some official guidance.

I have emphasized throughout this book that the correct definition of 'purpose' is essential. Without a clear definition of both the beneficiaries and the benefit we do not know who is to judge the organization, nor on what grounds, nor can the management evaluate any proposed strategy; this supreme aim must be shining there far above them to guide their every step.

Imagine, for example, that a new scheme of criminal justice is proposed designed to treat criminals more humanely *and* to reduce the crime rate; plainly that would be as welcome to the Howard League as it would to society in general. Now imagine a scheme which improves the treatment of criminals but does nothing for the crime rate; that, I assume, would accord with the Howard League's objectives, while society would be largely indifferent or even hostile. Now imagine a third scheme which reduced the crime rate but did nothing to improve the treatment of criminals; that might be welcome to society at large but would it be to the League? I suspect not, but how can we tell unless we know what it is for? Without the aim, we cannot evaluate the means.

My assumption that criminals, not society, is their concern is strengthened by the League's close association with other organizations like NACRO (the National Association for the Care and Resettlement of Offenders). If so, what is the League trying to do for them? Achieve a more humane and caring criminal justice system, presumably. And so we have:

Corporate purpose for the Howard League
The intended beneficiaries   Criminals
The intended benefit   A more humane and caring criminal justice system

A CPI for the Howard League

How should this be measured? We can surely reject membership and subscription income, or expenditure, as meaningful BPIs for the Howard

League. However, I did raise the possibility (on page 142) that a rapidly rising membership, or income, might be a useful CPI for the managers of an NPO; if income was rising strongly that would surely indicate that the members recognized that the managers were pursuing an acceptable set of strategies; conversely, if income was in decline, as it is for the Girl Guides, for example, that might warn the managers that their members were dissatisfied. It is interesting to note, then, that in the past decade the Howard League's total income has risen by 11 per cent Aarrog (due largely to rising donations) and its expenditure by 10 per cent—a very rapid rate, the fastest we have seen, suggesting outstanding success.

But, surely, the crucial figure that marks this organization's true success or failure is the prison population? Not only would this reflect prison conditions (which must closely parallel overcrowding) but also the League's other aim—the use of non-custodial alternatives to prison. If we assume that 'prison population' is indeed their BPI then I imagine that Tmin would be 'any increase in population over a period of years' while Tsat would be a perceptible decline, say 2 or 3 per cent per annum until our prison population had fallen to, say, the level of other European nations.

A BPI for the Howard League

Alas, as everyone knows, our prison population has risen inexorably (by nearly 2 per cent per annum) for the past two decades. Does that mean that the Howard League is a failure? If 'prison population' is indeed the appropriate BPI, then—and to my personal surprise—that is exactly what it means. I regret to say that not only has the prison population increased, but almost every other aspect of the prison service in Britain (overcrowding, sentencing, sanitation, educational facilities) —virtually everything for which the Howard League has been campaigning over so many decades—has steadily deteriorated. Apparently the Howard League has just not convinced the public, or government ministers, or the judiciary, or the media, sufficiently to have had the slightest effect. Meanwhile, just to demonstrate what it is possible to achieve in this area, in Germany the prison population has declined by 20 per cent in the past decade.

Even by the minor criteria—the number of prisoners slopping out, the time banged up, the number of non-violent criminals in prison, the number of 15-year-olds, the mentally ill, those on remand (up an amazing 5.5 per cent per annum over the decade, and nearly half are not sent to prison when they eventually get to court after months *in* prison!)—all these and more have moved relentlessly the wrong way. Every one of these issues is the subject of a dozen papers, reports and conferences by the League over the past 50 years.

I can only conclude that this organization (and about a dozen with similar aims) is a failure. Once you employ a relevant BPI you soon see that its generously rising income sends entirely the wrong message. As noted before (page 95) BPIs do not always move the same way as CPIs. Because prison reform is such an obviously good cause in Britain there is a tendency to support this, and other similar, organizations, just as it is churlish not to contribute to the blind or children when a collection box is rattled under your nose. Yet, and this is one of the central themes of this book, there must be occasions when one should demand that organizations like this radically overhaul their strategies (such as merging with other prison reform organizations to achieve more clout) or, if that fails, change their management, and if that fails, that they be closed down. I make some further, perhaps more constructive, remarks on page 153. Meanwhile, I cannot help remarking that the fastest growing organization we have met so far is the worst performer.

(Within the last few months the government has made some significant assurances regarding the Prison Service, though whether these will prove any more effective than all previous pledges, of which we have all lost count, time will tell.)

Local government

I have already explained (page 68) that the normal method of comparing one town, city, or village with another, namely by means of an array or index of MPIs, is useless. You cannot compare a town whose streets score 50 (out of 100) for cleanliness with another town (or the same one at a different time) whose street crime scores 50, because no one knows how much weight to give either factor. Moreover, to describe a town adequately you would need dozens of such indicators and confusion would quickly kill the idea stone dead. Everyone can play pick-the-winner with endless trivial statistics, indeed, that is precisely what politicians love to do.

Two further problems appear with this approach; one is the problem of the intangibles, such as the architectural quality of the town or the availability of cultural activities. If you cannot measure these, and I do not think you can, then they cannot appear in the index at all. The other is the trade-off between standard of living (SOL) with quality of life (QOL) indicators; even if we could devise a QOL index by adding together all its constituent factors, so that Northtown scores, say, 670 out of a possible 1000 for quality of the environment, we somehow have to include the average wage (or whatever other indicator you wish to use to measure SOL), and I do not know how to do that. Imagine that the average wage in Northtown is $12 391, now what are you going to do? Add the 670 to $12 391? And if next year the figures become 596 and $13 432 what does that say about the new pleasures of living in that town? I have no idea.

Even if we could add everything up into some glorious super-index you cannot judge a town on one year's performance, you need a run of several, so how do we interpret a town which scores 57, 71, 61 on this super-index over three years compared with its neighbour which scores 71, 57, 61? You cannot use DCF on an index.

What is a town for?

The purpose of a town (or village or city) is to provide a pleasant place for the residents to live in. It follows that you can judge a town's government by whether it is a better place to live than it was last year, five years ago, or than a similar neighbouring town. So we have:

Corporate purpose for Northtown
The intended beneficiaries   The citizens of Northtown
The intended benefit   A better place to live

How are we going to judge whether Northtown is any better than it was a few years ago, or than Southtown? Is there an overall BPI which includes everything?

If we used average income per head this surely would be unequivocal? Everything is included in this indicator—the quality of life factors, whether quantifiable or not, as well as the standard of living factors. Thus if Northtown's government fails to attract a balanced mix of new industry, if discarded syringes lie deep in its public parks, if facilities for the aged are meagre, if its planners permit unseemly buildings, if local companies are not expanding, if its museums are closed on Sunday, then income per head will fall relative to nearby Southtown because better-off inhabitants would decide to live in Southtown rather than Northtown.

A possible BPI

In Britain local income per head statistics are not as readily available as in other developed nations who often use income as the basis for local taxation. I would, therefore, propose property values (readily available from building society and estate agent statistics). If the value of property per head is rising faster in Northtown than in Southtown then, over a period of years, that could only be because it is 'a nicer place to live'. Why have house prices in Liverpool fallen compared with Leeds? Answer, because Leeds is better managed than Liverpool and more people want to live there—in fact people are still (understandably) actually deserting Liverpool as they have for several decades.

So we have:

Corporate purpose for Northtown
The intended beneficiaries   The citizens of Northtown
The intended benefit   A better place to live

The BPI	Property value per head	
Targets	Tmin:	Values rising not significantly less rapidly than comparable towns
	Tsat:	Values rising perceptibly faster than comparable towns

'Property value per head' should include the total market value of all property; not just domestic housing, but also commercial offices, factories and civic buildings. Note that local government tax revenue is not a valid BPI, it is an MPI, an indicator of concern only to the management, not to the beneficiaries and, in any case, it can be manipulated by the government itself as part of a perfectly legitimate funding strategy. Nor would population movements do, these can also be manipulated and, again, population migration may also be a perfectly legitimate strategy for a town's government—an MPI, in other words, not a BPI.

But could 'property values per head' also mislead? If a local government stops, or materially slows down, the granting of planning permissions this will create an artificial market price for property, thus distorting this indicator. But would it? In due course these property prices would be perceived to be higher than could be justified by the delights of living in that area compared with a neighbouring one. Fewer would wish to live there and prices would fall back.

And note this: the beneficiaries of a town are its *existing* residents, just as it is the existing shareholders for whom a company works. Many of these residents would welcome a slowing down in the physical growth of their town (many attractive towns and cities have adopted exactly that strategy). Physical growth is, as we have seen before in so many contexts, an aim much desired by managers, much less so by beneficiaries; physical growth is often a CPI, seldom a BPI. It might well be, then, that rising property prices resulting from a policy of highly restrictive planning approvals would accurately reflect, rather than distort, the opinions of the residents as to it being 'a better place to live'.

But it turns out to be invalid

Moreover, not only could we use property prices to measure each house-holder's return on his or her capital while living in a town, if you aggregate all the residents' returns you get the DCF return for the town itself. In this way local government officials would at last have a single criterion by which to evaluate all their proposed projects; a project costing $10m, say, would be justified only if it enhanced the net present value of property in the town by more than $10m.

155

Recall why we want these measures. We want to compare one town with another (and with any other organization); we wish to measure how well the town is being managed; the managers themselves wish to use the BPI to evaluate strategies and projects, and for their own performance payments. The movement, over a run of years, in the value of property per resident, compared with similar towns, would reflect this very well, I suggest.

What about windfalls? Perhaps property in Northtown has risen faster than Southtown because, say, it is nearer a new motorway? These anomalies may occur for any organization at any time. What is required is a calculation to take account of this once and for all (such as accountants do routinely when 'reconciling' after a change in accounting procedure) or, in the extreme, it means suspending the use of the BPI until the anomaly has worked itself through. Companies experience exactly this sort of episode which temporarily distorts their profit record (a merger, a factory closure, an exchange rate gain) and deal with it in accordance with strict accounting rules—and remember, all we are trying to do is to devise a BPI that mimics and emulates the ones that companies use; we do not seek perfection.

A key requirement of any BPI is that it measures the benefit to each beneficiary; recall that one of the most satisfactory features of EpS is that it measures the return on capital for each individual shareholder—each share receives an identical return. Now one of the duties of the governing directors of any organization is to ensure that each individual intended beneficiary receives a fair share of the benefits that the organization delivers (page 216). It would be a function of the governing directors of a town to ensure that all property owners, and non-property owners, such as the disadvantaged, were equally served. This requirement takes us back to my opening proposal, that income per head would be the best BPI for local government, were the figures available, for while they may not own any property, even the disadvantaged have an income which can be measured.

Property values, it turns out, are only a lamp-post proxy and might not be valid to measure performance for all the town's beneficiaries. Even I have been seduced by a lamp-post.

National government

The same aim is valid for national government. What a national government should be doing is 'making this nation a better place to live'. We want Britain to become 'a better place to live' than it was over the last 10 years compared with France, Germany, America—wherever. That is what a modern national government is *for* (a concept entirely, wholly and completely foreign to political philosophers down the ages until very recent times, see page 273).

How do we measure this? We normally judge a nation by two criteria; its quality of life and its standards of living.

Defective indicators of government

Typical of a long line of attempts to measure these aspects is one published in the United Nations Development Programme (report for 1990) called the 'Human Development Index' (HDI) in which three indicators are added together. These are life expectancy, adult literacy and gross national product per head (GNPH). I do not propose to describe the complex system of scoring but I do intend to record just one of its conclusions: America comes out seventeenth among the nations of the world, below Ireland and Spain, just above *East* Germany (as it then was) and Israel! How many of America's huddled masses are planning to emigrate to East Germany, I wonder.

And so once again we see the frailty of such indices (as we did on page 69 and again on page 70, both of which came to equally outrageous verdicts). What has gone wrong here is that, judged by GNPH alone America ranks second after Switzerland—a conclusion that would surprise no one. But as soon as you try to add those quality of life features you distort the index. Why? Because they are either causes or effects, or both, of the GNPH of a nation; all the HDI does is to double-count those items that it happens to include (namely, in this case, health and education), while ignoring those it excludes, such as liberty, say, or housing standards, or unemployment or pollution which also go to make up the quality of life of a nation.

The condition of all these factors—freedom, architecture, facilities for the disabled, public transport, the countryside—everything you can think of that makes up a nation—reflects how each nation chooses to spend its income (i.e. its GNP). In some less developed countries the government spends most of the nation's income and, as the personal priorities of its successive presidents swing one way or the other, so that nation's educational facilities, or its roads, or military might, rise and fall over the years. In democracies the movement of these features shift with the cultural fashions of the electorate and other vicissitudes, but they, too, wander around more or less at random.

More apples and plums

Just at present, for instance, as a result of Mrs Thatcher's political legacy, Britain would do well in any index which includes house ownership and badly in any that contains education. The French would score 'badly' in any index which includes fast food facilities. The Japanese are quite incapable of defending their nation against an armed attack, yet defence of the realm is a capability many politicians would rank very highly as an indicator of government competence (I have never seen it as a constituent of any such index because, I presume, the academics who devise these things could not bear to include anything so sordid as armaments).

The only way to ensure that the disposition of resources exactly matches what the citizens wish for is to do what Switzerland does: have a referendum for every tiny detailed decision. But even this will yield only the predilections of that nation and could not be taken as a norm for an HDI-type index—in other words you cannot use it to compare one nation with another which is exactly what it is supposed to do!

And so we have the same huge problems here, on a national scale, as with all attempts to add a number of MPIs to form a BPI: no one will ever agree either on the items to be included in the list or their weighting. Whatever weight the HDI gives to literacy against health, and both against GNPH, is arbitrary to a degree that renders the HDI nugatory, meaningless and useless for any purpose but cocktail party chatter. As for the weighting the HDI gives to housing, defence, liberty, pollution, etc., (namely nil!) well, what can one say? And moreover, all those features that are measured by MPIs are items every government may wish to adjust for strategic reasons; they are tools of management not indicators of success. Every tax that has ever been imposed, for example, will distort these MPIs and they are distorted for a second time when tax is abolished. No, we have just witnessed yet again that a BPI cannot be devised by means of a battery of MPIs however cunningly it may be contrived.

A BPI for national government

I suspect that, as we have seen for all other organizations, there is only one valid BPI for a national government; all other indicators are MPIs, valid only for sections, departments and ministries of government. You cannot measure a national government by adding up all its departmental MPIs, you have to devise a separate and quite different BPI for the government of a nation, one that embraces everything (you just cannot add unemployment to subsidies on pig food divided by closure of coal mines).

The only indicator we require to judge a government is steady, long-term growth (measured in decades) of GNPH—gross national product per head. What matters to people is not what the government spends their money on, but how much is available to spend per head either by the people themselves or by the government on their behalf. Except for the occasional cataclysm we judge governments by the state of the economy. Public opinion polls show repeatedly that this is what wins and loses elections, not schools, attacks on children by fierce dogs, or the latest sex scandal. We do judge our politicians' general competence by how they handle such issues, but the only reason we wish to gauge this is to reassure ourselves as to their fitness to run the economy.

Growth of GNPH is not merely the top item in a list of innumerable public concerns, it is in a list of its own: what matters to the modern citizen is whether the economy is growing at a respectable rate or not. Nothing else comes near (except very occasionally and quite temporarily).

A BPI must be valid for the organization and its beneficiaries

Note that GNPH is, like all the BPIs I have recommended, valid as an aggregate (GNPH is GNP for the nation divided by its total population), and also as an indicator for each citizen individually where it becomes each person's after-tax income plus any services received from the government—effectively each person's standard of living. Mathematically, if a nation's GNPH is rising at 3 per cent so will the average citizen's standard of living. This does not mean that *all* citizens will enjoy this rise—obviously one whose tax rate has increased, or has become unemployed, will not, while others will have gained disproportionately from government grants or services. It is part of the role of government, as it is for all organizations through the good offices of the Governing Directors, to regulate the benefits equitably to each individual beneficiary.

Some will complain that this continual emphasis on material things in this book is obsessive, but I am merely reporting as I find: the vast majority of people do place this emphasis on their material well-being. This most certainly does not mean they are ruled by money, still less are they greedy for it, but it does mean that it is of central importance to them, not for itself, but for what it brings. Contrary to those who rail against modern materialism, money does not deliver just a bigger car and a second bathroom, but personal satisfaction and self-regard, access to the arts, status in the community, privacy in an increasingly intrusive world, education and knowledge, leisure facilities, protection from crime, power, a brighter future for their children—virtually everything that modern people desire for themselves and their family. Whether this will always be so, and whether, even in a thousand years' time we will still be quite so concerned with wealth, I have no idea; I speak only for today, but I do so with great confidence.

Wealth or freedom

I find it instructive that the Russian people mutely and passively accepted communism—complete with torture, massacres and a total loss of freedom—for 70 years, yet as soon as they took on board, as they did towards the end of the eighties, that it had failed to raise their standard of living they overthrew it; moreover, I believe, they will judge their new political order, whatever it turns out to be, not by the extent of their freedom at all, but *solely* by whether it delivers a higher standard of living.

Am I really arguing that wealth matters more to the average citizen than, say, freedom? Alas, and contrary to all romance and to the protestations of liberals everywhere, it seems to be so—even if for no other reason than that, along with everything else that wealth can buy, is freedom itself.

We must take note of this and what it says of the priorities of modern society. Do people still believe that money is evil, that poverty is noble? I do not think so—still less that the poor will be rewarded in the hereafter. They never admit to this predilection for money; indeed, when questioned they vigorously deny it (surveys of undergraduates regularly show that 'intellectual challenge' is listed by 50 per cent as the top requirement of their first job, while 'salary' comes bottom with 20 per cent. Well, they would say that, wouldn't they?).

I suspect that materialism is not a character defect in modern society at all; it has ruled us from the very start, as soon as barter began. Those who sneer at materialism are, I notice, those whose standards of living are already among the highest in the world (go and ask the Ghanaian peasants, whose GNPH has actually been falling for many years, what they think about it). The only difference between us today and our predecessors down the corridors of history is that we know it is now possible to do something about our standard of living which, until a couple of hundred years ago, it was not. We know it; what is more we are not going to argue about it for our minds are made up, we are simply going out to get more of it.

Tmin and Tsat for governments

Setting a target for growth of GNPH is easy. Tmin for a developed nation is a rate that is barely perceptible over a run of years, or, alternatively, a rate significantly below the average for OECD nations; Tsat is a rate above this norm. So, since the OECD has grown at 3 per cent per annum for the past several decades, any prime minister who allows the nation's economic growth to drop below, say, 2 per cent for more than say, a year or two, should be unceremoniously sacked. A government whose average rate falls significantly below 3 per cent over its five-year term should be unre-electable. Britain has been below Tmin for several decades, dragging along at 2 per cent while other OECD countries have averaged 3; as a result their GNPH has trebled in 30 years while ours has doubled.

But, you may persist, what about unemployment, inflation, the environment, the arts, equality, and everything else that makes life worth living, including peace itself? Surely these are the true aims of a government? But these are the mere concomitants of economic growth; none of them can be enjoyed unless growth is secured; all blossom as wealth increases and, for many of them, if they are lost growth itself will die. If we damage the environment, growth must be reined back; if we control inflation, growth can be accelerated; if we are healthy we can earn more; if we are not free, we will be less creative. Everything we value—everything—comes with wealth and ultimately dies without it. Freedom, leisure, the arts, health—everything is either a result of the growth of wealth or a necessary condition for it, either a cause or an effect of it. The last war grew out of a depression; thus even peace itself is, if I may paraphrase von Clausewitz, 'nothing more than the continuation of economics by other means'.

Chandeliers and flag-poles again

Politicians loudly proclaim their objective as being 'to achieve a balanced economy', meaning they intend to trade off the various economic aims: inflation, unemployment, growth, a stable exchange rate, an equitable tax regime. But this is sheer nonsense. There is not one list here; this is not one long list of economic goals where the game is to place the items in order of priority or importance or to 'balance them'. It is not one list, it is two. List number one contains just the one precious aim: growth of GNPH. The other comprises inflation, unemployment, exchange rates, fair taxes—and all the other devices of political and economic management. One aim, many means. We are back to the single flag-pole and many guy-ropes; one end, many means; one purpose, many strategies.

It is all just another example of the mix-up between aims and means, purpose and strategies. And we have again the same consequences of this error just as we have seen so many times before in this book: select a means as an aim and it leads to disaster. Aim for full employment as we did in the sixties and it leads to inflation; aim for a 'fair society' and the lack of pay differentials leads to a weakening of the skill base; set a minimum wage and you get unemployment; aim for zero inflation (as our Prime Minister John Major decreed) and you get recession. All these economic policies fail because they do not aim for the top purpose, the corporate one, the one that brings benefits to all, whatever their various desires may be. There can only be one economic aim: growth of GNPH. To achieve that many variables have to be skilfully adjusted. From it all the other desirables follow. As always: a single purpose, a multitude of strategies.

Just like all our other organizations, when you think it through there is one performance indicator which towers above all others, which indeed is not merely superior to them, but in a different logical category altogether, the link at the end of the chain, the hook on the chandelier: and that is the BPI, the one on which all the others depend and which embraces everything the organization is aiming to do. All organizations are the same; if you think yours has more than one corporate objective that simply means you have not yet thought out what it is.

It is rather like those irritating IQ tests: 'Spot the odd one out: window, floor, roof, house, ceiling or door.' The answer is 'house'. Why? Because all the others are *parts* of a house. So try this one: inflation, exchange rates, GNPH, unemployment, foreign debt. I hope you got it right—I even put it in capitals for you!

An unequivocal BPI for government

The BPI for government, then, is long-term growth of GNPH. Most of what a government does or does not do should be part of a strategy designed to achieve that one aim. Bills introduced into parliament, discussions by civil servants, decisions by ministers—all should be geared to enhancing the GNPH. The greater the contribution to GNPH of any proposal the more priority it should be given. If a bill will generate an extra £20bn of GNP then it should be introduced before one which generates only £10bn. If any bill cannot be evaluated in terms of its effect on GNPH the presumption should be that it has none and it should be dropped as a waste of parliamentary time.

(Of course all this reckons without that other class of actions and legislation not considered until Chapter 14, namely those that regulate how a government should behave towards its intended beneficiaries (its own nationals) and its interest groups (foreigners). Thus, while acting to benefit one class of citizens a government must obviously take care not to damage the interests of another; the no harm principle certainly applies here as elsewhere. And so must the principle of engagement. Many of the actions of government will naturally be devoted to these conduct considerations as well as to achieving economic growth.)

Summary

Neat and succinct though the mission statement of the Prison Service undoubtedly is, it is defective. It ascribes two duties to the service but fails to define which is prior. The annual report contains dozens of pages of MPIs with not one CPI or BPI among them.

The Howard League displays *par excellence* the distinction between a CPI and a BPI, for its income has grown faster than any we have seen while the prison population—the BPI—has remained as dismal as ever. Judged by that harsh criterion this organization is a failure.

Turning to government, both local and national, I conclude that income per head of the relevant population is their sole criterion. Alas, this conclusion is so at variance with modern liberal thinking that it will be ignored in favour of the multitude of socio-political banalities—freedom, a fair society, equality, fraternity—with which modern society deludes itself. For all these may be bought if you have the money. Without that we are but slaves.

CHAPTER TWELVE

The police. Architects

$\mathbf{I}$ shall continue to try to apply the purpose sequence to two final NPOs.

The Police

The mission statement for the Metropolitan Police runs as follows:

The purpose of the Metropolitan Police Service is to uphold the law fairly and firmly; to prevent crime; to pursue and bring to justice those who break the law; to keep the Queen's Peace; to protect, help and reassure the people in London; and to be seen to be doing all this with integrity, common sense and sound judgement.

The reason I deplore this statement is partly because it is long-winded and pompous, but chiefly because it seeks to persuade us that policing London is a multi-faceted task (notice the long list of duties and the words 'all this'), and this is contrary to my belief that the purpose of every organization should be simple and singular. Surely to the average person 'pursue and bring to justice' and 'uphold the law' means exactly the same as 'prevent crime', which is well-nigh identical to 'keep the Queen's peace' and 'protect the people of London'? It is all the same thing, is it not—but here deliberately and pretentiously hand-embroidered?

Or again; a Chief Superintendent was recently quoted as saying, 'Industrial managers are lucky, they have one target: profitability. I have issues way beyond economics to bother about'. A typically self-important viewpoint held, not just by police officers, of course, but by almost every manager of every NPO I have ever met. We love to believe that our jobs are distinctive and portentous, that we are dealing with some vast enigma, quite beyond the ken of ordinary folk.

Defective indicators

Be that as it may, in an explicit desire 'to move away from crime statistics as indicators', there is a small unit ('Component 9') at Scotland Yard which is charged with developing performance indicators for the five key elements of this mission statement. It is therefore preparing indicators to measure (1) the extent of the cover the police give ('street-man-days per available officer', for example); (2) traffic safety and flows; (3) crime statistics; (4) public order statistics; and finally (5) public reassurance, which will be measured by complaints from the public and so on. But all these are plainly mere MPIs measuring what the police do, not one of them measures what they are *for*. Which is what? What should be the corporate purpose of a police force?

Surely the aim of the Northtown police is to 'protect the people of Northtown from crime'? (Any crime: traffic, theft, riots; who cares which legal category it falls into, so long as it does not happen?) How should we measure this?

The clear-up rate

Let me eliminate one popular suggestion, the 'clear-up rate'. Its first defect is that this is not a purpose, it is a strategy, an MPI not a BPI, for obviously one way to protect the good people of Northtown from crime is to catch criminals. Alas, the catching of criminals is not what the citizens want; what they want is less crime. Catching criminals is certainly a means, but just one of many. It is not the aim. Flag-poles and guy-ropes again.

Worse, one of the most neglected means of reducing crime is crime prevention; notice how the clear-up rate not only completely fails to measure the effects of this strategy but, as with all defective BPIs, turns management attention away from strategies other than the one it specifically measures. In other words, this aim is not strategy neutral and any police force which adopted clear-up rate as its aim would be sure to neglect all other paths, including crime prevention, encouraging parental responsibility, etc. That seems to me a terrible price to pay for selecting the wrong indicator, yet it merely reinforces what we have learnt over and over again in the past few chapters: select the wrong corporate objective, especially a means instead of an aim, and you hog-tie the management and render your organization dramatically less effective for the beneficiaries.

The second problem with this indicator is that it can be fiddled by means of 'TIC'—previous crimes 'taken into consideration'. Imagine the Southtown police chief sending his detectives out to arrest burglars; each one they catch counts as one crime cleared up (the police call this 'primary clear up'). But the Northtown police chief cunningly instructs her detectives to remain at the Northtown police station to interview any burglars who happen to be brought in. Now it is a fact that most burglars have committed a number of previous crimes (I read recently of one who confessed to 3000!), so if these detectives just sit there obtaining confessions Northtown could claim dozens of crimes cleared up ('secondary') for every one of South-town's! Another splendid demonstration of how a CPI can distort rather than measure; it certainly illustrates how careful one must be.

I notice the Audit Commission uses clear-up rate per officer as its key indicator of police effectiveness. Alas, as mentioned earlier, this worthy organization is so obsessed by efficiency that it is blind to the more significant measures of corporate performance.

The crime rate

What about that other popular indicator of police performance, the crime rate? There are a number of problems here. First, each crime counts as one—it does not matter whether it is the foulest murder or a youth pinching a chocolate bar, a £10 burglary or a £10m one, it still counts as one crime. So if the 'crime rate' goes up it may merely mean that more petty crimes have occurred while the most distressing ones, the ones that really matter, are unaltered (indeed, in practice it almost certainly does mean that because petty crime accounts for 96 per cent of all crime).

Simply to add up crimes—to add petty theft to murder—and call this the crime rate is perfectly absurd; it must be the ultimate in apples and plums lunacy; it is hugely unprofessional and terrifies elderly people into think-ing they are about to be murdered in their beds while, in fact, the murder rate has no more than doubled in the past hundred years. The grossly misleading crime rate has, in my view, done as much to drag the police down in the eyes of the public than any actual incompetence on their part. They have to get this right. Their failure to do so is an excellent illustration of my thesis in this book: we must spend more resources measuring the performance of our socially significant organizations. It is shameful for the police to demand more resources to tackle a major social crisis that does not exist.

But there is another oft-quoted problem. The police say they spend only 15 per cent of their time on crime because they also have to search for lost children, rescue cats from trees, attend court, type reports, help old people across the road. So what are they, an anti-crime organization or a social service or, contrary to everything I believe, both?

A BPI for the police

If it was true that the police spend only 15 per cent of their time on crime then they would have plainly completely lost their way and should be funda-mentally re-formed; police are clearly supposed to be a crime-related organization, not an everything-on-earth organization. But it is not true. What they mean when they quote this figure, which they do with considerable frequency, is that this is the time they spend actually catching criminals. All these other activities—typing reports, rescuing cats—are either directly associated with crime (their aim), or with improving relations with the public the more effectively to fight crime (a very sensible possible means).

A recent suggestion is that their aim should be widened: not 'protect society from crime' but ' ... from trauma'. I would be quite happy with that so long as it was possible to define trauma and to measure whether they were protecting us from it, but as it includes almost everything that might occur in a community, including domestic squabbles, it would be even more vexatious to measure than crime. (And see Chapter 17 where excellent reasons are advanced for preferring small, specialist organizations in today's world rather than large general ones; 'crime' is a much more focused and more specialist aim than 'trauma' and so is a far more sensible aim for any modern organization.)

There has even been (in 1991) talk of the police providing 'services to the public': another giant step in the same wrong direction, in my view, not just because 'services' is even more general, less specialized than 'trauma', and thus contrary to the modern trend to specialization, but because it will be even more difficult to measure (remember the problem we had with the AA and Barnardo's who claimed, too broadly surely, to be providing 'services'?) And services 'to the public'? 'The public' is just a generalization. I want beneficiaries to have names and faces. A measureless aim for a boundless generalization? What a way to enter the next century!

Hiving off some of their duties

No. The police should reduce the span of their duties, not widen it (a company in trouble would retrench, not expand, surely). One activity that does take up a significant volume of police time and which is not related to crime is traffic (except, of course, for traffic-related crime). I cannot see how controlling road traffic meshes with the duties of a crime fighting organization, any more than, say, controlling air traffic would, and I would prefer to see a roads authority (see page 269) responsible for the design, financing, construction, maintenance *and* policing of roads. I imagine their roads police (together with the traffic wardens who would obviously join this new authority) would condescend to allow the crime police to use the roads in the course of their duties and they in turn would find it possible to cooperate with the roads police for road-related crimes, just as they do with the customs and excise officials for contraband and with tax officials for fraud and so on.

Several other marginal duties might be shed: missing persons, perhaps, could be hived off to a separate agency such as the Salvation Army. One might even have a new and entirely separate community service to rescue cats from trees and tell neighbours to turn down their noisy radio (remember that 96 per cent of crime is trivial, not requiring the full majesty of the law).

So, the first stage is to ensure that the police spend most of their time on crime-related activities and not on anything else. I trust that would end the '15 per cent' spoiler. And notice this: I am not the first person to recommend that the police hive off some of their activities, but while other people wish 'to improve efficiency' or 'streamline the management structure' the reason I want these changes is to permit the police to measure their performance; to me that is the prime reason for radically altering any organization. To be able to measure the performance of an organization is the first principle of its design.

Useless lamp-post figures

But the crime statistics themselves need even closer attention. As we have seen so many times for other organizations, police statistics measure what the police want to know, not what the beneficiaries—the public—want to know. When they discuss 'the cost of crime' the police mean the cost of policing divided by the number of crimes; what the public mean is the cost to *them* of crime.

What we need is a new method of measuring the personal and social losses due to crime. This would distinguish between a serious crime and a less serious one judged by what *we* think, not by the value system of the police. I have the impression, for example, that if a police officer is tapped on the shin in a riot this is considered more serious than a rape. If we do not insist on placing our values on to the measurement of crime we must not be surprised if the police apply theirs (and so, once again, we note the astonishing and all-pervading extent to which we have all allowed managers to usurp and pervert the running of *our* organizations to *their* ends).

So how would we evaluate crime? The losses from a robbery with violence, for instance, would presumably include the cost of replacing the goods, the cost of hospital treatment for the injured, plus their days off work, plus their trauma (see below), plus the relevant cost of the police, the courts, the prison and other services. Could these be calculated? I have no illusions about the expense of doing so; it would require someone laboriously to track each crime, totting up all the actual costs that the victims and the state incurred. Moreover, as noted above, I repudiate the methods of cost/benefit analysis as being too theoretical; I dismiss all proxies; I want the actual, real, tangible costs as shown on invoices and in cheque-books.

In its early days such a scheme would be prohibitively expensive, even if we could persuade a number of voluntary organizations to make the calculations (or, more salutary, to supervise the criminals while *they* made the calculations) but, after a time, the learning curve would allow a substantial

167

drop in cost; the costing of some common crimes would become routine (to insurance companies such sums are already trite, they must have enough data in their computers to evaluate almost every crime in history).

Even such trauma as rape might become quantifiable if we encouraged private prosecutions by victims (who would know what it meant to them), as opposed to public prosecutions by the state. As I said above, crime statistics should reflect how society—the victims—values any given crime, rather than how the police or the state values it, and we will never discover how to make these calculations so long as the state is the sole actor in the performance. (Why *do* fines go to the state, not to the victims, I wonder? Another case of the managers pinching the beneficiaries' dues?)

The monetary value of crime

Is it really possible to place a monetary value on crime? I do not know but it would surely have some huge advantages:

1 It would provide a rational basis for compensation to victims and to society by the perpetrators. Assuming they are judged guilty and fully responsible they would pay back everyone affected by their acts either from their earnings, or from community work, or in prison at market pay rates. The punishment thus *exactly* fits the crime, not a penny more, not a penny less. There would be no need for a tariff of fines; the fine would equal the cost of the crime *to the victims*. If they were judged, say, only 30 per cent responsible then they would pay 30 per cent. The rate at which these fines were paid off should be related to the perpetrator's means.

2 It would provide crime statistics in money terms. You simply add up the cost of crimes, of all sorts and severity, for each period in each area (the cost of *crime*, notice, not the cost of policing, nor the number of crimes, neither of which are valid BPIs). We could see at a glance whether the volume of crime had risen or fallen over any given period, taking its severity—as valued by society, notice, not by the police or the state—fully into account, corrected not just for inflation but for the constantly changing ranking that society places upon the various classes of crime (and thus automatically adjusted for the propensity to report them).

3 Given these figures it would become possible to calculate how much it was worth spending on policing (indeed on each *method* of policing) in order to reduce the cost of crime by each marginal pound (we might even find that it was simply not worth fighting some crime, while it was immensely worth fighting others). Project appraisal using DCF would become practical at last in criminology and jurisprudence.

4 It would be possible to set targets, related to other policing areas and nations, for annual rates of improvement in the cost of crime, and we could

even set target rates of return for expenditure on policing compared with expenditure on other social projects.

5 We could offer rewards to police officers (and their collaborators) related accurately to the severity of the crime they prevent or solve.

What prizes are to be won, if we could be bothered to get this right!

It has been proposed by local authorities (in 1991) to link chief constables' pay with 'budgeting ability, detection rates, force workloads and community relations'. It really is hard to restrain one's contempt for such handfuls of meaningful indicators (page 66). You have to pinch yourself to make sure you are in this century. The police are there to do something about crime. Get on with it. If they succeed in *this*, not in some daft trivial irrelevance, such as their budgeting ability or how shiny their tunic buttons are, then pay them handsomely.

Comparability eliminates one spoiler

Suppose the police protest, 'Ah, but the crime rate depends upon all sorts of factors in society, not just the police, and none of these are within our control'. But remember, a central theme of this book is that it is only possible to judge the performance of one organization against that of others. Now either these factors are the same in each comparable police area, or they are not. If they are the same, then the performance of those police forces are directly comparable and one may be judged better or worse at policing than the other. If the factors are not the same, then one must measure the differences and adjust the performance record accordingly, thus making the two areas comparable.

For example, I am sure that unemployment is a factor in crime. If Northtown's crime rate is rising while Southtown's is falling against the same trends in unemployment in both towns, well that will take some explaining away by the Northtown police. Statisticians have some powerful tools for sorting out multiple variances these days. No company would *ever* complain, 'Oh, we cannot make more profit because we do not control our market-place'. Of course they do not. Nor will the police ever control all the factors that affect crime—at least I hope not—but that does not mean they can just wring their hands in impotence.

The Royal Institute of British Architects (RIBA)

RIBA was granted a charter in 1837 which declared it was 'for the general advancement of Civil Architecture, and for promoting and facilitating the acquirement of knowledge of the various arts and sciences connected therewith ... '. It is governed by a council of 62 members and managed by a director general through 200 staff and a management team of nine, and financed by subscriptions from architectural firms and partnerships.

I am uncertain whether this is an introvert or an extrovert organization. The charter surely implies the former: RIBA exists, as the senior staff emphasize, for the advancement of architecture, it is not a trade union for the benefit of architects. Of course, I reject this concept of an organization; organizations are for *people*, I believe, and so either RIBA is a trade union for architects (and therefore introvert) or it is extrovert and supposed to be advancing architecture for British people. If the latter is true I confess to feeling a sense of wonder that so many architectural firms should so generously contribute to this worthy cause, out of their own pockets.

I have to say that many people in Britain believe that post-war British architecture is appalling. If the advancement of British architecture is indeed its aim, then RIBA is an evident failure. Even though it is not possible to measure this 'benefit' the failure is so abject that, alas, quantification is barely necessary.

The purpose of RIBA

My view is that the sooner RIBA transforms itself into a professional trade union the better and I would then define its aims as follows:

Corporate purpose for RIBA

The intended beneficiaries	Members (architects)
The intended benefit	To maintain the interests of architects

But why should it become a professional trade union, you may protest, when it could equally well follow the National Trust and become an association for designing attractive new buildings for the nation just as the Trust preserves attractive old ones? The answer is that the National Trust enjoys practical and effective control over what they do—they actually own, inalienably, the properties they are preserving, and moreover can be seen to be preserving them, even if it is hard to measure how well they are doing this. RIBA does not have control over the appearance of the buildings their members design, nor over town planning processes. Nor, even if they did, could any system of measurement be devised by which to determine whether our buildings are better designed today than those of previous years. The beneficiary doctrine demands that organizations like that, which stand little chance of ever being seen to deliver their aims, let alone measuring them, should be reformed or closed down.

As a matter of comparative interest, RIBA's membership has risen by 0.4 per cent per annum in the decade to 1990. Total income has risen by 0.6 per cent and expenditure by 2.3 per cent in the past four years. However, although these figures are much lower than those we have become familiar with above, and which may well have a message for the managers (especially as they cover a period of astonishing boom in the British building industry), they do not directly measure the benefit the organization has delivered to the beneficiaries (membership and income are MPIs, remember, not BPIs).

Turning to possible targets, I imagine they would be exactly the same as for any other trade union, namely, Tmin is 'the long-term annual increases in architects' remuneration must not fall significantly below the average of similar professions (such as lawyers and chartered surveyors)', and Tsat is 'ensuring that growth of architects' remuneration is consistently in the top quartile' or words to that effect. No doubt the relevant figures are readily available.

Growth rates

I explained in Chapter 7 how managers in companies are obsessed with growth, even though, as I also explained, growth is not even a necessary element in the concept of return on shareholders' capital. I now wish to ask the question: should managers of NPOs also pay homage to growth?

Note first that whether they should or not, they do; most of the NPOs I review in these four chapters draw attention in their reports to the growing number of members recruited, children helped, prisoners held, and so on. Success and progress are seen as synonymous with more and bigger, not only in annual reports, of course, but wherever managers are gathered together. Faced with two projects, one that improves service to fewer clients or one that offers the same to more clients, most managers would choose the latter every time, whether in a company, a hospital, a children's charity, or whatever.

But we have seen repeatedly how mere volume or numerical growth can damage the interests of beneficiaries: when an insurance company increases the number of policy holders this can damage the returns on existing policy holders' funds; when a town encourages the influx of new inhabitants it degrades standards for existing residents; and, in general, almost any 'empire building' enhances the standing of the managers but at the expense of the beneficiaries. We saw that the fastest growing of our earlier examples (Howard League, AA and Barnardo's) were the ones which yielded the lowest growth of benefits per beneficiary, while the lowest physical grower (Girl Guides) gave among the highest rewards to their beneficiaries.

While physical growth may be a thoroughly defective aim from the point of view of the beneficiaries it is universally popular with managers in companies and NPOs alike and, since it is the managers who run these

171

organizations, growth wins. Without doubt growth is often a useful and valid strategy: it generates new jobs and promotion, it leads to cost reduction through the scale effect, it offers more clout in the market-place. Growth, then, is a valid CPI; it is seldom a valid BPI (few beneficiaries see it as having any clear benefits for them). Moreover, almost any physical growth is also liable to damage the environment. I see this as a major conclusion from this book: the attitude to physical growth which beneficiaries feel on the one hand and managers on the other reflects the stark divide that lies between them.

Growth of benefit per beneficiary (BpB)

But there is a form of growth that may well be a valid indicator for NPOs: growth of benefit per beneficiary (BpB). Note the subtle distinction; recall the difference for companies between growth of sales (something physical, desired by managers but of scant interest to the shareholders) and growth of EpS, something not physical, but of profound interest to the beneficiaries (money, more of it every year for each and every shareholder).

So, growth of help (more of it every year for every motorist); growth of remuneration (more of it every year for every architect); succour (more of it every year for every disadvantaged child); crime (less of it every year for every citizen of Northtown); accidents (fewer for travellers); GNPH (more for every citizen). What the managers of every NPO should be asked to do, then, is to discover exciting new ways to deliver more and more benefit to their beneficiaries every year. This is the format in which most targets should be set, in Aarrogs (for most organizations, not all; growth may not be valid for many project organizations, for instance).

The rate of growth of BpB, then, should be a prime measure of the competence of the managers and, judging by the effect high rates of achievement have on company managers, managers of NPOs will welcome the challenge of doing it better every year for their beneficiaries, year after year, better than most of their comparators.

No magic figures for NPOs

But whereas with companies I was able to suggest two 'magic figures' (3 per cent and 7–10 per cent to represent 'just perceptible' and 'satisfactory' target growth rates respectively) the spread of rates is far wider in the case of NPOs, naturally so, since the variety of their activities is so much greater. Thus we see life expectancy in Britain rising from 55 years in 1920 to 77 in 1988, a rise of a mere 0.5 per cent per annum; compare that rate with the decline in the accident rate on American airlines—a staggering 11 per cent per annum, where the number of fatal accidents has dropped from one accident in 10 million passenger miles in 1935 to one in 3000 million miles in 1985.

TABLE 12.1
Varying examples of rates of growth

	Growth per cent per annum
UK car reliability	+5
Road accident rate	−5
Passenger miles by car	+3.5
Journey times on British Rail	−1
Traffic speed in London	−2
Wheat yields per acre	+2
Cost of computing	−33
Visitors to Lourdes	+5
Visitors to National Trust properties	+7
Grocery outlets	−5
Heart attacks (USA)	−3
Heart attacks (UK)	−1
Population of UK	+0.2
Population of Zaire	+3
GNPH in Zaire	−2
Decay-free teeth of UK youth	+3
Women's/men's pay in UK	+1
Human embryo	100 000 000 in 9 months

Table 12.1 illustrates some interesting, amusing and contrasting rates of growth over the past many years or decades. But notice that most of these figures are *physical* growth rates. MPIs or CPIs, not BpBs. The BpBs are likely to be much lower, a fact which confirms that the growth of benefit to the beneficiaries of the average NPO seems to be well below that of companies (although, alas, we do not know how their BpBs have really moved because few NPOs have ever measured them.) In view of this huge variation I doubt if any 'magic figures' would be valid as targets for the whole range of NPOs; each type must be evaluated on its own merits. Thus to improve our life expectancy by 11 per cent per annum, instead of 0.5, would have us all living to the age of 219 by the end of this decade! Conversely, if air accidents had only improved by 0.5 per cent, instead of 11, and if air travel had flourished as it has (which, of course, it would not have), most of us would be dead.

But forget the actual target figure; that is for the governing directors to decide for each distinctive organization. What matters here are the implications of the conclusion that physical growth is contrary to beneficiary interests; growth of BpB is what they really want. The first implication is that managers should abandon all physical growth targets at the corporate level (though not necessarily at the MPI level); no more sales turnover targets, no more of those countless efficiency targets, such as cases per social worker, at least not as *corporate* targets. Instead companies should aim at more EpS; NPOs should aim at more BpBs. This may even mean *fewer* clients, but more benefit for each. Many organizations spread their benefit so thinly that we cannot measure the effect on the beneficiaries at all; these should cut the number of beneficiaries until the benefit delivered to each reaches a measurable threshold, just as a company in trouble would retrench until it starts to make profits again.

So, lift the benefit to existing beneficiaries until the effect on them is such that, at the very least, it may be measured. If performance is around Tmin, no expansion of the number of beneficiaries should ever be attempted. Only when the level of benefit is satisfactory should any organization expand the number of its beneficiaries, just as successful companies occasionally issue new capital if they are confident they can serve the new shareholders as generously as existing ones.

But normally, more for the same. Exactly the opposite of what most NPOs aim to do.

Summary (for Chapters 9, 10, 11, and 12)

In these four chapters I have discussed possible corporate objectives for 10 widely differing NPOs. Without exception every single one currently uses MPIs or CPIs to measure their corporate performance (highlighting what these organizations *do*) as opposed to BPIs (what they are *for*)—a vivid confirmation of the dominance of management over governance.

Moreover, while 'growth of membership' (of children, motorists, architects or whatever) or of income, or of expenditure, is often a valid CPI and may inform and warn the management of trends in the success (or popularity or vogue) of their organization, this is not always the case; thus the impressions of a previous chapter—that physical growth is a poor indicator—are confirmed. It may even be a poor strategy too, leading to a fall in the benefits per beneficiary; the faster managers force an organization to grow, the more attenuated the benefits may become. If this is so the practice of 'empire building' is revealed as one of the most damaging effects of the dominance of management over governance it is possible to imagine.

Valid indicators would include any which quantify the benefit actually delivered to the beneficiaries or which measure the annual increase in benefit to beneficiaries, especially if these make it possible to calculate how well *each* beneficiary, individually, fared over a significantly prolonged period (not less than several years). Growth of benefit to beneficiary (BpB), then, a sort of earnings per share (EpS) for NPOs, is a universally valid BPI.

Even more acceptable are those BPIs which measure a financial return to each beneficiary in terms of a discounted cash flow. This would allow every organization in the world to be compared with every other and with any given 'hurdle rate' of return (such as the universal 4 per cent return—or whatever it should be for the debt-laden nineties). The return could be calculated for each beneficiary individually or aggregated for the organization as a whole. Using this approach, very significantly, a 'satisfactory return' may be defined without any element of growth at all.

None of the above organizations set themselves corporate targets. Few show any significant figures for more than the current and the immediate past year (except for membership figures, which are sometimes shown for decades)—a ridiculously short period in which to be invited to judge their performance. Companies nearly always display a five-year record.

Turning to the application of the purpose sequence, we identified the intended beneficiaries of most of the selected organizations fairly swiftly, although we did have some difficulty with prisons, the Howard League and RIBA. Defining the benefit was no more difficult either, once we had rejected 'services' and accepted the critical role of money, salary, income and material well-being to the modern person (all criteria that are comparatively easy to track). We had especial difficulties with a BPI for the police where a massive reappraisal is obviously required—a revision far beyond anything currently under consideration by the authorities (I saw the 'crime rate' as a prime example of how not to measure performance to *beneficiaries*). Tmin and Tsat did not present many difficulties once a satisfactory definition of the BPI was proposed for each given organization.

But the main conclusion of these chapters is surely that physical growth, the first choice of almost every manager, is virtually certain to be deleterious to the beneficiaries, and that the best strategy for all organizations is to aim to generate more benefit to the same or fewer beneficiaries rather than the same to more. This appears to be as valid for children in homes as for criminals in prison and citizens in towns and nations.

Managers are not going to like that.

CHAPTER THIRTEEN

The stakeholder theory

Up to now I have limited my detailed discussions to the first, and most important, part of the beneficiary doctrine—performance—and have said little about the other two members of its trilogy, conduct and governance. The main point to emerge so far is that the purpose of every organization is to strive single-mindedly to deliver a verifiably satisfactory benefit to its intended beneficiaries. But it has become obvious that, because single-mindedness can lead to excess, we need a set of rules to restrict, constrain and govern over-enthusiastic managements. Indeed, the whole philosophy so far propounded, centred as it is on performance to the beneficiaries alone, could be distinctly unattractive without some form of moral mitigation.

So now we turn to this second part of the beneficiary doctrine: corporate conduct. The need for a code of conduct is axiomatic for all individuals and all our organizations; it is not just companies who misbehave. Far from it; at least most companies do not torture and murder their own employees, as most governments (over half of them, according to Amnesty) do their own citizens, so while we certainly need to curb the greedy business executive, we must also curtail the false witness of the over-eager police officer, the officious social worker, the drug-enhanced athlete. The last thing modern society needs, in its search for improved performance, is any further decline in standards of morality.

I use the term corporate conduct to mean 'how an organization behaves itself in society while pursuing its purpose', or 'how organizations should treat their various interest groups while aspiring to serve their intended beneficiaries'.

Well, how should organizations behave?

Many types of ethical theory

According to the Board for Social Responsibility of the General Synod of the Church of England (in a 1989 report on acquisitions and mergers), 'social goals should take priority over economic objectives in the conduct of British business'. I would not care to estimate how long British business would last under that code of ethics! Or you can try this approach from Yorkshire:

See all, hear all, say nowt
Eat all, sup all, pay nowt
And if tha does owt for nowt
Allus do it for thissen

which translates, 'Watch and listen but say nothing, eat and drink whatever you are offered but do not pay for anything; if you do anything for anyone without payment, make sure it is for yourself'. And we would not last very long that way either!

By far the best known and most widely accepted code of corporate ethics is provided by the stakeholder theory.

The stakeholder theory

As mentioned many times before I believe the stakeholder theory (also known as the consensus theory) is a curse that lies heavily upon all our organizations. As it has been so widely accepted throughout the world, across all shades of political opinion, over so many decades, I shall have to spend a little time explaining my distrust of it.

As I understand it, the theory notes the obvious fact that every organization comes into contact with a variety of groups of people in the pursuit of its aims. It goes on to claim that some of these groups have such a close and mutually important relationship that they must be deemed to hold a 'stake' in the organization, and they are therefore entitled to have a right to a claim upon, some of the benefits that the organization generates.

In the most popular version of this theory (the 'equity' version) these rights are equal not only to each other—all stakeholders are equal—but also to the rights of the intended beneficiaries themselves. Thus a company's shareholders are not seen to stand in any special relationship with their organization; their bond is no stronger with their company, and no more privileged, than that of the employees, the managers, the customers, or the local community; they should be shown no more and no less consideration than any of these. The European 'supervisory boards', for example, whose role it is to lay down how each stakeholder is to benefit from their companies, are just one of many formal manifestations of this belief around the world.

By this same argument a school should benefit, or meet the aspirations of, not only the students but also the teachers, the local community, the student's parents and employers and the education authorities (indeed, New York's state schools are given formal, written 'system goals' for all these stakeholders).

A hospital is there not only for patients but also their families, doctors, nurses, the ancillary worker's union, the government, the hospital managers, the local community and health insurance companies. All should benefit—equally if the equity version is accepted. Hospitals in every corner of the globe issue mission statements enshrining this philosophy.

The distributive role of the managers

This, then, is the central theme of the stakeholder theory as it is perceived and practised throughout the world today. It is further asserted that an organization's managers should take responsibility for 'holding the balance' between its various stakeholders, to act in 'the interests of all the community', for the good of all, and to ensure that everyone receives their just deserts. The stakeholder theory thus requires all organizations to work for the common good of all the participants. It is a concept of delightful generosity of spirit; its philosophy is liberal and caring, typical of many similar self-deceptions with which modern society beguiles itself.

I see a number of insoluble problems with it. First, I suspect that it is based on false logic. While it is perfectly true that when a school teaches a student, a hospital cures a patient, or a company makes a profit, the relevant communities do benefit. But that is not why any of these deeds are done; we teach students for the students—even if it could be shown conclusively that no benefit whatever had accrued to anyone else we would still teach them. Would a hospital give up healing the sick because the nurses and doctors, the relatives and the local community were discovered not to be deriving any benefit? Do you really believe that a hospital is there in any sense whatever to provide jobs for nurses or as a platform for the exercise of the surgeon's skills? No, one beneficiary is sufficient justification for any organization; no organization needs more than one.

But there are many other puzzles here.

Who are they?

It is not clear to me who may and may not be deemed a stakeholder. No one would dispute that the lives of long-serving managers, employees and customers, for example, are so intimately bound up with their organization that they unquestionably have a most profound interest in its future. Yet many have not; employees come and go, some are part-time; while some customers develop and cherish a lifetime's loyal relationship, others perform but a single fleeting transaction. Are there shades and gradations of this relationship depending upon its depth or longevity? Where is the cut-off? Is there a grey area where one is a sort of 'associate' stakeholder?

Again, many suppliers are even more dependent upon the organizations they serve than some employees and customers are, yet Britain's leading food retailer, Sainsbury's, lists only four stakeholders: the local community, the customer, employees and shareholders. It says nothing whatever about its suppliers while our leading high street retailer, Marks and Spencer, who also publicly embraces a stakeholder approach, would emphatically include their suppliers in such a list.

Who else is or is not to be deemed a stakeholder? What about competitors, tax collectors, passers-by, auditors and bankers who also have a relationship with these organizations, some of very great duration and profundity, do they qualify as stakeholders? I have never seen them mentioned (certainly not tax collectors). IBM has recently recognized 'the community' as a stakeholder to add to their employees, customers, shareholders and 'business associates' all of whom they have long since recognized; what suddenly enticed them to yield this new favour?

For a British company the state (Britain) is surely a stakeholder; for a French company France is a stakeholder. But is the European Community? I have seen 'the environment' listed as a stakeholder implying that organizations have a duty to preserve it; I have seen 'technology' listed, to indicate a duty to advance technology for the good of mankind. Some protest groups are listed as stakeholders; others are not.

So, I am not sure who qualifies as a stakeholder, nor what the qualifications are; the theory does not say.

What rights do they have?

What rights does this stakeholder status confer upon these people, and what are the rules for deciding when rights should be granted and when withheld? Should stakeholder-employees receive extra wages or enjoy more job security than temporary, and presumably non-stakeholder employees? Extra discounts for stakeholder-customers? If the equity version is correct (that is, if all stakeholders—including the intended beneficiaries—are equal), then presumably when profits rise by 20 per cent the managers, the employees, the customers, as well as the shareholders, should all receive 20 per cent extra. Do you know a company which behaves like that?

Five years ago the profits of British Petroleum (BP) amounted to one-third of the total wages bill; profits are now (1990 figures) equal to the wages bill; that does not sound to me like equal rewards to equal stakeholders. Some stakeholders are more equal than others, it seems. Sainsbury's profit margins have doubled in the past decade. I can see how their shareholders benefited from this, but how did their employees and the community? Equally? And I cannot see how their customers could have benefited at all.

I must not put words into these companies' mouths; neither BP, nor Sainsbury's, so far as I know, have ever claimed allegiance to the equity version of the stakeholder theory, although their public pronouncements seem to imply they do. Be that as it may, note the implication of all this for the credibility of the stakeholder theory itself. If stakeholders are equal it has some meaning; if not then, presumably, they can be pampered or ignored at will. In practice, quite evidently, some are indeed favoured above some others. They are not treated equally. The core of the theory is thus severely damaged.

Again, it is sometimes proclaimed that organizations are 'working for a common cause' or 'towards a common goal', implying that all the stake-holders want the same thing from their organization, but in fact the goals or aims of the various stakeholders are not only not common, they are sometimes irreconcilable or diametrically opposed. When a charity raises its employees' salaries the beneficiaries inevitably suffer; when a company raises its prices the shareholders will be pleased and the customers furious. It is said we all want efficiency—but a rise in produc-tivity means some employees will lose their jobs—hardly one of *their* aims.

One big happy family

It is claimed that everyone wants growth. But that is not true either: managers want physical, or volume, growth (their empires and salaries expand with it), so do the suppliers; but shareholders want financial growth, customers want value-for-money growth and neither of these cares, or even knows, whether the organization is physically growing or declining; environmentalists do not want growth at all. So, if the stakeholders do not all want the same things, what are the rules governing the nature and distri-bution of their rights? By how much should the hopes of one set of stake-holders be dashed in the pursuit of the goals of another set? What is the coinage of these trade offs?

So much for a chairman's pompous claims that 'We are all pulling together in one big, happy family'. I realize he or she has to say such things but we are not compelled to believe these claims. Those who promote stakeholder-like theories should recognize the difference between what companies actually do and what they would do in Utopia.

And note what happens when a company goes bust. Are the employees given the same priority as the shareholders, the customers and suppliers? No, they are all treated differently (broadly, it is bankers first—because they usually 'secure'—shareholders last). It is quite clear that, in this case at least, the shareholders are (in fact and in law) merely the residual legatees and stand in a wholly different relation to the company from the other 'stakeholders'. How agreeable for those other stakeholders to receive equal benefits when things are going well but avoid equal penalties when they go wrong.

In general then, exactly what are the rules by which any claim that any stakeholder makes upon the organization may be resisted?

Who decides who gets what?

Everyone agrees that it should fall to the management to hold the balance between the various stakeholders, to act in 'the interests of all the community', for the good of all, and to ensure everyone receives their just deserts.

But by what right do managers trade-off the benefits of any one interest group against another? What mandate is given for this either formally or informally? Is it anywhere encoded in law? How, for instance, should it be decided whether an organization should donate, say, a $1m swimming pool to its local community or a $1m sports facility for its own disabled employees? Or should both receive $0.5m? Or, since there may be five (or 10) stakeholders, should they all get $0.2m (or $0.1m)? Should a bank close on Saturday in deference to the wishes of its employees, or open in deference to its customers?

As if all this was not already highly suspect, legally and morally, we are also to believe that the managers are entitled to trade-off the *intended beneficiaries'* share of the rewards—all stakeholders are equal, remember, not just with each other but with the beneficiaries as well. The managers of a company are invited, apparently, to seize whatever portion of the profits they judge to be appropriate and hand it over to the employees, the local community or whomever they deem to be worthy recipients. By what conceivable principle may this treatment of the assets of the legal owners be validated? (In practice most companies vigorously sack their employees and raise prices to customers rather than see a fall in the dividend. If employees and customers really were much-loved stakeholders, they would not do that, surely?)

And this equity argument similarly dictates that the needs of children in a school should be sacrificed for the benefit of the janitors if they have somehow become 'unequal'. Patients' needs sacrificed for nurses'. Is that really how it works?

Positive discrimination

Consider this example: in the interest of preserving the Welsh language certain local schools in Wales insist that their children are taught in Welsh. But some statistics show that these children do less well in exams than those taught in English. Do you think these children should be used to benefit the Welsh community in this way? Or again: I have just heard a local politician claim that a new college 'has certainly reinvigorated the city centre'. Is that good? I just dared to wonder what is has done for its students.

And what about other forms of 'affirmative action', such as positive discrimination, where organizations recruit employees on grounds of ethnic, minority or other qualifications rather than on their suitability for the task? Would it assuage your irritation, on waking up in hospital with the wrong leg chopped off, to be told that one of the criteria for the selection of your surgeon at medical college was ethnic background ('we were a bit short of Polynesians that year')? No, the idea that organizational performance is secondary to the needs of employees is entirely contrary to the beneficiary doctrine. Positive discrimination also breeds resentment in those who are discriminated against—by definition, the majority—which further damages performance.

If we really want to help minorities then let us—or, rather, them—set up organizations devoted to doing exactly that with single-minded vigour. Such as, just to give one small example, the Windsor Fellowship which helps black people move up into managerial jobs by showing them how to compete effectively with white applicants.

Father Christmas on the gift list

And does the fact that 'management' is always listed as one of the stakeholders arouse any doubts in anyone's mind over this task? Here we have a Father Christmas who makes sure his own name is on the gift list. And recall this, there appear to be no agreed rules for the distribution of the gifts! Are we mad? Do we seriously expect managers not to take advantage of this unrepeatable offer? Is this not an open invitation to pervert the resources of the organization in their own interest—an invitation that, very clearly, not all managers find it easy to resist?

Nor am I talking only of companies here. Certainly we see company managers paying themselves huge bonuses even when profits are falling; we see them 'fighting for the company's independence' against a bid when, manifestly, they should be gratefully accepting it in the interests of the shareholders. But ministers also battle tooth and nail for larger departmental budgets when the public good obviously requires a reduction (just listen to all our Western defence ministers now the Cold War is over!); scientists falsify their results to gain additional research funds; and so on. We are all mortal; the last thing any of us needs is any quasi-intellectual theory to justify awarding ourselves a little bit more.

I actually believe that the managers and employees of some organizations have stolen so much of their organization's resources that they have rendered it entirely useless for the beneficiaries—that this occurs in virtually all the nationalized industries of the world is incontrovertible. And we need a theory to encourage these people to believe they are entitled to such perks, do we?

The community

One of the alleged stakeholders is 'the community'. Most companies claim to be working for the community. BP proudly tell us in their annual report that they spent £18m on 'community programmes' last year. That is a huge sum by charitable standards in Britain but it actually turns out to be about 0.06 per cent of BP's turnover (£29bn) — rather less than you or I contribute to charity from our salaries, I would guess. Sainsbury's has managed £1m out of a turnover of £4bn for their community—0.025 per cent of turnover—and devoted two full pages, complete with photographs of smiling children, in their annual report telling us all about it. (I notice they did not take a full page to tell us about any other item of that magnitude, such as stationery, for instance; we do not get any glossy photographs of envelopes and compliment slips. And nothing about the disbenefits that any supermarket brings to its locality either—such as the little shopkeepers who go bust.)

Let me make clear what I am saying. If these companies are so concerned for their communities as to list them as stakeholders, equal in importance to employees and shareholders, then these contributions are quite out of proportion to the magnitude of these groups. It is true that BP and Sainsbury's expend much time and managerial endeavour as well as this actual cash on their communities, yet still the total effort is trivial: how will £1m (or ten times that) have the slightest effect on 'the community' surrounding Sainsbury's 400 stores in Britain? How will £18m (or ten times that) affect BP's global 'community'—that is, the population of the entire world, about five billion people? It must be perfectly plain to anyone who looks beyond the glossy annual reports, that they do not, in fact, rank this stakeholder very highly. Nor, in my view, *should* they.

Misguided do-gooders

We get calls from kindly people, such as 'Business in the Community', for companies to take a much closer and wider role in society; the Church constantly snipes at local business for not doing enough; Prince Charles calls on industry to clean up the inner cities. I say they should learn to clean them up themselves. Rather than business in the community being blessed, I see it as thrice cursed: it distracts senior managers from their true jobs; it encourages all those awful NPOs to postpone putting their house in order; and it allows unelected, patronizing business people to interfere in local affairs. To put it crudely, these managers should mind their own business (or are they so ashamed of making profits that they must don sackcloth one day a week to make amends?).

I see most statements proclaiming that the community is an important stakeholder as little better than humbug. We have all come to believe that organizations should be 'caring'—which is absolutely correct, they should—but this manifestation of concern does not seem to me very helpful; worse, it is often very patently insincere; the community is dropped like a hot brick as soon as profits are threatened. Marks and Spencer proclaimed a 'Buy British' policy a few years ago; since then the volume sourced in

Britain has dropped from 95 to 83 per cent of turnover. Laura Ashley earned wide approval for its undying loyalty to manufacturing in Wales; that is going. All large, 'socially responsible' companies employ specialist lawyers to limit the tax they pay to the community by diligently searching for loopholes; they should not be doing that, surely, if the community was such a much-loved stakeholder? Etc., *ad nauseam*—and I use that term deliberately.

And are companies really expected to behave in the interest of the nation at the expense of their profits? If so we had better nationalize the entire private sector. While certainly not suggesting that companies *must* not act in the interests of other people (that would be disgusting), and while certainly not recommending that companies should ever act *against* the local or national interest (that would be contrary to the no harm principle, see page 188), I see this oft-quoted, much milked, and highly seductive, aim, as entirely unattractive and inappropriate. Some writers note that it can be an advantage to a company to contribute to the community. Well, of course it can—but that is why they do it; they do it for their own advantage, not for the community itself. This is not what the Church and Prince Charles are saying; *they* are saying, categorically, that companies should do it *for the community*.

Companies should 'come out'

No. This 'social market' is a contradiction in terms; it cannot exist. My view is that companies should 'come out' and admit their dreadful secret, they should stand up tall and say, out loud, to society, 'Look, we are here to make a profit. Is that OK?' If they did so I believe society would (after getting over the shock of such unaccustomed honesty) look them firmly in the eye and say, 'Yes. That is all right. But . . .', and here it would wag a stern finger '. . . but you had better behave yourselves'.

I suggested on page 57 that society does not object to organizations making profits—indeed it does not object to the aims of any organization, only to the means. Everyone knows perfectly well that profit is what companies are for but, because we persist in the charade that they are for something else less base, because we perpetuate this big lie, we fail to tackle the root of the problem, which is not making profits but companies' awful behaviour in pursuit of them. Let us get company morals right so that they can hold their head up in society, rather than skulking around in that moth-eaten old sheepskin; everyone knows there is really a wolf underneath. We should house-train the wolf, not pretend it is a sheep.

I admit that 'We are here to make more money for the shareholders' is not an attractive company mission statement. Perhaps we are waiting for some innovative public relations genius to come up with a slogan to describe companies in more positive terms such as 'wealth creators' or maybe 'enhancing shareholder value' is marginally happier. Perhaps we should accelerate the spread of share ownership. Or we could be adult enough to accept the truth here, just as we are willing to talk openly today about other brutal facets of human existence such as death and sex.

And I cannot see why it is so much more morally uplifting to claim to be working for employees and customers when, in the modern world, all of us are not just employees and customers but also shareholders directly or indirectly through pension and insurance funds.

I am often told that Japanese companies do not adopt my recommended capitalistic attitude; they are truly 'working for Japan'. Oh really? When Toyota builds a factory in Britain do they not study the return on capital of the project? I bet they do, and if it is not above their hurdle rate they quite simply do not go ahead. At least I hope so; for if Toyota is not aiming to make a profit—and is not therefore a proper company—what is it? And what is it doing here? Is it an arm of the Japanese government, masquerading as a company, on foreign soil? *Here*? In Britain? For whose benefit? It is beginning to sound thoroughly sinister.

You may not go all the way with Dr Johnson ('There are few ways in which a man can be more innocently employed than in getting money'), but profits are surely not quite at the bottom of the ethics league of corporate objectives.

Back to the single beneficiary

But the community is not the only spurious stakeholder. Look at Sainsbury's annual report. They list their objectives (in bold print on the first page) as:

*... contributing to the public good and to the quality
of life in the community
To provide unrivalled value to our customers ...
attractive and friendly shopping environment
To offer to our staff outstanding opportunities ...
career development ... and remuneration
To generate sufficient profit to finance ... growth ...
and an excellent return on shareholders' investment*

It looks very like the list I showed on page 39 where I suggested that there was only one true aim—to make profits—and by that single criterion Sains-bury's have done remarkably well over the past decade (shareholders have seen the value of their shares rise sevenfold. How have the other stake-holders fared? We do not know. There are no figures in the annual report to show how they got on (compared with 20 pages of figures for the share-holders), but I very much doubt if the employers, the customers or the community benefited sevenfold. There are no indications whatever that customers enjoyed 'unrivalled value for money' or employees obtained 'outstanding opportunities for development'.

Now suppose there were some figures, suppose Sainsbury's discovered a way of quantifying what they do for each stakeholder. Let us imagine this company scores 50, 60, 70, 80 (out of 100) for shareholders, employees, customers and the community respectively for 1990. Then, in 1991, the scores became 80, 70, 60, 50. Is that better or worse? We do not know because we do not know whether the various stakeholders are equal in importance. (Oh, and by the way, suppose Marks and Spencer scores 50, 60, 70, 70, 80—five stakeholders, remember, not four as for Sainsbury's—so now how do you judge between these two companies?)

In fact, the above calculations yield only nonsense. If any organization ever attempted to quantify the benefits they give to all their stakeholders they would not have the remotest idea what it all meant—the multiple nature of the calculations eliminates all hope of ever judging an organization's performance or comparing it with rivals (and imagine trying to audit 20 pages of figures each not just for the shareholders but for the employees, the customers, the community, etc!) Perhaps we have now uncovered one of the reasons why the stakeholder theory is so popular with some managers: it is a splendid spoiler! Adopt the stakeholder theory and it is goodbye for ever to the perpetual threat of being judged by results! For companies it has the added attraction that it buries 'profits' among a welter of liberal-sounding idealism.

No, the only rational way to evaluate an organization (or a project) is to use a single criterion (as demonstrated on page 75 and yet again, as we will see later, on page 199 below). By that standard Sainsbury's performance has been magnificent. I, personally, take my hat off to them—I hope they do not mind.

Widespread managerial confusion

I believe a number of wholly evil consequences flow from the stakeholder theory.

This belief among managers—that their organization has *several* beneficiaries (nearly always including themselves)—can only lead to confusion, not only for the managers but for everyone else in the organization all the way down the line, as to exactly what they are supposed to be doing. Often it leads to those huge committees at which everyone's views have to be represented. I believe this lack of singleness of purpose has a highly significant cumulative effect on the performance of countless NPOs. Moreover, it can lead to an organization being run by default, for the benefit of whoever is in a position to influence its decisions, most often the managers themselves. Thus some colleges are run to please the education officials, hospitals are run for the prestige of their consultants, charities for the convenience of governors, research laboratories for the vainglory of scientists, companies for managers.

I see the stakeholder theory as a lure, inviting our organizations to care for all humanity, but, alas, if they fall into this trap they fail the very people for whose succour they exist. Today the world's problems are far too severe to allow us to indulge in this bleeding-heart management style.

Summary

The stakeholder theory purports to describe how organizations should behave in society. Yet its rules are vague and impractical; it fails to clarify who the stakeholders are, or what rewards an organization should bring them, nor is it clear who should determine the allocation of benefits to each stakeholder nor by what criteria, and it fails to provide any test by which any of their claims may be rejected.

Worse still, this theory provides a formal, quasi-intellectual excuse for managers to pervert the aims, strategies and resources of their organization to their own interest—and this they do to an extent not generally appreciated, even sometimes to the point of rendering their organization useless to its beneficiaries.

Pronouncing the rule that organizations must have more than one beneficiary (a demonstrably false premise, in any case) blurs the focus of management and employees alike as to the true aims of their organizations; it confuses them; in attempting to be all things to all people it satisfies none.

The stakeholder theory also precludes the measurement of corporate performance, an appalling and devastating defect in the context of this book.

I believe this theory is responsible for the dismal levels of attainment of many of our NPOs. It is a curse upon society. Moreover, because of its popularity, especially with egalitarians and socialists, it eclipses the far more productive 'principle of engagement' described in the next chapter. Mercifully, most organizations have more sense than to follow its precepts.

CHAPTER FOURTEEN

The principle of engagement

If we reject the stakeholder theory as our model for acceptable corporate conduct, by what rules should organizations behave? I shall suggest that there are two: the 'no harm principle and the 'principle of engagement'.

The no harm principle

The 'no harm principle', which must surely be the simplest, most venerable and most basic of all human rules of behaviour, valid down the countless centuries and across all our various civilizations, firmly established at the very centre of all our religions, true for individuals as well as organizations, states: 'No organization should knowingly cause any significant harm to any of its interest groups'. It could hardly be simpler!

I need to define some of these words a little more closely. First, an 'interest group' is any person or group of people who come into contact with an organization: customers, employees, the local community, the state, passers-by, tax collectors, suppliers, shareholders, and so forth, even perhaps relatives of some of these, and, not least, the beneficiaries themselves.

Next, the word 'knowingly'. Most of us would excuse an organization which caused us harm if we were satisfied that its servants could not reasonably have been expected to know that their actions might be injurious. We normally do not condemn an act which harms us if previous similar ones had not done so, or if the perpetrator had taken reasonable care, or faithfully followed an established code of practice, but we come down heavily on those who damage us deliberately or negligently. In stating this I hope I am doing no more than drawing upon well-established legal principles enshrined in such common phrases as 'duty of care'; I hope I am not putting forward anything new; as I said above, this principle is as old as humanity.

Centuries of detailed experience

The no harm principle simply summarizes the way most of us behave — indeed, virtually our entire body of formal law, built up over the centuries, is nothing more than a complex list of what constitutes 'harm' in the eyes of society at any given time in its development, together with the rules by which to judge culpability, penalties and compensation. Most legislation on, for example, product liability, safety, quality, labelling and so forth are essentially attempts to define what 'harm' means, when it is 'significant', when it is culpable and what should be the penalties.

So, in practice, the definition of 'harm' for almost any given circumstance is minutely described and known in detail throughout the length and breadth of the land. And every day the media, ombudsmen, protest movements, and above all government legislation and statutory regulatory bodies, tell us how individuals and organizations should respond to this or that new possible or potential cause of harm as it appears.

There are variations of this rule for every conceivable corporate situation: the Quakers have their special definition of harm, the Jews theirs, Muslims theirs. The Jains, an Indian sect, take the no harm principle rather further than most of us: they wear silken masks to ensure they do not ingest flying insects and sweep the path in front of them with a cotton brush to avoid stepping on any of God's lesser creations.

Naturally, in this complex world of ours we sometimes mistake what 'significant harm' is, and, in the last analysis, the courts will have to decide what it means in any given case, but, as a general rule, we know very well indeed what is and is not acceptable behaviour; compared with most of the rules by which we try to live our lives mistakes in this area are difficult to make. In effect this rule says you can do whatever you like, so long as you do not hurt anyone.

No harm and compensation

In an ideal world, 'no harm' would mean *no* harm—or, at any rate, no *significant* harm. It would be much better for ICI not to pollute the environment at all, ever, in any circumstances. But ICI is a chemical company and, unless we shut down all such enterprises and revert to pre-industrial revolution standards of living (and the organic filth that went with that), it is hard to see how a chemical company can *practically* avoid doing us some damage from pollution.

There seem to be three lines of defence: stop all pollution (by installing equipment, reformulating and so on to achieve what is called 'clean production'); next, clear it up if you do make a mess; third, if you cannot do either then compensate the victims. The principles of 'polluter pays' and the more general 'full social-cost pricing' are entirely in accord with the no harm principle, and my examples from the chemical industry are nothing more than particular applications of the no harm principle which, in general, says to all organizations: either do no harm, or neutralize it if you do any, or compensate the victims if you cannot.

189

There are, however, many permissible exceptions to the no harm rule. The act of punishment is certainly one; most organizations (notably governments) legitimately act in apparent breach of the no harm principle when they impose punishment and penalties on citizens for wrongdoing, but even here there are limits to the 'harm' a government may mete out to its citizens—most advanced nations draw the line at capital punishment, for example, or chopping off the hands of thieves.

Further modern exceptions

Competition may be another exception. What is the position of a company which deliberately sets out to damage the business of a competitor? Is that a legitimate breach of the no harm principle? Up to a point it must be, because all companies aim to beat their competitors, but is it 'fair competition' when, for example, Japanese companies deliberately and systematically target a named competitor to force him out of business?

Dismissing employees is another act that causes injury but which we accept as an inevitable concomitant of employment (not everyone accepts it: IBM, Barclays Bank, and a few others, had a no-redundancy policy for decades and, in many nations, compensation for this event is generous to a fault). Exceptions exist at the individual level too: in some competitive sports the 'no harm' rule is suspended, boxing being an obvious one, where, unlike most sports, injury to the opponent is administered knowingly and deliberately. Thus many exceptions to the no harm principle are recognized by society. However, as we become more civilized we progressively tolerate fewer of these; not long ago a teacher would think nothing of tapping an indolent child with a ruler—today the teacher would be sacked. (The American woman, who tried to sue a whisky company because the health warning on their bottles was too small for her to read when she was drunk, was probably a little ahead of her time.)

'Positive-sum' organizations

It might be thought that every organization inevitably breaches the no harm principle because, whatever it does, and however careful it is, so interdependent are we all that it is bound to cause significant harm to someone somewhere. No one could lift a finger without someone suffering; if I get a job, you lose yours. This must often be true, but it need not be. Take a company which sells a product to 10 customers and makes a profit of $10 000—apparently each customer has been 'cheated' out of $1000, thus breaching the no harm principle. But suppose that same product would have cost $11 000 had it only been available from a non-profit organization; in that case each customer would have actually benefited by $1000 as well as the company by $10 000. That such a miracle is possible is due to capitalism being a 'positive-sum game'. It 'creates' wealth.

In fact, and contrary to this commonly accepted cliché, it is not only companies that create wealth, many other organizations do this: a charity which applies 'positive therapy' to disabled children so that they can earn their own living surely creates wealth; those United Nations scientists who have recently eliminated the screw-worm from North Africa (indeed any organization that 'adds value' for its beneficiaries without taking it from anyone else), all these must be positive-sum organizations. Civilization itself is the accumulation of all humanity's positive-sum activities over all the previous centuries. 'Progress' is the rate at which humanity's positive-sum activities exceed the negative ones. If we are making progress positive gains must, by definition, be being made, and humanity progressed long before there were any companies.

Satisfied beneficiaries and unharmed interest groups

So a 'no harm organization' is a perfectly viable concept—indeed, it should be the norm for every organization to strive to benefit its beneficiaries without hurting anyone else. If a hospital nurse can bring succour to many patients throughout a 40-year career without harming anyone in his or her private or professional life (a massive personal positive-sum existence) why cannot the Northtown Widget Company do likewise? All organizations, surely, should aim to bring benefits to their beneficiaries without harming anyone, ever. It would be hard to imagine the National Trust, for instance, knowingly causing any significant harm to anyone under any circumstances. Seen in that light, a positive-sum, no-harm organization must surely be among humanity's brighter conceptions.

But alas, there are also 'zero-sum' and 'negative-sum' organizations. A zero-sum organization is one where the benefit to the beneficiaries is balanced by an equivalent volume of harm to other interest groups, as when, in a game of tennis, if there is a winner there has to be a loser and the amount by which the one wins is exactly the amount by which the other loses. Whether it is possible in real life to calculate the actual amounts by which benefits equate with harm, as it always is in games, I do not know, but mercifully the no harm principle does not call for quantification. It simply says *no* significant trauma shall be caused to any interest groups in pursuit of benefit for the beneficiaries. No harm means no harm; we do not need to know whether the actual volume of harm is less than, equal to or exceeds the benefit; the rule is *no harm*.

'Negative-sum' organizations

Turning briefly to negative-sum organizations; these are usually illegal. Where the damage inflicted on an organization's interest groups exceeds the benefit to the beneficiaries it would be outlawed; thus crime is outlawed because it is negative-sum; so is terrorism. The very word 'gang' implies that its members intend to do 'more harm than good'. War is a negative-sum device for settling international disputes and, I suspect, the British legal system has become a negative-sum process for settling personal ones.

Not all negative-sum organizations are illegal, though. I am sure many companies would be found to be in that category if we could estimate the harm they do: making a profit of $10m for their shareholders is laudable only if, in doing so, the company does not perpetrate $10m worth of damage to society—if it does then that company becomes a zero- or even a negative-sum organization. I suspect there are many instances; the handsome contribution which companies used to make to humanity's progress is in jeopardy, I believe, due to a decline in their ethical standards (the execrable conduct of many companies is, of course, a major theme running through this book).

But even some religions are negative-sum organizations. Collectively over the centuries, our various religions have no doubt brought much benefit to humanity yet they have also wilfully frustrated the march of science and deliberately and knowingly hindered the alleviation of the poverty of their flocks. The damage to our world from the growth of its population has been engendered, at least partly, by the Catholic Church's attitude to birth control, a result which exceeds any good that Church may have accomplished over the past many decades. Finally, the attitude of many religions to women has helped to deny humanity half its potential energies and abilities for the past 2000 years.

Benefits not equated with harm

Mercifully, however, we do not have to answer such bruising questions as 'which organization has caused humanity more distress over the past century, Catholicism or capitalism?' because the no harm principle does not ask us to set distress off against benefits; it simply says no harm. Any significant injury to any interest group is contrary to this principle, regardless of how this equates with the benefits generated. However, although the no harm principle itself does not call for an estimate of the balance of benefits and disbenefits from any organization, society does sometimes wish to know what this balance is in order to determine its attitude to suspect organizations.

(By the way, if society does wish to make this calculation it must not forget the lessons that DCF taught us on page 100 about cash being worth less in the future for, by the same token, so is harm. An action which makes us $100 richer today but causes $300 damage in 50 years' time is a good deal at any realistic interest rate, not a bad one. Thus the cost of clearing up the mess of Britain's industrial revolution is trivial today compared to the wealth it created for us. It is a lesson that only the more professional environmentalists have so far learned.)

Because of its verifiable simplicity the no harm principle seems to me to be extremely valuable. If an organization suspects that it is causing damage to anyone then it must either desist or neutralize the damage or offer full compensation. The more affirmative application of this law would lead to a number of quite remarkable, and hugely advantageous, changes in our society similar to those brought about over the past few decades by consumerism and environmentalism, but applying to all interest groups including employees, suppliers, the community and so on.

So vital is this no harm principle that we should incorporate it into the definition of the word 'organization' which now becomes:

> An organization is a group of people working together to yield a satisfactory benefit for its intended beneficiaries while causing no significant harm to any interest group.

I see the no harm principle as a floor under the behaviour of organizations, a sort of ethical Tmin, a guide to minimum ethical behaviour. Fine, but what are the guides to superior organizational conduct? Are there any practical systems of higher corporate ethics? In answer, I would commend the 'principle of engagement'.

The principle of engagement

Contrary to the stakeholder theory, the 'principle of engagement' says that organizations do *not* have to benefit everyone in sight; it recognizes no stakeholders of any sort and rejects all the claims they say they have. What it does say is this:

> Organizations should treat their interest groups in whatever way best engages their enthusiastic cooperation to increase the benefit delivered to the intended beneficiaries.

This principle turns the stakeholder theory on its head: 'ask not what your organization can do for its stakeholders; ask them what they can do for its beneficiaries'.

I see this as an entirely pragmatic, as opposed to ethical, code of behaviour. It is the principle of enlightened self-interest, strengthened and brought up to date. The principle of engagement invites managers positively, actively and systematically to reach out to anyone who can contribute to the success of their organization and deliberately enlist their enthusiastic help, to immerse them, to delight them, in delivering more and more benefit to the organization's beneficiaries.

Let me give a few examples of this philosophy.

Employees

These are obviously among the most important of all interest groups; for an organization's own employees not to be fully and enthusiastically, even joyfully, engaged would surely be an emblem of failure on the part of its management. But, the principle of engagement declares, the sole criterion of the most effective style of human resource management is that it results in the highest level of benefit to the intended beneficiaries—no, not to the employees (that is what the stakeholder theory requires), to the *beneficiaries*.

Such engagement is achieved today by, for example, paying employees generously, treating them with respect and humanity, providing them with superior working conditions, consulting them widely, delegating liberally, providing health care, training them lavishly, rewarding them for excellence.

Note that such rewards to employees could, under the principle of engagement, sometimes go far beyond anything demanded by the stakeholder theory; management would offer these enhanced inducements because they wished to heighten corporate performance, rather than with the grudging, resentful, reluctance that the stakeholder theory invokes where managers feel they have to reward employees simply for being stakeholders rather than for any evident contribution they may be making. This is a sentiment not unlike that which some trade unions engender among employers, where the managers would welcome the chance to reward distinction in the work of their employees but dare not do so lest the trade union demands the same reward for all in the interest of 'fairness and equity'. Thus, to return to it for one moment, not only may the stakeholder theory deflect managers from the single-minded pursuit of the interests of their beneficiaries, as noted earlier, but it cramps the whole-hearted motivation of employees as well.

Hugely motivating

The difference in productivity in organizations which have and have not understood the value of engagement has to be seen to be believed. Just a simple example: nurses used to be the silent, servile helpers of the hospital consultant, ordered about and absolutely never asked their opinion. In a well-run hospital today, however, they are fully engaged in the decision-making process for their patients right up to the limits of their competence. The effect on the cure rate for the hospital is quite remarkable (not to mention the secondary, but highly desirable, increases in job satisfaction and material rewards for the nurses).

Moreover, and contrary to all the textbooks, the creation of this culture does not appear to be impaired by the profit motive. I can take you to a company owned by one of the wealthiest families in Britain—hardly a compelling social cause to work for, one would think—yet the effort applied by the employees to the organization is just as energetic and enthusiastic as that displayed in, say, ICI (indeed, figures suggest that family firms are, as a general rule, the most profitable type of company). And how strange that those employed by Hanson, the company most strident in its assertion that the shareholder is king, seem to work no less strenuously than those who work for more 'worthy' companies such as Marks and Spencer.

The community

How should organizations treat their local community and the state, for example, under the principle of engagement? They should treat them in whatever way best engages their enthusiasm for the greater good of the organization's beneficiaries. If making donations to local charities, serving on local committees, sponsoring local teams, is going to do that more effectively for a company, for instance, than some other strategy, then that is the way that company should behave. If an amateur dramatic club wishes to raise funds from its community then it must put on a play which brings in the audience. If the government wishes to build a power station in Northtown then they must offer Northtown some inducement to welcome it.

Thus sometimes the two theories, stakeholder and engagement, might predicate exactly the same behaviour, while at other times the deductions would be quite extraordinarily different, for in the one case you do it because they are stakeholders and in the other because it helps your beneficiaries. As mentioned earlier positive discrimination is one such test case.

Barnardo's has 4000 employees. It also draws on 26 000 voluntary workers. The Order of St John has 300 paid employees and 200 000 volunteers world-wide; just think how the work of those organizations must be elevated by this army of helpers. Nor are they mere well-meaning do-gooders, but highly trained to perform vital and sensitive jobs—working with children and with the sick are not mere fun-jobs these days, but serious, skilled and disciplined. Just consider what impact 'engagement' of this order might have on our many social ills. What might happen to crime, for example, if the police could engage anywhere near that sort of commitment from you and me?

Customers

I mentioned that Barnardo's engages 26 000 volunteers. You may say, 'Ah, but you would never generate that kind of enthusiasm for a selfish introvert organization such as a company'. Oh no? What do you think you are doing when you shop at a supermarket? You are being engaged. In a supermarket the retailer has cunningly persuaded the customers to work as shop assistants and, remarkably, to enjoy it. The idea has swept the board; retail shops not engaging their customers simply go bust. All companies have to treat customers in such a way that they willingly help to improve profits, coming back time after time for their irresistible product, paying more and more for its quality, the integrity of the services on offer, and so on—engaging the customer is as old as marketing.

Another recent manifestation is 'relationship banking' in which the banker builds a long-term, far more sympathetic and helpful affinity with customers (as the German banks are said to do), instead of frantically lending as much money to as many clients as possible, regardless of the consequences to the unwary customer; positive engagement instead of negative exploitation.

Again, there is said to be an improvement in health when doctors invite their patients to monitor their own health for themselves, especially when they give them simple, foolproof gadgets for self-diagnosis and treatment at home (and hats off to the American surgeon who sells videos of their operations to patients, not only enlivening their subsequent dinner parties but, apparently, greatly improving the cure rate). Another example is that of Boeing, the aircraft manufacturer, which is inviting its customers to help it design its new 777 airliner. Engagement, it seems, takes many forms.

The intended beneficiaries

Recall that an organization's intended beneficiaries are also numbered among its interest groups and so the principle of engagement also applies to them; organizations should therefore treat their beneficiaries in such a way as to engage their enthusiasm to enhance their own benefit. A good school will not only electrify the teachers, parents, janitors—everyone—in the achievements of its pupils, it will also, and not least, arouse the delight of its pupils themselves.

Again, rather than just locking them up in dingy dungeons, issuing pious mission statements about 'treating them with humanity', a successful prison service would surely take infinite care to engage its inmates and their families to help themselves not to return. And what would happen to the success rate of Alcoholics Anonymous, and all similar organizations, if they did not engage their clients in their own cause? Answer: it would plummet.

Other relationships

Under the stakeholder theory the parents of a delinquent child would have to be brought into the discussions by the social services dealing with the case—or rather, the stakeholder theory provides no grounds on which to refuse their participation; parents are plainly stakeholders in this situation and have a 'right' to attend. Under the principle of engagement, however, the criterion is whether their participation would benefit the child; in most cases it would—and their enthusiastic engagement should certainly then be sought. But if not, then it should not.

The criterion under this philosophy is absolutely clear; whether it would benefit the intended beneficiaries is the *sole* measure of how to treat any interest group.

Indeed, this is a general rule with wide application. Many organizations are funded by sponsors—all charities are, for example, as are all state-funded providers of services. These organizations should not view their sponsors as stakeholders as they currently often do, but as interest groups to be 'engaged' for the benefit of the beneficiaries.

Non-employees

I particularly want to draw attention to these people. Professional managers in large organizations have recently learnt how to engage the enthusiasms of at least some of their employees ('Our people are our most valuable asset' declaims the chairman). Maybe, but what managers have not yet grasped is the vast potential pool of helpers and volunteers outside the organization who might be engaged.

If only someone could devise an effective means of harnessing the energies of all those people out there a vast new source of power would be unleashed. The employees of every organization would become little more than the permanent core supervising an external work-force of vast dimensions and wondrous enthusiasm. Surely there can be no better test of the quality of the management of any organization than the extent to which they harness the energies of all their interest groups—including this new class of potential enthusiasts, the 'external employees'.

The principle of engagement spreads the net of potential assistance far wider than the stakeholder theory; anyone and everyone could be, should be, enthused and engaged under the former, not just stakeholders.

The two theories compared

What I have been trying to do in this chapter is to lay down some rules for the moral behaviour of organizations in the modern world. While the no harm principle is rather basic it has very successfully guided personal and organizational behaviour for many centuries past; it is entirely valid today, and will be till the end of time. But it merely tells organizations how they should *not* behave towards other people—they should not harm them. That is far more than can be said for the behaviour of many organizations today, especially companies, but on its own it is quite insufficient, even though the definition of 'harm' is being tightened continually as our civilization progresses.

To lift corporate behaviour on to a higher plane we need a more positive attitude to the people who come into contact with organizations. That may be provided by a number of ethical systems, one of which is the stakeholder theory, and another is the principle of engagement.

One reason I dislike the former is that it does not tell us who may legitimately claim to be a stakeholder, what they may claim, who should decide whether to give it to them or what are the rules by which any claim may be refused. Another is that it confuses managers: the aims of their organization becomes diffuse; they forget whose interests they are supposed to be serving; they take their eyes off the ball. Single-mindedness, the essential ingredient in corporate success, is explicitly and systematically discouraged, leaving organizations weak and ineffective, all things to everybody but of sparse value to anyone. And, in any case, most organizations today are highly specialized, and few have the skills required to act in the interests of people other than their own intended beneficiaries, in whose service they need to be pre-eminent. Nor can I see any moral superiority in serving many groups of people moderately over serving one group outstandingly.

A plethora of defects

Yet another defect of the stakeholder theory is that it encourages managers to grant themselves favours — as if they are not in a position to do enough of this already without this quasi-intellectual rationalization for what sometimes amounts to plain theft. Another is that it is a negative philosophy: organizations are told to distribute favours to all and sundry without really knowing why and with no return to the organization itself on this largess. The tasks of many organizations today are far too serious to allow them to be hog-tied by positive discrimination and similar sanctimonious handicaps. But worse, it is simply not true that organizations work for all and sundry; the surgeon does not, in fact, cancel an operation on a patient on hearing that the local community will not benefit from it.

One test of the distinction between the two approaches is that while the stakeholder theory permits, and even encourages, such practices as positive discrimination, race-norming and quotas, the principle of engagement clearly rejects these on the grounds that they damage the performance of the organization.

No, the stakeholder theory takes us a notch too far up the moral scale; organizations do not behave in accordance with its precepts, however much they pretend to do so in public. Finally, in demanding more than one beneficiary the stakeholder theory renders it impossible to evaluate an organization's performance—a defect of commanding significance in the beneficiary doctrine, in which inability to measure corporate performance is seen as tantamount to failure.

No wonder the stakeholder theory is so popular with managers; even though my own experience in the privacy of the board-room suggests they do not believe a word of it, they embrace it in public. It sounds so caring and benevolent and, miraculously for them, precludes measurement of their performance so that, under its protection, they can turn the resources of their organization to their own ends. And who is it who decides whether any given organization should follow the precepts of this theory? Its managers do.

An intensely positive approach to people

The principle of engagement, on the other hand, calls upon anyone and everyone capable of improving the benefits to its beneficiaries to be enlisted to enhance its performance. The mark of real skill in a manager is the ability to encourage, enthuse and excite these people, to harness everyone with relevant abilities—not just their employees, but suppliers, bankers, neighbours, everyone—in the interests of the intended beneficiaries. However, unlike the stakeholder theory—and this is a vital distinction—the principle of engagement imposes a strict limit to what an organization should do to enlist this support, namely, not to exceed the long-term marginal net increase in benefit accruing to the beneficiaries from any such action.

The principle of engagement meshes exactly with the beneficiary doctrine in placing the intended beneficiaries at the very centre of every organization, thus allowing management to act single-mindedly in their interests. Moreover, it solves one well-known conundrum: how to evaluate organizations (see the next section). Thus, the principle of engagement says to organizations 'Ask not what you can do for the stakeholders but what they can do for your beneficiaries'. I believe that its positive attitude is immensely powerful. As organizations progressively take its precepts on board I believe it will often be found to double their performance.

Evaluating organizations

Imagine that it was possible to score (out of a possible 100) an organization's performance from the point of view of each stakeholder. Which is the best organization in the league table represented in Table 14.1?

It is obvious that organization 1 gives a better deal to stakeholder D than it gives to A, and A would be happier with organization 3, but, since all the organizations score a total of 200 points, and since we do not know which

TABLE 14.1
Performance league table (stakeholders' viewpoint)

Organization	Stakeholder				Totals
	A	B	C	D	
		(points out of 100)			
1	20	50	60	70	200
2	50	50	50	50	200
3	80	40	40	40	200
4	60	60	60	20	200

TABLE 14.2
Performance league table (intended beneficiaries' and interest groups' viewpoint)

Organization	Intended beneficiaries	Interest group		
		A	B	C
		(points out of 100)		
1	20	50	60	70
2	50	50	50	50
3	80	40	40	40
4	60	60	60	20

stakeholder is the most important, we cannot say which organization is the best overall. That is odd, surely, for the scores differ wildly; one must be better than another, I would have thought, yet we cannot tell.

Now the principle of engagement looks at all this quite differently. It does not see four sets of people at all. It only sees two: one is the intended beneficiaries, the other (in this example) is composed of three interest groups (who work for it, supply it, live nearby, or whatever). The performance league table from *their* point of view is represented in Table 14.2.

Completely different

In this second example it makes no sense to total the scores—the intended beneficiaries are in a class on their own and cannot be added to stakeholders. But we can see at once that organization 3 is the clear winner because it is delivering more benefit to its intended beneficiaries than the others—and it would still be the winner even if it scored 80, 0, 0, 0! Why? Because, like the robot school I invented on page 36), what matters is performance towards the intended beneficiaries; the fact that none of the interest groups received any benefit at all would not count against it (the principle of engagement does not demand that any organization *has* to engage anyone, merely that doing so may enhance its performance).

If any of the scores were negative, however, that would indicate a breach of the no harm principle and this would certainly count against it—indeed, strictly applied, it would not even be allowed to continue to operate.

Look at the scores for organization 1. The stakeholder theory did not know whether it was better or worse than the others because they all scored 200 points; but we can now see that, even though it is obviously very generous to its stakeholders, its performance towards its intended beneficiaries is dismal and, by the beneficiary doctrine's criterion of organizations (benefit to intended beneficiaries) it is therefore unequivocally and indubitably the worst performer of the bunch. (My suspicious mind would further conclude that these two facts were linked—the managers have perverted the organization against its beneficiaries and in favour of its interest groups.)

Which is the better hospital? One which scores 50 for its patients and 60 for the doctors or 60 and 50? The answer has to be the latter. It would still be the better even if it scored 60 and 0 (although it might not be for long because the doctors would soon become disaffected, their motivation would decline and the patients would suffer). But that is the correct relationship—the hospital must treat the doctors better so they get better results for the patients.

Summary

The beneficiary doctrine does not recognize the term 'stakeholder' at all; instead it acknowledges two distinct categories of people: intended beneficiaries and interest groups.

The no harm principle states that, in pursuing the interests of the intended beneficiaries, no organization may cause significant harm to any of its interest groups—a rule which, ruthlessly applied, as it increasingly is today, will greatly enhance the behaviour of all organizations. But this precept forms merely a floor for corporate behaviour—it often requires nothing more than care to avoid negative effects upon those who come into contact with an organization: something more positive is also required.

The principle of engagement is a far more positive philosophy. It demands that managers should actively and systematically search out every group of people who would be willing to contribute generously and enthusiastically to enhance the benefit delivered to the intended beneficiaries. Not only will this lead to a marked improvement in affinity with those who normally enjoy a close relationship with their organization—employees, suppliers, customers, the local community—but it may bring to bear substantial new forces, as when a traditional corps of employees is augmented by volunteers. Indeed, in some cases, the traditional employees might become a minority, a trained, central core, whose sole task is to engage these external enthusiasts and supervise their work.

And, crucial in the context of the beneficiary doctrine, the principle of engagement allows an unequivocal evaluation of the performance of any organization to be made—something rendered impossible by the stakeholder theory.

The principle of engagement, then, stands the stakeholder theory on its head and sees just one passenger in the coach: the intended beneficiary; everyone else should be out there—the employees, the suppliers, the local community—delightedly oiling the wheels, grooming the horses, polishing the brasses in the interests of this very important passenger. By contrast, the stakeholder theory sees everyone in the coach, including the horses—why, even the management is in there, tucking into the passenger's steak and kidney pie.

A school should not be asking itself, 'What should we be doing for the children, the teachers, the parents, the community?' but 'How should we be asking the teachers, the parents, the community, to help us do more for the children?' The police should not ask 'What additional services should we perform for the community?', but 'How should we behave towards the community so they help us cut crime more willingly?' Completely different.

It is the duty of the governing directors to determine the extent to which their organization should observe the precepts of the no harm principle and the principle of engagement, and to use these criteria to monitor the behaviour of their organization in society. This and their other duties will be described in Chapter 16.

CHAPTER FIFTEEN

Defective systems of governance

We now turn to consider the third and final component of the beneficiary doctrine: governance.

We have seen how the other two constituents, corporate performance and corporate conduct, both deserve far more careful attention in the modern world than they have so far received. I have explained how most organizations have managed to get one of these wrong, many both of them; the plain fact is that NPOs keep letting us down over issues that matter to us profoundly—the education of our children, the fight against crime, and on and on endlessly; meanwhile we cannot trust companies to behave themselves to the standards most of us demand today. I believe that all these defects spring from our failure to recognize the distinction between the roles of governance and management.

Because this has not been properly understood we have consistently ascribed the wrong duties to our so-called governors and have drawn them from the wrong pool. What we need is a new breed of professional, whom I call 'governing directors', elected by, and representing the interests of, the intended beneficiaries; they should sit aloof, above the hierarchy of management, as internal observers of the performance and behaviour of their organization.

In this chapter I shall first explain how profound is the distinction between governance and management. Then I shall illustrate why so many of our current systems of governance—non-executive directors, supervisory boards, councillors, Members of Parliament, school governors, and so on—are so ineffectual and why they continually let us down.

In the next chapter I shall describe how my new governing directors should be elected, remunerated, organized and what their duties should be.

Governance and management

I define governance as 'deciding and monitoring corporate performance and corporate conduct'. I hope the previous chapters will have made this very brief sentence thoroughly meaningful: it means that governance is, first, the act of moving through the purpose sequence to devise Tmin and Tsat for an organization; second, deciding how it should conduct itself towards its interest groups; and third, monitoring—making sure that their organization is actually matching these two desiderata.

Many organizations—certainly most companies—leave these matters entirely to their top managers. It is they who decide both the performance targets and the code of conduct for their organizations and, incredibly, they are also held responsible for achieving them. Thus they act as judge, jury and executioner in their own case—a notoriously dangerous thing to ask anyone to do, and doubly so where huge financial rewards depend upon the verdict.

Thanks partly to half a century of self-congratulatory books and seminars on management we have allowed company managers to usurp the role of governance—we have even permitted the job of company chairman and chief executive (see Glossary on page 283 for my precise use of these titles) to be merged in one person, leading repeatedly to company failures of spectacular size and stupidity, as became clear several decades ago when the practice first became common (Argenti, 1976) in our publicly quoted companies. I shall misquote Lord Ashburton (who was actually debating the power of the Crown in the House of Commons in 1780): 'The power of the manager has increased, is increasing and ought to be diminished'.

Squeezing the genie back in the bottle

Throughout history we have searched for some way of harnessing the power of managers which allows them to take vigorous action in our interests, while at the same time constraining their excessive ambitions. In the case of most companies this has failed because governance has been too lax and we see the result in their over performance and disgraceful behaviour.

In the case of many NPOs, however, the opposite has occurred. There, governance has been too assertive and we see the consequence in their weak attainments. In the case of government the separation of powers is either so complex that the management of nations has become a nightmare of checks and balances, or has degenerated into autocracy (see Chapter 19). Wherever you look, across the entire range of human organizations, the balance between governance and management is defective.

I explained above what a governor should do: he or she should represent the interests of the beneficiaries. What does a 'manager' do? Managers decide, execute, achieve results, and, in general, cause actions to be taken which have concrete effects in the real world: factories are built, employees sweep floors, letters are posted, dollars are converted.

Governors define corporate aims. Managers decide the means. Allow these functions to overlap, to merge, cross over, become blurred, and one or other will dominate, vastly to the detriment of either the performance or conduct—or both—of the organization.

The modern world is characterized by specialization. To pretend that top managers are a sort of governor or a governor is a kind of part-time executive is like claiming a neurosurgeon is a sort of hairdresser.

Defective systems of governance

Failure to appreciate the distinction between the job of governance and that of management is responsible for the absurd and useless essays into governance that we have seen in recent decades in which the two roles have become inextricably confused. This is all the more regrettable because, in the modern world, managers and organizations have become progressively more powerful while we, their supposed beneficiaries, have become progressively disenfranchised—an extraordinary and damaging trend in view of the fact that most of us have become more insistent and idiosyncratic in our demands.

Among our futile attempts to supervise the managers of our organizations are a number of defective procedures. These are examined in the remainder of this chapter.

Non-executive directors

In many of the larger companies in Britain and America, boards of directors are composed of executives and non-executives sitting together. In Britain the non-executives are virtually always in a minority; typically there are only one or two, occasionally as many as four, on a board of six to a dozen executives.

The problem with these 'non-executives', who are invariably part-time, is that they do not appear to know why they are there! The reason for this bewilderment is that there are, in fact, a number of quite different roles that non-executives should legitimately play:

1 As experts who may have been invited on to the board so that their wide experience or specialist advice is readily available to the company's senior executives.

2 They may be there because their names are well-known in the community or in a relevant industry, or in order to lobby for the company in Parliament or elsewhere.

3 They may have been appointed to watch over the interests of a stakeholder or shareholder especially, for instance, where an investor such as a bank has taken a significant stake in a company.

The first two roles explicitly call on the non-executives to act in the interests of the *management*—advising them and acting for them as their expertise allows—while the third role invites them to act for the share-holders, not for the management. No distinction is normally made between these very different intentions and no rules exist anywhere to guide these people on their duties and loyalties nor when to switch from one role to the other.

In practice most of those appointed to these posts are themselves execu-tives; typically a senior executive from one company is appointed as non-executive to the board of another of similar ranking. Because of this background, and regardless of the reason for the appointment, the appoint-ee's natural and inevitable attitude is not 'How can I protect the interests of the shareholders?' but 'How can I protect the reputation of my fellow directors?'. Thus the appointee 'goes native' and the relationship quickly becomes cosy and ineffective. Moreover, non-executive directors are nor-mally not elected by the shareholders but appointed by the executive directors, to whom they thus owe allegiance and on whom they have to rely for every scrap of information (and, judging by the surprised look on their faces when their company 'suddenly' goes bust, they are not always very well informed).

Gamekeepers playing poacher

Just a trivial, but significant, example of the uselessness of these non-executives: in recent years, because of public disquiet in Britain over escalating executive pay, many top companies invited their non-executives to form special committees to determine the executive director's pay (and in America they are obliged to do so). Since then public disquiet has actually accelerated! Why? Because these gamekeepers are themselves also poachers! It is hard to control one's mirth at the current level of thinking on the subject of governance.

Here are all these supposedly wise and experienced people who appar-ently have never been informed that you cannot be a player and a referee in the same game. Needless to say we are now regaled by cries (from the 'Cadbury Committee' on the financial aspects of corporate governance, for example) to 'strengthen' the powers of these non-executive salary commit-tees still further when, in fact, they should be abandoned as being the patently wrong solution to a small component of a quite different problem. The problem is supervising managers. The solution is hardly likely to lie in the direction of inviting more managers to do it.

In view of their evident self-interest in this useless but remunerative defensive farce it is not surprising that British executives are so keen to preserve it, aided and abetted by their Institute of Directors. However, we British are not alone in this self-serving charade: 60 per cent of non-executives in America are chief executives in other firms (although the American system is slightly less vulnerable because non-executives often outnumber executives on the board). It does not matter how many there are, however, for it still does not work. This is partly because so many of these non-executives also work for companies that already have some other pivotal relationship with them—bankers, suppliers, customers—and these other interests, sometimes quite manifestly and blatantly in conflict with their non-executive duties, mar their effectiveness as watchdogs for shareholders or for anyone else.

Shareholders have thus become disenfranchised and the only action they can take in protest against an incompetent management is to sell their shares—another contribution to the disease of 'short-termism'.

And so, here are these non-executive directors, all busily exploiting their priviliged positions, just at a time when each shareholder, whether it is a large institution or a mere individual in the street, expects closer and stronger, not lesser and weaker, representation.

Supervisory boards

Unlike the practice in America and Britain, larger companies in Europe are legally obliged to form supervisory boards. Although the pattern varies widely throughout the continent, in general half their members represent shareholders while the remainder represent the employees, the local community, suppliers and so forth. This is the stakeholder theory given flesh (other Europeans have long been devotees of this theory and are far less capitalistic, and infinitely more corporatist, than we or the Americans are. This predilection is not yet widely appreciated in Britain).

German supervisory boards used to include the same wide variety of stakeholder representatives as in the rest of Europe, but in the 1970s the unions took over one entire half of the membership leaving the boards split equally between workers and shareholders. In Germany, then, the worker and shareholder representatives are together responsible for looking after the interests of all the other stakeholders; while in the rest of Europe the various stakeholders themselves are actually directly represented on the board (and in Britain the board of directors supposedly safeguards the interests of the stakeholders).

Which of these Euro-boards works best? No one knows. Nor do I know anyone who believes that European companies behave better than British, or that European companies are more successful because of these boards. If the River Seine was less polluted than the Thames or the Mississippi, if Dutch product advertising was less misleading than British advertising, if German arms' and chemicals' companies had not supplied Iraq even more enthusiastically than the British—in short, if corporate performance or corporate conduct was better anywhere than anywhere else and verifiably so because they have some superior system of governance—then I would have no more to say. But as all are equally defective and none of them are superior to any others, or not noticeably so, I feel entitled to declare the

European machinery no more successful than British or American non-executive ones in limiting the excesses and incompetencies of corporate management. (At any rate I notice that neither we nor the Americans have adopted the European device, nor they ours.)

Irreversibly locked into the past

Notice too how the Germans have locked their employees into the pre-eminent position that employees had in the sixties and now, 30 years later, neither the environment nor the consumer—both now considered of massive significance by most other organizations—is represented on these boards thus rendering them outdated and irrelevant to modern demands. No wonder the German coal and electricity industries are the most virulent polluters in Western Europe.

But this phenomenon is universal. Any attempt to represent the views of any specific stakeholder directly on a supervisory body will fail because, over time, the weighting society gives to stakeholders changes (I know one board of governors in Britain where 12 of the 49 governors represent organizations no longer active in the relevant field; meanwhile a dozen organizations who have recently become active are not represented at all). To fall behind in a culture-change is just as dangerous today as losing touch with technology.

And when one learns that the retiring chief executive of Europe's largest insurance company (Allianz) is to take up the post of chairman of that company's supervisory board, one wonders just whose interests this device is supposed to be protecting. Is it conceivable that anyone can suddenly turn from chief poacher to head gamekeeper? This example suggests that most people believe there is not much difference between being an executive manager and being a governor. A governor, everyone imagines, is a sort of manager. A non-executive is a kind of part-time executive. For example, the Cadbury Committee's draft report defined governance as 'the system by which companies are run'. What, then, is management if it is not 'to run companies'?

School governors

Here is a version of governance seen specifically in schools and colleges since the 1988 Education Reform Act in which the British government, in an attempt to wrest education out of the hands of local government, provided for the appointment of governors to take over much of the responsibility for schools and colleges under 'Local Management of Schools' (LMS).

The Act requires that the board of governors for every state school be composed of (amongst others) five parents (at least two of whom must have children currently at the school) and two teachers (both to be teachers at the school) plus the head teacher. This seems to me quite outrageous; I would have thought that to appoint parents with children actually at the school, and teachers actually teaching there, would incur such myriad conflicts of interest as to render objective governance impossible. (Two teachers have a row, one is a governor; who wins—and who decides who wins? Or, the governors are in dispute with the union; both teacher-governors are members of the union; now what? Or, the mother of one of two children fighting in the playground is a governor; the other is not. You can think of 10 conflicts of interest per minute for this scenario.)

Notice that the duties of these governors bear no resemblance whatever to my concept of a governing director who, as I explained, should reside far above the sound of battle, ready to deliver an unbiased judgement on the performance and conduct of the school as a corporate whole. The one thing I would have been perfectly certain of if I had been drafting this act would have been the principle that neither parents nor teachers *at* the school should have anything to do with its governance whatsoever. I see this act as simply perverse. (And by the same token, one-third of the membership of local police authorities in Britain are magistrates. The General Medical Council, which hears complaints against doctors, is staffed mainly by, guess who, yes, doctors! Who are the naïve ignoramuses who make decisions of this calibre on our behalf? Are the words 'conflict of interest' mysteriously missing from their office dictionaries?)

Steam-hammers crushing flies and gnats

Worse is to come: these governors are not there to monitor the school's performance (judging a school's performance is not mentioned anywhere in the act), but to deal with practically everything from contracts to investing funds, arranging ballots, deciding the curriculum, settling staff disputes, and so on for 50 pages, including the appointment of every member of school staff. What is left for a head teacher and the senior management team to do after the governors have done all this for them, I do not know; I do know that no private sector executive would even consider a management job like this which requires inaugural castration—everything of any management significance whatever is apparently to be performed by these governors. One school governor said he attended 34 meetings in one year, during which much time was spent deciding details of the school uniform. No wonder it is now (in 1992) proving difficult to find candidates for this officious task.

In truth, of course, these governors are not governors, they are managers—and very low grade managers too, judging by another provision in the act which states that, if they appoint a teacher, even a junior one, this has to be discussed with the chief education officer (CEO) of the local education authority, and even where they make a non-teaching appointment of more than 16 hours a week (that is a civil service euphemism for a part-time cleaner, I suppose) they must inform the CEO—in other words these governors have about as much authority as a third-rank supervisor in a minor subsidiary in a second-rate division of a heavily over-centralized company. This concept is pure civil service; it stresses trivial administration; it champions barren bureaucracy. It is barely even 'management', let alone 'governance'. (I had to pinch myself when reading this act to make sure it was really dated *1988*.)

The universal, cosy, coalition of governance and management

In local government too, I find it extraordinary that the person I vote for in my local elections goes off and starts *running* my town. I thought he or she was going to represent my views, not get involved in the location of traffic lights and the provision of leisure centres. To whom do I complain if I do not like the new traffic lights or the leisure centre if my own representative was on the committees that decided to put them there? This is 'democracy' is it? Just try complaining; all you ever get, on the rare occasions you have felt moved to do so, is a defence of what the management has done, rather than a careful consideration of your complaint. It is not difficult to see why; your representative has switched sides!

Meanwhile, what are all those local government officials doing? They are also managing the town! Why do we need two types of manager—an elected amateur layer and a parallel, but lower, professional layer? If this system of management, employed as it is for every single one of our counties, cities and towns as well as all our schools and universities, is so superb and effective why have companies not adopted it? I would like to see a list of all its advantages, especially how these two management teams—elected officials and appointed officers—welded into enormous committees, often of 50 people, work better than the purely executive 'lean teams' (seldom consisting of more than five people) that successful companies use (see page 251).

The reason for these huge committees is to ensure that everyone's views are taken into account in any decision. But I do not want everyone's views taken into account. The only views I want heard are those of the intended beneficiaries—it is for us that these organizations exist and it is in our name that its decisions are supposedly made!

And the same goes for national government. The person I elect to represent me in Parliament suddenly becomes the Minister of something, quite incapable of listening to me. If I had wanted to elect a manager I would have voted for someone else—the personality traits required to manage are entirely different to those required in a representative. I pursue these thoughts further in Chapter 19.

It is the same everywhere: a squirming mass of governors and managers, all intimately entwined, wriggling about at the top of every organization, all under the impression they are supposed to be making managerial decisions and barking out executive instructions to each other. Meanwhile who is looking after the interests of the intended beneficiaries?

Charity governors

Most charities boast huge boards of governors. Typically, for instance, the BMA has 80 councillors, the National Trust has 52—not to mention the General Synod of the Church of England with 574! Some of these so-called governing bodies meet 12 times a year, which can only be because they are managing, not governing.

Sainsbury's, on the other hand, has *four* non-executive directors. To put these figures into perspective, the BMA's income is £10m and they have 400 employees; the National Trust's income is £50m and it employs 3000; Sainsbury's income is £6000m and they employ 60 000! The ratio of employees to governing directors is 5 to 1 for the BMA, 60 to 1 for the National Trust and 15 000 to 1 for Sainsbury's.

Once again this points to the fearful confusion between governance and management; if NPOs want to catch up with companies they must drop this absurd practice of appointing a massive part-time amateur shadow-management on top of the hierarchy of professional managers. The world today is much too complex and it moves far too fast to allow organizations to be controlled by part-time amateurs. For a committee to examine any matter of any weight it must be small, skilled, knowledgeable, active; if its membership is either numerous or part-time—let alone both—the discussions take so long that the problem will have either exploded or disappeared before the committee has had its second meeting. The world has accelerated far beyond the levels of urgency that obtained when all these voluntary committee systems were developed a century or more ago.

But large committees break another sensible rule, too; the fewer the members the more each feels responsible (and indeed *is* more responsible) for collective decisions. No company would dream of ordering its affairs by part-time discussion in groups of specialists coming together once a month in a vast number of sprawling committees. Most NPOs, then, have this problem of wholly excessive numbers of governors, many of whom are amateurs play-acting at being part-time executives. In today's rapidly spinning world, an amateur finance committee is a fatuous substitute for a skilled finance director, a part-time general purposes committee a clumsy surrogate for a professional executive team.

And, as with the non-executives described above, many of these governors do not know why they are there; many are appointed for their special expertise, not to represent the beneficiaries at all. Often their relevance declines over time but, like those antediluvian German worker-directors, they are not replaced.

None at all

Many organizations have no governing board of any sort: British trade unions do not, they have a committee of which the general secretary is their boss not their servant. Partnerships do not have one—the senior partner is often chairman and chief executive rolled into one, thus making it difficult for a junior partner to complain about the management. British companies do not have governing boards, as we have seen. The British constitution incorporates no bar of any sort to the power of the Prime Minister. The Catholic Church is headed by the Pope who is a chief executive; there is no chairman (not an earthly one anyhow) to circumscribe his power; nor does any archbishop or ayatollah have one (and where any body that might be mistaken for governance is found, such as the Curia and the General Synod, one discovers that the Pope and the Archbishop is the boss of that too and, as usual, it turns out on inspection to be a part-time amateur management body, not a governance one).

Many of the organizations which have no governing boards, and some that have, are supervised by watchdog bodies either set up by the state or by interest groups. Serious practical difficulties attend these watchdogs. They find it hard to obtain information about the organizations they are watching—sometimes the management makes it impossible for them to get this and the more sensitive the data the more difficult it is to extract. They are seldom given teeth (the more teeth they have, the more red tape is generated, the more freedoms are eroded) and so they seldom even bark, let alone bite (except when the popular press get hold of some trivial corporate peccadillo and then the relevant watchdog snaps out wildly at the offender just to show it is still there).

The powers of the watchdogs are often set out in law and, as with most laws in the modern world, they become outdated quickly, soon after that they become ludicrous and eventually downright damaging and contrary to the public interest. If you want to know how effective watchdogs are ask yourself where was the Bank of England, the Securities and Exchange Commission, the Department of Trade and literally hundreds of other regulatory bodies around the world—not forgetting the ever-vigilant financial press—during the countless major corporate débâcles and scandals in recent years; Maxwell, BCCI, Polly Peck, junk bonds, Blue Arrow, ...

Summary

I have reviewed a number of alternative designs for the governance of organizations. None of these systems seems to work any better than the others and all are defective in three crucial respects:

1 They do not protect the interests of the intended beneficiaries, who continue to occupy a less than prime position in the minds of the managers who blithely continue to pervert the resources of a wide range of organizations

for their own benefit (see the daunting list in the next chapter). In spite of the wide differences in their design there is no obvious correlation between the level of performance in organizations and their form óf governance.

2 The concerns of interest groups do not seem to be any better protected under one rather than some other scheme—not even where they have direct, specific and explicit representation on a governing body (as they do in European supervisory boards). The relevance of any specialist representative erodes as times change but they are seldom replaced. There appears to be no correlation between the design of their systems of governance and the behaviour of organizations in society.

3 In every one of these systems the governors habitually usurp the role of the managers causing an additional layer of bureaucracy. Or the managers usurp the role of governors leading to the perversion of the organization for their own ends.

Governors will perform far more effectively once they have shed any pretence to manage. Managers will perform far more effectively once they are relieved of governance.

CHAPTER SIXTEEN

The governing directors

In the previous chapter I explained why I thought that all our current systems of governance were defective. Let me now describe a pattern, a prototype, for a system of governance suitable for all our modern organizations.

The duties of the governing directors

I hope it is now clear what I do not want governors to do; I do not want them to act in any way as managers, advisers to the management, defenders of the management. I want them to have nothing whatever to do with the processes of management.

I do want them to act as internal watchdogs on behalf of the intended beneficiaries and the interest groups, to determine the performance to be achieved for the former and to designate the desired conduct towards the latter, and to ensure they both get what they are supposed to get.

Thus the governing directors would have a, deliberately, very limited number of duties to perform as follows:

 DUTIES OF GOVERNING DIRECTORS

1 To define who the intended beneficiaries of their organization are to be, the nature of the benefit they should receive, the BPI to measure it, and the long-term Tmin and Tsat targets (all as described in Chapters 4 to 6).

2 To define the organization's code of corporate conduct, including its relationship with all its relevant interest groups (as described in Chapter 14).

3 To monitor the organization's performance in respect of these two and to report annually upon them to the intended beneficiaries.

4 To appoint, remunerate and dismiss the chief executive.

5 To wind up the organization if it persists in falling below Tmin.

They would have no other duties of any sort—indeed they would be strongly dissuaded from undertaking any other tasks whatever and, above all, they would be required to keep well out of the day-to-day management of the organization. Thus they would be strictly non-executive; they would hardly ever actually *do* anything except in their official dealings with the chief executive and, in the extreme, closing down the organization.

I have already described in great detail over many chapters how the first two duties are to be performed and I have a few more miscellaneous comments to make later; the other three duties are now described in the following sections.

Monitoring

Monitoring means not only watching the facts and figures which record the organization's immediate past and present performance but also testing what confidence the governing directors feel for the long-term outlook. In the rapidly changing world today knowing the past is not enough—you have to anticipate performance in the future to be able to take corrective action in time. Companies have known for some decades that historical information, such as the traditional accountant used to provide, comes far too late to be helpful and that is why they take so much trouble to make forecasts, often for several years ahead, to try to predict trouble before it strikes; many NPOs do not yet do this. The governing directors would therefore have to ask themselves, on a virtually continuous basis, the following questions relating to short-term performance, long-term performance and conduct:

1 Do we really know how much benefit our organization delivered to each of its beneficiaries over the past few months and years compared with the targets we set, and are we reasonably sure that the next few months will not bring any unfortunate surprises?

2 Are we confident that the strategies the management are now pursuing will ensure that our organization will achieve Tsat for the next few years and that, above all, we are not heading towards Tmin?

3 Are we confident that all employees, especially the managers, understand the code of corporate conduct we have laid down and that they have not taken, and are unlikely to take, any actions that may run counter to it?

Intended beneficiaries are the prime source of data

To place themselves in a position to answer these questions they would have to maintain an intimate and continuous contact with the intended beneficiaries who are by far their most important source of information, since, of course, whether the beneficiaries are actually receiving a satisfactory benefit is what the organization is all about.

I have described the concept of beneficiary tracking (see pages 43–44) and I now repeat that it should be the governing directors who should be directly responsible for the efficacy of the method employed to evaluate the organization's performance towards its beneficiaries. While this does not mean they would actually physically have to operate the system themselves— the use of independent specialist agencies would soon become the norm among major organizations—it does mean they should be granted a suitable budget to cover the cost of tracking and of research into continuously improving its technology. As I also noted, tracking would initially be very expensive.

I have stated repeatedly how important it is to ensure that each individual beneficiary receives a fair share of benefit. Just as the governing directors of a company would have to verify that each category of shareholder received the same return, so the governing directors of, say, the BMA, would need to ensure that each of the many categories of medical practitioner (consultant surgeon, general practitioner, hospital junior) received a fair share. Why is this so important? Because today many of us in the developed world are prosperous enough to indulge our individual differences, to ensure that each unique beneficiary receives a fair share from an organization, we need a closer and more attentive form of governance.

Back to BPIs versus MPIs; governance versus management

I also noted that beneficiary tracking is wholly and totally different to monitoring MPIs. Today most so-called governors spend much of their time monitoring the operational performance of their organizations—sales per day, nurses per patient, capital adequacy. But this is what the *managers* are supposed to do; my governing directors are not to do this. They should monitor BPIs—to each individual beneficiary or class of them, moreover— not MPIs. Governing directors are not in any way like schools inspectors or quality controllers who should all be watching *management* performance; governing directors are there to observe the effects of their organization on the beneficiaries.

And note this: one of the most severe problems non-executive directors experience is obtaining information from their executive colleagues concerning the intricate workings of their company. But this is not material information for governing directors—the key information they require relates to and springs direct from the beneficiaries, via the tracking system, not from the executives, via the management information systems, at all.

Thus the task of monitoring is *wholly* different to what most governors to today and wholly different to the monitoring that managers should do.

Strategic monitoring

Next, to accomplish the second, strategic, forward-looking monitoring task, they would need to know what strategies the management have proposed in order to achieve the long-term Tsat targets and would have to decide whether they thought them adequate. Now it is plain that to carry out this task the governing directors would need to possess substantial knowledge of their organization's affairs, a capability reflected below when I discuss their qualifications. I describe the extremely revealing 'gap analysis' technique in Chapter 17 by which this long-term strategic monitoring procedure may be carried out and I describe below a format by which an organization might report its long-term performance.

I started this book by bemoaning the fact that most organizations could not answer the question 'How are you getting on?' from the point of view of the intended beneficiaries. This is what I want these governing directors to be able to do. *This is their job*. Once they have laid down the standards of performance and conduct, monitoring is their sole task. It is their responsibility to know what the organization is supposed to be doing for whom and whether it is actually doing it. They must be the leading experts on this topic, both short-term and long-term, past, present and future.

A wakeful watchdog

Finally, to monitor conduct the governing directors should maintain close links with all the interest groups—employees, suppliers, local community, environmentalists and the rest, to ensure that they are being treated in accordance with the no harm principle and the principle of engagement.

While the governing directors specifically represent the beneficiaries, not the interest groups, it is quite clear from the above duties that they must also keep themselves continuously informed of the views of all relevant interest groups and must weave these into the organization's code of corporate conduct; governing directors must know what these people consider to be 'significant harm', for instance, and what behaviour is most likely to engage them.

These governing directors, then, would be expected to maintain close communications with all interest groups to verify that the management is behaving in accord with the norms of corporate conduct they have laid down, including, in certain cases no doubt, strict and detailed codes of practice and the enforcement of the duty of care. While I certainly do not see governing directors as a form of secret police or KGB, I do see them as an internal regulatory bulwark and watchdog against wrongdoing in which task they will be aided by professional auditors. These should be appointed for a fixed term by the governing directors *not* by the managers (another outrageous example of how, nowadays, management always seems to outflank governance) and also, of course, report to them. The conscientious governing director will doubtless also scrutinize the monthly management accounts and cash flow statements.

While all this would never completely obviate the need for independent inspection of especially sensitive organizations (such as children's residential homes), it would certainly provide a dedicated first line of defence against such corporate misdemeanour as abuse, theft, fraud, corruption and so on. These governing directors would be more concerned than any imaginable outside inspector or statutory regulatory body to safeguard the good name of the organization in which they have such a prominent role of professional guardianship. Remember that, unlike any other governor or director or watchdog, they uniquely have no management responsibility at all in my scheme of things, no conflicts of interest of any sort, while they do have access to privileged information. Moreover, their *sole* responsibility is to ensure that their organization is conducting itself effectively *and* ethically. That is their job.

The annual report

The highlight of the governing directors' year will be the publication of their annual report. In addition to the usual details currently found in reports of companies and NPOs, I would like to see a central double-page spread, entirely separate from all other figures, showing the following crucial items, not one of which currently appears in any annual report I have ever seen. Few quoted companies show their EpS record, for example, fewer still display their share price over the past five years, and I have never seen ROSC mentioned; not even by those companies who declare that earning a satisfactory return on shareholders' capital is their main aim. Should not they tell us whether they have done it?

Annual report
From the governing directors to the intended beneficiaries

- Statement of corporate purpose defining the intended beneficiaries and the nature of the benefit the organization intends to generate for them (just two brief sentences as on pages 89, 90, 121 and elsewhere).

- The long-term target, including a definition of the BPI and the Tmin and Tsat currently set to the management for at least the next five years.

- A statement of performance showing the actual BPI out-turn (in real terms) for each of the past five years together with that of selected comparative organizations (as on page 103).

- A statement of conduct outlining the organization's current attitude to its various interest groups.

- A signed declaration by the chairman, as the senior representative of the intended beneficiaries, that he or she is satisfied with the performance and conduct of the organization over the past five years (or not, as the case may be), and expressing confidence that long-term strategies are in place to take the organization to Tsat and avoid Tmin up to year five.

● A signed declaration by the auditors that the method of measuring the BPI which the organization is using adequately reflects its actual performance.

A real, distinctive task

It should be very clear by now that there is a major role for these governing directors. They are to be the fountain-head of knowledge on what their organization is trying to do for whom and whether it is actually doing it. They are the guardians of the *cui bono*, the definers of the 'Why are we here?'. What is required from them is accurate, verifiable statistics, of transparent honesty and probity, relating to their organization. A foundation of robust data whose veracity can be seen to be unimpeachable, promulgated by people who can authoritatively correct misstatements and rumour such as appears so often in the press.

As experience grows in the gathering and interpretation of the statistics that lie behind BPIs for NPOs, I visualize these governing directors becoming acknowledged experts in their field, capable of providing convincing evidence of the validity of their published figures, within the limits of the most up-to-date technology. I hope a major new academic industry will arise to study improvements in measuring corporate performance to assist them in this task.

The governing directors and the chief executive

The last two duties of the governing directors were listed earlier as:

● to appoint, remunerate and dismiss the chief executive

● to wind up the organization if it persists in falling below Tmin.

Appointing, remunerating and dismissing the chief executive (CE) are the only official executive duties the governing directors need ever normally undertake. They appoint the chief executive, who in turn appoints all the other senior executives. They fix the CE's pay and conditions, and the CE determines everyone else's. When things are going well, and the organization's performance is above Tsat, the CE will no doubt earn a performance bonus based on the BPI. If the organization is tending towards Tmin, or if serious breaches in conduct occur, the governing directors will issue warnings, cut the CE's pay, leading finally to the CE's dismissal.

Very occasionally a governing board will need to consider closing down, re-forming, selling off or merging their organization. I hope I made it clear in Chapter 6 that Tmin reflects a level of performance that would, if continued for a number of years, demand the termination of the organization as an autonomous body. Long before that stage is reached the governing directors should have replaced the chief executive and long before that they should have issued a warning or sanctioned pay-cuts, so, if they do their job conscientiously, closure would be very rare indeed.

How the governing directors may be organized

Although I have suggested that only the most socially significant organizations would need to appoint governing directors, so valuable do I feel this concept to be that I imagine many smaller organizations might well decide to adopt it as a safeguard; even quite small organizations, especially such sensitive ones as children's charities, might recruit a single governing director whose vigilance on behalf of the children would provide a rugged (and apparently much needed) defence of their interests. Or again, one of the problems in family businesses is the divergence of views that gradually widens over the generations between the founders and their successors; a single governing director to hold the balance might be useful even in quite small concerns—and so on across a whole range of situations. As these small organizations grow, and as their circle of interest groups widen, so this one governing director would gradually be joined by others.

I also see the need for legislation to enable any significant body of intended beneficiaries, or interest groups, who feel threatened by the performance or behaviour of their organization, or who believe it to be essential to provide themselves with a safeguard (perhaps against an autocrat), to apply to the courts for the compulsory appointment of a governing director.

Few organizations would ever need more than a dozen governing directors, although very large national and international organizations—governments, for example, and organizations spanning many nations—might well require several hundred if they are accurately to reflect the views of their diverse constituencies.

Qualifications and remuneration

I would expect to see many of these governing directors drawn from the ranks of the middle-aged and retired, because this job requires wisdom, knowledge, experience, incontrovertible probity, judgement and common sense rather than energy, drive and skill in the technologies of modern management. Energy and drive are highly desirable in a manager but very definitely not required in a governing role where interference with day-today management must be strictly proscribed. While they certainly need to know what modern management can and cannot accomplish, they do not need to be specialists in its techniques. What we want here are sensible supervisors not dynamic doers. And let us learn from the non-executive débâcle noted earlier; these governing directors must not be employed as executives in any other organization, although, of course, they may be governing directors of other unrelated organizations.

Not all these posts would be part-time; unlike most governors, many of whom spend less than a dozen days a year on their organization's affairs, most governing directors would need to spend 50 days a year and the chairman of any large organization would almost certainly be full-time. All would be appointed for a fixed term and salaried, substantially in the case of major organizations, in view of the qualities required and the fact that they are legally responsible to both the beneficiaries and the interest groups.

Completely independent

It would seem sensible, in order to fortify still further their independence from the management, for the governing directors to be paid not directly by their organization but from a trust fund set up by it, which would also meet the premiums on their professional insurance as well as the fees or salaries of the tracking and monitoring and other specialist staff that some of them would need, together with the fees for the organizations' auditors who would also report to them. (A new breed of auditor will be called forth who, rather than verifying financial data, will comment upon the method employed to measure performance—see the item 'Auditor' in the Glossary.)

A well-known public figure, governor of one of our famous institutions, has recently proclaimed that the highest qualification for a governor is devotion to his or her institution. He was utterly, completely and hopelessly wrong! What is required is devotion to its intended beneficiaries not to the institution itself; we have far too many organizations whose continued existence is based on nothing more helpful than a sentiment of loyalty for past glories. The last thing the beneficiaries need is a clique of 'old boys' bent on keeping everything the same for yet another dreary generation.

The question often raised over this sort of proposal is, 'But where will we find such people?'. But we have hordes of them! Almost every NPO in Britain has dozens of governors, far more than they require (does the BMA really need 82?), many of whom would be eminently suitable if redeployed in this new role. I acknowledge the problem in developing nations, where an educated middle class has yet to emerge, but all we need in Britain over the next decade or so is an average of a dozen people for each of the top couple of thousand NPOs and companies—a total of about 20 000 souls. Surely we can manage that.

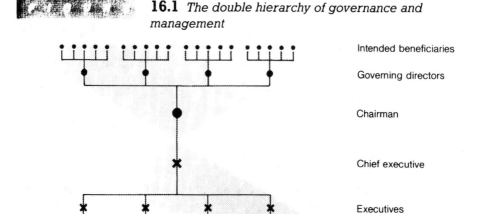

16.1 *The double hierarchy of governance and management*

Intended beneficiaries

Governing directors

Chairman

Chief executive

Executives

Employees

The double hierarchy

The intended beneficiaries will elect the governing directors and they in turn elect a chairman. Thus in every major organization I see two hierarchies facing each other in a distinctive double triangle: governance versus management, separate and distinct (illustrated in Figure 16.1). At the top of the upper triangle are the intended beneficiaries each of whom is represented by a governing director who, in turn, are led by their elected chairman; facing them is the chief executive with the traditional hierarchy of managers stretching down to the individual employees.

The chairman will act, as most good ones do, as the spokesperson for the organization. This will, for example, involve facing the media, correcting, vigorously and frequently, all the misconceptions that will inevitably arise over the performance and conduct of the organization (while the chief executive will be the expert on its operations and activities). The chairman is expected to be the leading expert on the 'How are you doing?' question, to know the answer from day to day, month to month, year to year and decade to decade.

The other duties of the chairman are to ensure that a consensus exists among the governing directors on all matters of significance and if it does not, either to cast a vote to break a deadlock or to initiate a re-election by the intended beneficiaries. He or she will be strictly forbidden to act in any executive role, other than to carry out the duties listed above. It will not hurt to say it again: a key cause of corporate failure is the fusion of the role of chairman and chief executive (sometimes referred to as 'executive chairman'); this is an aberration that must be avoided at all costs in the proposed regime.

The 'Institute of Governing Directors'

I visualize the formation of an 'Institute of Governing Directors' (IGD) which would take its place alongside other major professional bodies. I see it regulating the profession of governing director, licensing its members to practise, setting standards, publishing model job descriptions, training them in the legal and financial aspects of trusteeship, disciplining unprofessional conduct, operating selection services and generally acting as many similar professional bodies do around the world.

No doubt it would also issue advice on technical standards for setting corporate objectives, corporate conduct, BPIs, and so on for the various types of organization its members represent. It would encourage the convergence of the standards of corporate conduct for companies and NPOs (desirable because we will not be able to determine whether we want certain services performed for us by companies or by NPOs until we level the ethical playing field), until both adopt similar corporate conduct benchmarks. The existence of this institute would hasten progress towards this single standard, since many professional governing directors would sit on the governing bodies of both types of organization.

I would expect the institute, among its other services, to operate a 'current awareness scheme' for its members to assist them to keep pace with the constantly changing demands of society. It would also employ teams of specialists, auditors and adjudicators to advise and assist governing directors, managements, and the courts, in cases of dispute. It would propose lists of suitable candidates for governing boards and would supervise elections. It would license auditors and organizations specializing in beneficiary tracking.

This institute would be empowered to select a governing board for any organization whose intended beneficiaries cannot do so for themselves (children, the handicapped, and so on). Where a court orders an organization to appoint a governing board it would look to this institute for suitable nominees.

Would this result in a clique, an old-boy network, a *nomenklatura*? I wonder if it might be no bad thing for Britain, and other Western nations, for a new army of opinion-formers to join the entrenched 'establishment'; these governing directors, selected for their probity and wisdom, might provide a most welcome vein of fresh moral conviction.

The consequences for management

I hope there will be two massively beneficial effects on the management of organizations from the adoption of my new definition of governance, along with the appointment of boards of governing directors to all our more important organizations. First, it will shift some of the currently excessive power of managers back to governors, and second, decisions that are presently management-centred will become 'beneficiary-centred'. Before detailing these advantages I have to attend to one severe possible disadvantage.

The effect on managers

One of the most cogent reasons for not adopting a stronger form of governance such as I am proposing is the fear that it might dismay the managers over whom this apparatus is imposed, thus dampening managerial courage and initiative that is so essential to the success of organizations. This is an objection to be taken very seriously; I can hardly claim that the beneficiary doctrine is going to be a great boon to society if it is actually going to kill off the spirit of enterprise in all our top organizations!

But consider the changes I am proposing and note the marked divergence from current practice. I want governing directors to govern, not to second-guess the managers; this is wholly unlike all other current systems of governance, in which the governors meddle almost daily in absurdly detailed issues, such as the selection of junior staff, the approval of projects of puny insignificance, even the signing of cheques. I want my governing directors to stand right back from management, to intervene only if they believe that the management's strategies are heading towards Tmin.

Thus I am claiming that my governing directors will intrude *infinitely* less than all current forms of governance to the immense relief of those countless managers in organizations all over the world who silently curse their supervisory bodies for holding up essential change, delaying projects and endlessly raising issues of fatuous triviality.

Clear demarcation aids cooperation

What sours relations between people is when there is a grey area of uncertainty between their duties and, precisely because my job descriptions of governing directors and senior executives is so distinctive and so clear-cut, the relationship between them will in practice be much easier to manage for both of them.

Indeed, I would go further; recall that governing directors will be setting targets for BPIs. BPIs are strategy neutral. Thus top managers will be given absolute *carte blanche* to achieve the targets in whatever way they deem best (subject to conduct, of course). What a challenge! Surely this will arouse their enthusiasm far more effectively than either not setting them any targets at all, or, worse, setting them a mass of detailed MPIs which the present forms of governance invariably do, thus pre-empting so much valuable management innovation and initiative. None of the forms of governance reviewed in the previous chapter is anything other than thinly disguised amateur managers determined to second-guess the professionals.

There is, however, one class of manager whose activities would certainly be curtailed and that is the autocrat. There are two styles of management that really work; one is the entrepreneurial autocrat or dictator, and the other is the first-among-equals team leader or democrat. I believe there is no workable middle way—a truth elegantly demonstrated by the fact that, when either system fails, it fails suddenly and disastrously, collapsing into its opposite.

Polar management styles

We have here the classic 'catastrophe theory' situation where these two systems flip abruptly from one to the other across a 'cusp'; a smooth transition is not available, as is demonstrated repeatedly in every kind of human organization, because all intermediate styles of management are ineffective. We saw it recently when the autocratic command economies of Eastern Europe snatched so abruptly, almost greedily, at democracy; they did not select a middle way because there is none. We see the opposite when a weakly-managed company is turned round by a ruthless, autocratic 'company doctor'. There is no middle way, not for huge nations, for small companies, not for tiny charities or vast cities.

Contrary to popular opinion, and contrary to most management textbooks (who always seem to disparage autocrats, I suppose because they break all their neat management formulae), both these management styles are vital to organizational effectiveness, but in their completely different realms. The entrepreneurial autocrat is superb—indeed, unbeatable—when building up a young organization (Watson at IBM, Reith at the BBC, Lee Kuan Yew of Singapore), or for turning round an older one in trouble. The management team, on the other hand, under a first-among-equals leader, is superb at providing steady, reliable progress over a long period. The one problem is that autocrats take power not only as chief executives but as chairmen too—and then no one can get rid of them, not even when their task is done and so, alas, they go on and on until they make that inevitable huge mistake (can you imagine such people making small mistakes?) which brings the organization down in ruins.

Taming the autocrat

In well-established organizations governing directors will surely avoid these autocrats like the plague. But if their organization is tending towards Tmin then the distinctive services of an autocrat would be invaluable and, once appointed, such a person could be left to manage the organization until it starts tending towards Tsat again, at which readily identifiable instant (see gap analysis in the next chapter) the governing directors would terminate the autocrat's appointment, no doubt with grateful thanks and a handsome bonus.

And a further advantage, of inestimable value to society, is that these entrepreneurs would be free to build their empires up to the point where they begin to threaten their interest groups when, one may assume, these people would demand the appointment of a governing board to protect them from the autocrats' intemperance. To enjoy the soaring achievements of these remarkable entrepreneurs while also, at the critical moment, protecting society against their outrageous, and often painfully damaging excesses, would indeed be a triumph.

What I am suggesting in this section is this: far from management teams resenting my governing directors, most will welcome them with acclaim because they will not arbitrarily interfere in the detailed management of their organization and because they will hand down what all professional managers most admire, a BPI target to get their teeth into. Autocrats will be less enraptured, yet even they will have their opportunities, within clear-cut constraints, to work their special magic. Whichever style of management it may be, team or autocrat, positive governance breeds confident management.

Beneficiary management

I have coined the phrase 'beneficiary management' to distinguish the kind of management that these governing directors will foster—beneficiary-centred, as opposed to management-centred.

Managers in today's organizations act in their own advantage, quite routinely, without giving it a moment's thought, and unremarked by any of us. This is how they act today because this is how we have, after decades of manager-worship, come to expect them to behave. Academics refer to this as the 'agency cost' of running an organization (the cost to the principals of their agents failing to act in their interests) and while few of these misdeeds are individually of major significance, cumulatively they amount to such a debilitating drain on organizations that some are rendered literally useless to their beneficiaries. These acts occur in at least three areas of management: in setting corporate targets, in selecting strategies and in the misuse of resources.

I have suggested that managers should never be allowed to set corporate targets. But they do. Virtually all of them—even when the governing body apparently sets them they will have had 'suggestions' tactfully passed up to them by the management. Some managers deliberately pitch their targets too low (so they can easily achieve them), others so over-ambitiously high (to demonstrate their prowess) that they place their organization at grave risk from outlandish strategies or unethical practices. Many set targets over far too short a period, sometimes under pressure from impatient outsiders (short-termism), sometimes because their bonus is related to an inadequate horizon—even a year is far too short a time in which to judge an organization. We need someone who is not a manager to set targets over a much more meaningful period.

But, worse, managers also aim at quite the wrong objectives; as we have seen repeatedly in this book most managers aim for *physical* growth, because this satisfies their vainglory, their passion for size and empire, but, as we have also seen, what the beneficiaries want is growth of benefit, not growth of the size of the organization—and this defect holds true for every type of organization from the smallest company to the largest NPO. While managers aim for more beneficiaries, what the beneficiaries want is more benefit. The mismatch is universal and fundamental, built deliberately into the culture of the modern organization by its managers.

Managers' aims trump the beneficiaries' aims

Again, managers set themselves the top objective of 'remaining independent' or 'autonomous survival'. Yes, that is fine for them—I quite see how it suits them; might there not be occasions, however, when the beneficiaries would be better served by their organization being split up, taken over or closed down? Look at the former USSR and India; it must be blindingly obvious to everyone that these huge, heterogeneous nations should be split down into federations, yet it suits the politicians in Moscow and Delhi to hold them together. Millions of people's lives are stunted at the whim of a powerful few at the centre. (The former USSR disintegrated into separate republics in December 1991, an event which, in the long term, will greatly benefit all concerned.)

We have seen in previous chapters how many managers start their corporate plan with *management* aims ('we aim to be the biggest' or 'we aim to increase market share' or 'to be the technology leader' and so on) with the inevitable result that they select management-orientated strategies, not beneficiaries-orientated ones. And what about those well-meaning teachers who determined that their schools should bring about Utopia by 'promoting social equality' (Drucker, 1990), or 'a multi-racial intelligentsia' (one of the University of California's stated goals) or preserving the Welsh language, or 'reinvigorating the city centre'? Did the *students* benefit from these aims? When a manager sets the wrong top target for an organization its very purpose is perverted.

Management's strategies and use of resources

Company managers love to diversify—it excites them to do something new, it demonstrates their managerial prowess to show they can manage anything from ice-cream manufacture to helicopters. But the records show that most (well over 50 per cent) diversifications are disasters. These figures have been available for decades, every study ever undertaken shows the same thing. Yet managers go on doing it because it is fun for them. Much the same with acquisitions: most are failures, but what sport they provide! Again, managers of NPOs love complexity—most of our best brains go into the public sector—and so they set corporate objectives for their organizations of Byzantine complexity and snarl defensively when people like me ask what it all means for their beneficiaries. '*Who*'?

Some top managers decide their own salaries or bonuses. Others commit their organizations to special operations for their own enjoyment: the twinning of towns, for example (a transparent ruse for foreign travel for town councillors), or those monstrous week-long conferences in exotic resorts, or the building society in the south of England which, by coincidence I am sure, has several (loss-making) branch offices in Scotland and a salmon-fishing chairman. The appeal courts quite blatantly act to protect the dignity of the lower courts, not the liberty of the citizen. And so on to infinity: the agency costs have become intolerable.

External watchdogs a threat to liberty

But surely all these peccadilloes will be caught by more watchdogs, tighter legislation, tougher inspectorates, more vigilant policing? Well, they have been going on for many decades now and none of these has stopped them. I do not want our freedoms eroded still further by these repressive reactions; every time there is a scandal the system of inspection is strengthened—until the next scandal when it is strengthened again; no, that has been proven over and over again not to be the answer. We just go on tightening the wrong screw.

I want to break this cycle of failure; I want organizations to adopt a mechanism of governance that demands they put their *own* house in order. These governing directors will know, to the nearest millimetre and the latest split second, what their beneficiaries want them to do and how to behave towards their interest groups. Their sensitivity to how their organization is performing and behaving will be infinitely closer and more finely tuned than any watchdog. Their desire to see their organization perform well and behave better will be infinitely more forceful than any outside inspection system.

However imperfect the process by which they are to be elected (and sometimes, when representing children, for example, they may not be elected at all) these governing directors will fight more single-mindedly for the interests of their beneficiaries than any other mechanism yet devised. Even the most ordinary people take delight in the success of any organization with which they are connected; let us tap this deep, tribal instinct by inviting a few, sensible, committed people to act as internal watchdogs in this new, fully professional role. But we must not distract their loyalty to their beneficiaries by asking them to do anything else at the same time.

I believe we have missed the point again and again. Organizations must be endowed with separate, authoritative governance. In recent years managers have virtually taken over the world and have patently made a hash of it.

Less government

Now I hope that organizations which adopt these governing directors will gain such a reputation for high performance and benign conduct that they will encourage governments all over the world to spin off, over the next century or so, virtually all the operations they have accumulated in the past two centuries. I cannot see why government has to run the buses, housing, roads, children's homes, schools, hospitals, justice, book shops, museums, safety inspection—and on and on almost to infinity. Not quite all these are illegitimate, for some activities are of the essence of government. Making laws is (as opposed to administering justice which may not be), so is defence of the realm, control of the economy, the ordering of some aspects of society and so on. I do not wish to pretend to determine here what governments should and should not do; but it is widely recognized that most governments in the developed world have taken over far too many activities and most of these should be spun off (see Chapter 18).

One of the key reasons for not doing so, for delaying this desirable devo lution, is that we do not trust the organizations to which these activities would be allocated. But is it really beyond us to tame our companies and NPOs that we could allow them to take over the running of justice, the education system, the currency, food safety and so on? After all, the Germans gave the super- vision of the value of their currency to the independent *Bundesbank* many decades ago and inflation there has been exiguous, while here, where we entrusted this sacred duty to our government, they have somehow managed to lose 90 per cent (yes, *90!*) of its value within three decades.

If the Germans can trust an independent organization to look after such an important element of their national life as their currency, why not justice, why not road safety, why not a hospice? After all, even today, would you not trust Barnardo's to look after your disabled child—or would you prefer he or she went to a government-run home?

The idea that governments do things better than other types of organi- zation dies hard, so what is it that stops us handing all these duties over to those others? The answer is: we cannot trust them. Appoint governing boards to a few dozen of our major organizations and, within a couple of decades, we will wonder why we ever let our rulers get their hands on any of these activities.

Summary

In spite of decades, and even centuries, of trial and error, none of our so-called systems of governance has protected the interests of either the beneficiaries of our organizations nor of their various interest groups.

In view of the power of many organizations today, and the crying needs of society, we should place a layer of governance above the hierarchy of managers in all socially significant organizations. This requires the reformation of virtually all the governing bodies of all our schools, charities, companies, institutions—and even Parliament (see Chapter 19).

These governing directors will elect a chairman whose role is to lead them in their tasks of setting long-term Tmin and Tsat performance targets, deciding how their organization is to conduct itself in society, and monitoring its progress in these two areas. They will perform no management duties whatever—except to warn and then dismiss the chief executive if the organization approaches Tmin.

Thus the two functions, elected governance and executive management, will face each other in a double hierarchy; this unique structure being the badge of the beneficiary doctrine, the hallmark, the seal of approval, that signifies when an organization has achieved the nirvana of 'corporate democracy'—that it is managed in the interests of its beneficiaries. A double triangle design would no doubt make an elegant and appropriate logo for the Institute of Governing Directors.

CHAPTER SEVENTEEN

The management of organizations

$\mathbf{I}$n Chapter 3 I defined an organization as 'a group of people acting together to generate a satisfactory benefit for its intended beneficiaries', and I have spent most of the book expanding on the latter part of the sentence. I now wish to turn to the first part, to the 'group of people' who 'act together'. People who work for organizations perform three different functions which are closely interlinked in a hierarchical structure. I have already described what should be the function of the first of these, the governing directors, but I have only briefly mentioned the second—the managers—and now I shall describe what they do and how they fit into the overall structure in more detail. I need just to mention the third role—the operators.

I also want to explain what happens when the governing directors hand the organization's corporate targets down to the managers. What do they do with them? How do targets get turned into strategies? How can the governing directors or the management tell if their strategies are going to achieve the targets? In addition to the management tool specifically designed to develop these strategies, called corporate planning, I must also explain one other management technique which assumes particular importance in the philosophy of the beneficiary doctrine—'mall management'.

I end the chapter with an account of the various routes by which a management may re-form their organization to meet one of the central requirements of the beneficiary doctrine: that it should aim to satisfy but one set of beneficiaries.

The three functions

I have spent many pages explaining that, contrary to all other descriptions of how organizations work, I believe that two quite different functions have to be performed at the top—governance and management. I believe the practice of treating all senior members of an organization as if they were various categories of executive is a fatal error of many decades standing, and that the governance function must now be recognized as a vital duty quite distinct from management.

I defined governance as 'deciding and monitoring corporate performance and corporate conduct', and I have explained how I thought governors should pass performance and conduct goals down to managers. I define management as 'achieving given results through subordinates', where the word 'given' reminds us that the results to be achieved have been passed to the managers by a boss; it is essential to note that the results managers strive to achieve are not those they set themselves, they are handed down 'from above'.

The decline of megaphone management

Now, I know there is a school which claims that, in modern times, this hierarchical 'command structure' is old fashioned, has been superseded and that management structures should be shown as a circle or whatever, to emphasize their new democratic credentials. I can only say that, while it is pleasant to see the decline of megaphone management, the plain fact is that, in every organization, however informal, some managers are senior to others and that, however polite and deferential everyone is to each other today, and however thoroughly they consult together, the 'senior' ones are 'superior' to the 'junior' ones. They are in a hierarchy. There is an up and a down. If the boss says jump, you jump, even if you are told 'please' and offered a bonus if you clear the bar. In the final analysis, if two managers disagree, the senior one wins.

Management, then, should be a living, working hierarchy where, starting from the governing directors at the top, each boss hands targets down to his or her subordinates, who decide the best means by which to achieve them. They then pass part of these tasks down again to each of their subordinates, and so on down the chain, each manager's means becoming the subordinate's aims.

At the very bottom of the chain are the third type of person in any organization—the operators. Their role is defined as to 'get given results'. As they are not managers they have no subordinates to hand targets on to and so they are the ones who take the physical actions that actually get the results.

So this is the management hierarchy within any organization; there is a cascade of instructions trickling down the hierarchy to the workers at the base; one person's means are the next one's aims.

The management wiring diagram

There is a stream upwards too. Each person reports progress to the boss above and eventually, when these messages aggregate at the top, the governing directors can see how well their organization is progressing towards the corporate target. Figure 17.1 presents a simplified wiring plan of the management process which, unlike most such diagrams, shows what happens at the top and bottom of an organization.

Governing directors differ in two respects from all the other people at the

 **17.1** *'Wiring diagram' of the process of management*

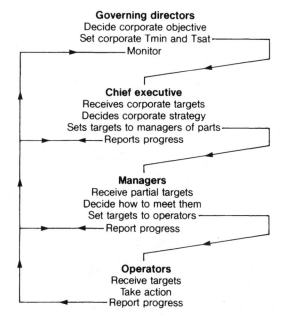

Governing directors
Decide corporate objective
Set corporate Tmin and Tsat
Monitor

Chief executive
Receives corporate targets
Decides corporate strategy
Sets targets to managers of parts
Reports progress

Managers
Receive partial targets
Decide how to meet them
Set targets to operators
Report progress

Operators
Receive targets
Take action
Report progress

top of a hierarchy in that (a) they are not called upon to decide the means, and (b) the targets they hand down are corporate ones BPIs or CPIs; everyone else decides means and hands down partial targets—MPIs.

Corporate planning

I do not wish to discuss management techniques in detail here—this book is about governance, not management—but I do need to demonstrate how these corporate targets are turned into strategies because this is the point at which governance actually meets management. The process in which the corporate objectives, as determined by the governing directors, call forth a set of corporate strategies specifically designed by the top managers to achieve the corporate targets is called 'corporate planning'.

A corporate plan consists of the targets, an analysis of the organization's overall strategic situation, a set of major strategic decisions and an action plan.

The corporate planning process

A variety of processes have been in widespread use for several decades. Many of these do not recognize 'deciding the corporate objective' as the

 **17.2** *Blackbird International plc: profit targets*

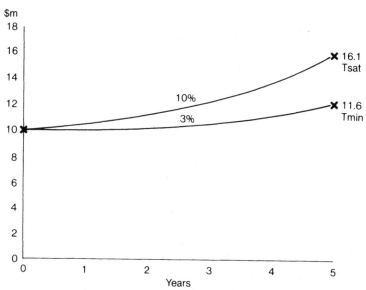

starting point, some omit parts of the analysis of the strategic situation, others are based upon quite different principles. All these are rejected here in favour of those which do include the above list of essential steps.

Corporate targets

Plainly, if the whole point of a set of strategies is to achieve the corporate targets, the corporate planning process must begin with them. It should start, then, with the governing directors moving through the purpose sequence as described in Chapters 4 to 6. Recall that this sequence ends with Tmin and Tsat. Let us imagine a company called Blackbird International plc which is currently (year 0) making a profit of $10m and where the governing directors have selected Tmin as 3 per cent per annum growth and Tsat as 10 per cent. Their aims are illustrated in Figure 17.2.

These are the targets they hand to the chief executive, perhaps with the words, 'achieve Tsat and we will give you a bonus; tend towards Tmin and we will sack you'—however politely they phrase it, that is what these targets mean.

Forecasts

Next, the senior executives will forecast what profits the company might make over each of the next five years assuming they pursue the corporate

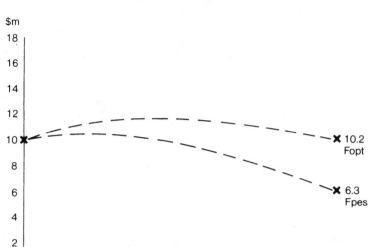

17.3 *Blackbird International plc: profit forecasts – current strategies*

strategies that are currently agreed among them—assuming 'unchanged policies', as it is often called. 'What would happen to our profits over the next five years', they would ask themselves, 'if we continued to run the company as we presently intend to run it?' But since it is impossible to forecast what is going to happen in the world over that time-span the process requires them to make *two* forecasts: a pessimistic forecast (Fpes), which assumes that many of the trends and events are unfavourable to the company, and an optimistic forecast (Fopt), which assumes many of them are going to be favourable. The result is two curves on a graph, illustrated in Figure 17.3.

Figure 17.3 suggests that, on present strategies, this company's profits will actually fall over the next few years if the pessimistic assumptions are borne out and, even if things go well for them, profits will fall back to $10m by year 5. Of course, the accuracy of these forecasts is abysmal, but the exercise is an extremely revealing one (and, on occasions, most exciting), for the mere act of quantifying all their hopes and fears for the future provides the managers with a forceful insight into their company's prospects.

Now what happens? The next step forms the actual moment of linkage between governance and management. It is called 'gap analysis'.

 **17.4** *Blackbird International plc: profit gaps – current strategies*

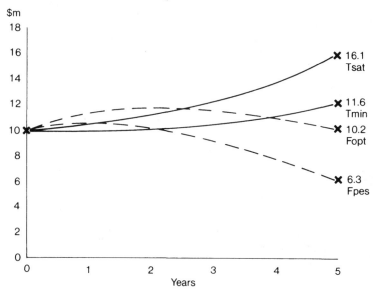

Gap analysis

Here the targets and the forecasts are placed together to obtain the 'gap'. A target, it will be recalled, is 'what you want to happen' while a forecast is 'what you expect to happen', so the gap is the difference between the two and shows you how powerful any new strategies will have to be, and how soon they must begin to work, to close the gap between what you want and what you expect. It is clear from the graph in Figure 17.4 that Blackbird's present strategies may *not* safeguard Tmin or achieve Tsat beyond year 2 (indeed, the present strategies are going to lead the company into decline within a few years). It is clear that the management needs to devise a set of strategies which not only stands a better chance of hitting Tsat but which— and this is urgent and vital—protects the company from falling below Tmin in year 2. So these new strategies must yield an extra, say, $7m profit by year 5 to take profits safely above Tmin and around Tsat.

The reason I said that gap analysis is the moment when governance and management come together is now clear: the function of a governing director is to 'determine targets . . . *and monitor*' the organization's performance; the role of a manager is to devise strategies to do this and what we have in Figure 17.4, on one simple graph, is a statement which shows both the target performance and whether the company is likely to hit it on present strategies. In this case it is not going to and both the governing directors and the management can see this very plainly.

This gap analysis technique is not limited to companies, although it is confined, naturally, to organizations that can quantify their aims; one can imagine, for instance, a road safety organization setting targets for fatal accidents per million vehicle miles and then calculating, on the basis of present plans for motorways and other strategic intentions, how the figure might be expected to turn out on pessimistic and optimistic assumptions. The gaps would show them whether, on present strategies, they would achieve their Tmin and Tsat improvement in the accident rate (of course, in this case, the targets will curve downwards, not upwards).

I have suggested that one of the key distinctions between a company and an NPO lies in their ability to quantify their aims but, in fact, the distinction really lies in their ability to perform this gap analysis calculation. Companies know when they have devised a suitable set of strategies because 'suitable' means 'capable of closing the gap'; until NPOs can make this extra-ordinarily helpful test they will remain second-class organizations. Companies can make such assertions as: 'To hit our targets we need to introduce a new product yielding $20m profits in year 3' or whatever—incredibly valuable revelations. Without the ability to make statements of this sort I question whether the word 'management' means anything at all in the modern, numerate, world.

The SWOTs

So, everyone at the top of the organization, governing directors and managers alike, know where they stand; they know what extra, if anything, they need to do to hit the targets, and how swiftly. The next step in the corporate planning process is for the management to examine their company's strengths and weaknesses and to try to match them with the threats and opportunities that they see as likely to occur in the next 5 or 10 years. This 'SWOT' procedure is standard today and I need not describe it fully here (Argenti, 1989).

Devising the strategies

The management should then devise a new set of strategies, to augment or supersede the current ones, designed to take advantage of the strengths and opportunities while avoiding the threats and weaknesses. As a very general rule strategies that work best in practice are those which rely heavily on the organization's key strengths or competitive advantages, while those that are most dangerous are those that lie some distance from these. How will the management know when they have found a suitable set of strategies? By making new optimistic and pessimistic forecasts, this time, of course, on the basis of their new strategies, to see if these will close the gaps.

237

I said in Chapter 16 that one of the questions the governing directors should ask themselves was: 'Are we confident that the strategies the management have devised will ensure that our organization will achieve Tsat for the next few years and that, above all, we are not headed towards Tmin?' This is how they can tell, from this new gap analysis, whether the management's new set of strategies convince them that the targets will be hit. Notice again the essential point that the strategies have to hit two targets, not one; they have to protect the organization from Tmin and, at the same time, have to hit, or preferably exceed, Tsat. Each organization requires a 'layer-cake' of strategies: a low-risk strategy to make sure of exceeding Tmin together with others, probably of increasing riskiness, to take them up to and beyond Tsat. And, remember, the strategies must also be in accordance with the code of corporate conduct that the governing directors will also have communicated to the management, as well as fitting all those strengths and weaknesses and threats and opportunities. This is a very demanding specification; there will not be many strategic proposals that meet all the desiderata; great ingenuity is required to find a suitable set but, thanks to gap analysis, the management can tell at once when the search is complete.

Evaluating the strategies

The new gaps, taking account of the new strategies, are illustrated in Figure

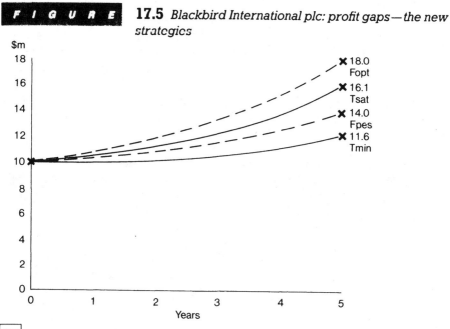

FIGURE **17.5** *Blackbird International plc: profit gaps—the new strategies*

17.5, where, if the future is favourable, profits will exceed Tsat through to year 5 while, even if the pessimistic scenario prevails, profits will not sink dangerously close to Tmin.

Monitoring

As time passes both the governing directors and the managers should monitor their confidence in the chosen strategies: perhaps something happens that was not foreseen and the gap widens; maybe they experience a windfall and it closes; perhaps they decide to raise the targets and so the gap opens again. At last, after a number of years, as the strategies run out of steam, as the world about them changes, as new threats and opportunities appear, the gaps for the later years will open, they will lose confidence in the existing strategies and, at last, the governing directors or the managers themselves will call for a new strategic review.

This corporate planning process is very difficult and absorbs much top management time, but it is the most reliable technique yet devised for placing an organization on track to hitting its long-term targets. It is equally valid for NPOs, and those that have learnt how to quantify their corporate objectives will be able to take full advantage of it—while those that have not will neither be able to generate a proper corporate plan nor use gap analysis to evaluate one. The sole purpose of a strategic plan is to achieve the corporate objective; if an organization has not got one of these then it plainly cannot plan or evaluate a corporate strategy (*pace* Hatten and others, see Hatten, 1982 and Wilson and Butler, 1990).

The big ideas

Notice what corporate planning does and does not do: it does not attempt to plan everything in sight in the most minute detail; it does lead to a few major decisions, decisions of such magnitude that they are unlikely to become outdated within several years even in this rapidly moving world. It provides the management with a few, robust 'way-points'. It gives them the handful of 'big ideas' they need to steer the organization towards its corporate targets.

Very often these strategies can be summed up in a few pages, or even a few sentences: 'We have become far too dependent upon bulk commodity chemicals; we need to develop or acquire a range of new, speciality products for world-wide niche markets. We are also far too dependent upon the UK economy; we must become a global operation', would summarize ICI's corporate plan some decades ago while today they might well decide, 'Our group has now become too large and diverse; it should be divided into several autonomous, specialized, global companies.'

A mental health NPO, for example, might decide 'Rapid growth over the past few years has resulted in lower standards of care and a greatly centralized bureaucracy. Head office staff will be cut from 110 to 27 and will concentrate on monitoring standards of care and on national fund-raising; the managers of our residential homes will be trained to exercise full authority over their region; the governing body will be cut from 73 to 22.' (And on pages 265–268 I attempt to sketch skeleton corporate plans for the police, prisons and the Church.)

Mall management

One of the conclusions that I hope has come out very clearly in earlier chapters is that an organization with more than one set of beneficiaries will be unable to judge how well it is performing from their point of view (which is all that matters), because it is impossible to evaluate an organization with two BPIs. I went further: I suggested that the benefit should also be homogeneous. Now this implies that the only organizations likely to meet the stringent standards of today's world are those which specialize—those which offer a homogeneous benefit to homogeneous beneficiaries.

How very interesting! Because it just so happens that one of the most striking strategic trends in the private sector is exactly that: companies are specializing. 'Stick to the knitting' is a phrase heard all around; the craze for diversification has moderated; 'synergy', a term once used to justify almost any diversification, has been replaced by thoughts of 'de-merging'; the words 'core business' have become current; 'cutting back to employ key strengths' has become fashionable—companies are actually shrinking in size (the average American company employs 20 per cent fewer people than a decade ago).

Every day a new 'core' announcement appears: in April 1992 British Airways announced its decision to sell its engine repair division along with catering, contract handling, avionics workshops—practically everything except the core business of running an airline. Pubs are separating from brewing, programme producing from broadcasting, transport and warehousing from retailing, and so on across a whole range of commercial activities.

The trend to specialization

Naturally, diversification has not entirely disappeared; there are a number of strategic situations in which it makes very good sense indeed, but the unthinking craze for it has run its course. The causes of this sweeping reversal in strategy selection are not far to seek:

Market segmentation

As we become better off we demand that our own individualistic foibles are met. Look at any product over the past few decades and see how it has become fragmented to meet increasingly meticulous demands: glossy magazines, steel, ice-cream—all now available in a bewildering diversity of colour, size, shape, price. Few companies can master the full range; they just have to specialize.

Competition

Intensified competition means that only those that are supremely good at what they are doing will survive. Now, quite simply, as a matter of practical fact, not many companies can beat their competitors in more than one significant activity, which suggests that they should concentrate heavily on what they do best—not only on the products themselves, as mentioned just above, but activities such as manufacturing, transport, negotiating, marketing, purchasing. If you are not superb at it, get someone else who is to do it for you.

Technology

To keep up with new technology (not to mention safety legislation), the cost of which is rising faster than general inflation, you have to specialize into a smaller and smaller area of endeavour; companies that used to build aircraft now only build components for aircraft, for instance (but often for a global market).

Diversification

And finally, so disastrous are so many diversifications (over half are failures) that, even though it is less exciting for them, many managers have at last been persuaded to 'stick to the knitting' wherever possible.

What a catalogue! No wonder companies are pursuing this specialization option so strongly after their flirtations with diversification. Typically, a British company, say, which produced five different products for the British market is switching to one product in five markets; narrower products in a wider area. But alas, NPOs are not following this trend. They have not yet caught on. They will simply have to do so because they are heirs to the selfsame trends listed above for companies. I visualize more and more NPOs specializing, spinning off their less pivotal beneficiaries, offering only those services to their primary beneficiaries that they do best. The result will be more and more NPOs each of which will be more specialized and, inevitably, smaller. Most will become better and better at less and less. Only the very successful will become better and better at more and more.

Smaller and specialist

I believe we will see more specialist courts, for example, to handle fraud only, children only, violence only, rape only, discrimination only, and so on,

241

with an increase in local, specialist, tribunals to deal with small claims, disputes between neighbours and so forth, outside the official legal system—a great surge of smaller, more specialized, less traditional, more flexible mediation and 'dispute-settling organizations'.

I forecast far more specialist hospitals: hip operations only, eyes only, skin only (already what few statistics we have demonstrate that the cure rate is higher in specialist clinics than in general hospitals).

We already have a few specialized prisons; let us have more—for women, for mothers with children, for youths, for remand, for violent offenders, for the mentally deranged, for sex offenders and so on—each with their own specialist facilities and specifically trained staff. And I am certain that children's charities should not try to help quite such a range of children as some do today—all the way from fostering normal children to the mentally disabled, physically disabled, the abused, young offenders, the disadvantaged; they are all 'children', but each requires such special treatment today.

Schools and colleges will specialize in music, science, sport, cramming, the hyperactive, the gifted. The larger the organization the less it can cope with diversity. The more specialized it is the more accurately it will be able to measure its performance.

But if this trend to specialization really does lead to more smaller organizations would not their management standards decline? Would they not become more vulnerable to unpredictable changes in their ever-narrowing field of activity? Would they not lose their 'clout' with government and other organizations? Yes, small may be beautiful but it is also more risky. So what should they do? They will have to join a group of similar organizations in a federation. There are many patterns in which organizations can huddle together under an umbrella. One is a 'mall'.

Yesterday's retailer

Enter a department store; there will be a fur department, a food hall, a café, men's shoes—and so on. Now visit a shopping mall; there will be a fur shop, a food shop, a café, a men's shoe shop—exactly the same. But the unseen difference is that in the first case all those departments were linked together through a lofty hierarchy of managers, each reporting to a boss in a level above, culminating in the chief executive right at the top. Just imagine how slowly it will react to changing needs and fashions; it will take weeks for each decision to be referred upwards, to be passed to the finance department for evaluation, to the legal adviser for vetting, and then the decision to close the fur department, or whatever, has to be tactfully passed back down, negotiated with the union, redundancy payments agreed, and so on indefinitely.

The need to speed up response-times is universal; the problem we have is not only that the rate of change is increasing but, just when that necessitates accelerated decision-making, managers have to spend *more* time consulting with more people because today they have so much more knowledge, so many more bright ideas, to offer.

What we need is to break the command hierarchy into segments so that decisions do not have to crawl up and down so many levels, but can start and end within a smaller, shorter hierarchy in a smaller but still autonomous organization. This is what a mall does: it allows smaller organizations to cluster together in a larger one while preserving their autonomy—i.e., they remain accountable directly and solely to their intended beneficiaries, not to some higher, intermediate manager. In the mall each shop is owned and managed by just a few entrepreneurs who, daily, or even hourly, know what the customer is saying and doing; they can tell, from the ringing of the till, almost from second to second, what action to take to improve their performance.

And so, for companies and NPOs alike, 'mall management' is becoming important. Mall management is valid wherever an organization needs to split itself into a number of smaller, specialized rapid-reaction sub-organizations. But, equally, it can form in exactly the opposite route: as an accretion of smaller similar units gathering together as if under an umbrella. Note that, unlike a management hierarchy, where decisions are centralized at the top of a command structure, each sub-group is independent with its own owners and managers (and, where appropriate, governing boards).

Depending on the terms of the contract, the mall owner will provide services (often trivial ones like cleaning, security, and so forth), but also where appropriate loans, management expertise, know-how, research and development, central purchasing, teams of trouble-shooters, or it may offer regulatory authority over the members to ensure high standards among them. Above all, it allows small organizations to achieve 'clout' in their negotiations with government, suppliers, customers and other interest groups. It is a symbiosis very like a franchise operation.

A very different hierarchy

Note the distinction between a mall, or federation, and the command hierarchy; the former is composed of *autonomous* organizations (i.e., with their own governing boards) who, by definition, may join and leave a mall at will. Units in a traditional management hierarchy are not autonomous, they do what their boss tells them to do and there is no escape from the contract. One is a hierarchy of free autonomous bodies, the other of tied subordinate managers. 'You will' becomes 'Shall we?'—a giant step into the modern world.

This federal structure could be a priceless concept for all types of organization. I see it as the end-point on a devolutionary path down which virtually all modern organizations are treading on their way to self-determination. The decades-old flattening of the hierarchy, the trend from centralized autocracy to teams of democratically-led managers, the surge to form profit-centres with devolved powers, the insistent demand by subordinates and citizens for wider 'empowerment', the declining size of organizations, their increasing specialization, all these trends, which may be observed in every type of organization today, point to this eventual mall-like, federal structure.

Unlike the master–servant relationship, which is unvarying in the traditional management hierarchy, a federation allows a wide range of contractual and informal relationships—everything from a tightly regulated franchise with negligible subsidiarity all the way down to a loose assemblage of fellow, like-minded, organizations—a 'confederation' (a federation with no or few central powers) such as a commonwealth. This generous, accommodating, format must be a huge competitive advantage in our modern, pluralist world.

Command and federal structures

Take an organization with a dozen different operations. In a traditional command hierarchy these might be broken into three divisions, each under a divisional director in a three-level management hierarchy as illustrated in Figure 17.6.

But in the mall arrangement all these operational units could be accommodated in only two levels because this is not a *management* relationship, requiring tight, continuous supervision, it is an assembly of autonomous units each with their own management and governance (see Figure 17.7).

I see this federal structure becoming the norm for companies and NPOs alike in the coming century. Not only does it reduce the number of levels required to manage a given number of operations, but it can accommodate

FIGURE **17.6** *A command structure*

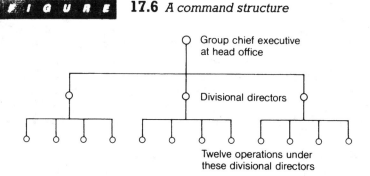

Group chief executive
at head office

Divisional directors

Twelve operations under
these divisional directors

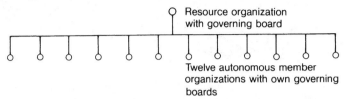

F I G U R E **17.7** *The federal structure*

Resource organization
with governing board

Twelve autonomous member
organizations with own governing
boards

as many levels as you like without increasing the response-time of the units themselves. And, because each unit is autonomous, and can join and leave its federation at will, it places the onus on the federal managers to provide meaningful added-value for the members; the members, equally, must conform to the federal standards. A most powerful symbiosis.

The size barrier

Another major advantage of this concept is that it allows very large companies to split themselves up into small units for the enhancement of human relations. Many experts believe there is a 'size-barrier': that once an organization exceeds 200 or 300 people it becomes increasingly difficult to engage its employees; it loses the 'family atmosphere' where the boss knows everyone (and even their families) and vice versa. A federal structure welcomes this limitation. As we grow more and more individualistic all, or most, organizations will eventually have to split down to segments of approximately this size to engage their employees and other interest groups. This means that factories, companies and NPOs will all have to be reduced to autonomous units of a few hundred people.

Perhaps nations too: nations are already broken down into states, provinces, regions, cities and towns so why not, finally, within each town or city, break the community down into what we British might call 'parishes' (and the Americans 'blocks') of a few hundred people each with their own autonomous local governing directors and chief executives or 'block captains' (no, not a huge new bureaucracy, just half a dozen part-timers). I wonder what would happen to crime, homelessness, poverty and so on if responsibility was floated down to these community associations? Might this not be an improvement on expecting the whole of Bristol say, or New York, to be managed by one single, gigantic, management hierarchy controlled from the town hall where no one roots for the average citizen any more?

And I see that research by the American National Institute of Justice suggests that major crime grows from minor crimes that are not nipped in the bud: nipping juveniles in the bud is just what the vicar, or a village constable used to do (and the beadle for a few hundred years before them),

245

and perhaps we need to re-establish parish-level authorities. I suspect, then, that an entire layer of government is missing from our democracies; our social tree has lost its root system, our political river has no tributaries.

Re-forming an organization

Once in a lifetime every organization may need to be completely re-formed. This will occur either when its corporate objectives have been, or evidently cannot be, completely met. Thus, for example, NATO, set up to deter the then USSR from invading Europe 40 years ago, and having manifestly succeeded in that aim, now requires a specific new role. (I have heard several politicians explain what its new role is but have yet to comprehend it. We do hate killing off organizations that have outlived their value, do we not?)

While success and failure are both stimuli for re-formation, then, the beneficiary doctrine provides another. It will be recalled that I see no possible justification for any organization having more than one, single, beneficiary—multi-purpose organizations are unmanageable. Yet many of our most venerable institutions believe they are multi-purpose—I mentioned the BMA, the Ministry of Agriculture, Fisheries and Food, TECs, the CAA and many more. I would like to enumerate some of the routes by which such organizations may be relieved of this burden. Since re-formation involves the redefinition of the corporate objectives, and is an event of major significance in the destiny of any organization, it should be overseen by the governing directors.

There must be dozens of routes to re-formation. Among them are: split into several single-beneficiary organizations, repudiate all but one of the intended beneficiaries, adopt a federal structure, redesign the eco-system (the environment within which any organization operates).

Split into two

Where an organization serves two or more different beneficiaries it could split into two or more, smaller, autonomous organizations each serving one. The British Ambulance Service currently offers two essentially different facilities: on the one hand there is the emergency service; on the other is a taxi service for ferrying out-patients to and from hospitals and clinics. On the face of it, it must have been a very sensible decision to run these two services in parallel, because emergency ambulances are only used part-time and elderly ambulances might be gainfully employed as taxis (especially since 90 per cent of ambulance journeys are of this latter type).

However, the first service requires speed, efficiency, advanced medical equipment and a highly trained crew, on whose skills the lives of accident victims depend so much. The second requires none of these—quite the reverse; patience and a kindly disposition in the crew, an atmosphere of comfort and calm in the vehicle.

The result of splitting these services (now being undertaken in Britain) will, I suspect, lead to a quite dramatic improvement in both. The first will gain new specialized equipment and very highly trained and motivated staff. The latter will become noticeably cheaper. But note this: when the service was mixed there was no possibility of measuring its performance; how can one add speed and life-saving to comfort and cost?

So this is what I mean by 're-forming'—in this case, by splitting an organization into two completely unrelated parts each serving a narrower, more specialized beneficiary with new specialized facilities. But splitting is right not just for organizations with two different beneficiaries but also those providing two different benefits.

The Ministry of Agriculture, Fisheries and Food should be split into two, one to serve food consumers, the other to serve farmers and fisheries. The Civil Aviation Authority should be cleft into its regulatory and operational aspects, and so on through NPOs without number. The National Rivers Authority, all adult colleges, universities, TECs, Scottish Enterprise—they all suffer from split personalities and must be re-formed into single-minded specialists whose performance can be measured.

More to one selected beneficiary

But in some cases splitting is not the answer. The Natural History Museum, for example, also serves two beneficiaries; it uses its unique resource, the collection of specimens (65 million of them!) housed in the Museum, to categorize and study animal life and it employs the same resources to entertain and instruct the public.

Now one alternative would be to emulate the ambulance service and simply split the museum's activities into two. The collection would go to the scientists (who must have the real thing, of course), while the public would get exhibitions of plastic replicas. This is undoubtedly one solution—critics call it the Disneyland Solution—yet it may well be viable (and might, incidentally, ameliorate the problem of the deterioration of the specimens when on display. Some of them are unique or extinct, remember, and must be preserved—literally for ever).

But another solution is to drop one of the intended beneficiaries and treat them as an interest group; either make the public pay or charge the research clients for advice so that the one subsidizes the other or helps to pay for the collection. The choice of which to drop and who should pay depends on a number of factors, including the original act of formation, the practicality of each alternative, the likely income from each, any legal barriers (such as covenants attached to gifts from collectors) and so on.

247

The point is made, I hope. Organizations with more than one intended beneficiary could split into two—or could simply drop one beneficiary entirely.

Then there is this route: an organization which serves a large number of beneficiaries, even if they are homogeneous, may find that it cannot measure its performance because it is spreading the jam too thin. This calls for reducing the numbers served and upgrading the service to each until its effects become measurable. A $1m charity which spends $100 each on helping 10 000 homeless people to find homes will be less able to demonstrate results than one which spends $1000 each to help only 1000 people.

Or again, imagine three charities which all help the disabled in three large towns; which is best? No one knows. But let each operate in just one town and we would soon see the difference between them (which is, of course, why this suggestion would not be favoured by their managers). The more an organization does for fewer beneficiaries the more likely we are to be able to measure its effect on them.

The federal solution

I have explained how the federal structure not only allows small specialized organizations to join a larger, umbrella, organization but also provides a framework into which large organizations can break down. Thus the Natural History Museum could also turn itself into a federation. This would entail breaking it up not into two but into three autonomous organizations: a 'resource organization' to own the specimens, and two to make use of them—one for the scientists and one as a display organization. For all we know, having broken the museum up like this, there might be a third, or even a fourth, use for the specimens which the present structure precludes.

I am sure the federal structure is the right one for general hospitals, towns, universities, colleges, and dozens of other multi-purpose organizations—not to mention nation states. Thus a general hospital could be split into a central resource-organization to provide facilities for all the other erstwhile departments: a hip replacement clinic, an eye clinic, a scan facility, and so on, where each would be truly autonomous, able to determine, on their own initiative, what facilities they require—even to opt out of the hospital entirely—and each with their own management and small governing board. It is interesting to note that the resource-owner would not then be a medical organization any more; it would be a 'services to medical organizations' organization. A specialist resource-owner or resource-manager would be the federal centre.

A universal trend

In the same way a typical adult college could split into three: the resource-owner, a vocational college for the youngsters, and a non-vocational college for adults (remember what trouble we had trying to measure the perform-ance of a dual-use college on page 49?).

Again, a railway could become a mall; there would be the resource-owner who acquires and maintains the track, and any number of service organi-zations (companies or NPOs) who run freight and passenger services on it. The complex accounting technology is relatively trivial with today's com-puters. (The Swedish railways have achieved substantial improvements since splitting into a resource-owning and several operating NPOs.)

Nations, too: far from being a cause for regret, as it is so often seen (especially by its political leaders), splitting up highly disparate peoples may be no bad thing. It is time we learnt more of how such federations should be designed and managed, for this is the way forward for many of our human organizations—not merely for vast ungovernable nations such as India, but any nation where diversity hinders its development. In Europe alone it may soon be time to split Czechs from Slovaks*, Flemings from Walloons and, yes, Celts from Angles. Federation may be the last and best answer for minorities everywhere, the peaceful way to realize our innate urge to tribal partisanship.

Federations, then, allow all types of organization to be big and small at the same time; autonomous yet influential; fleet of foot yet low in risk.

Redesign the eco-system

The more organizations specialize, the more they break up or spin off into specialized self governing units, the greater is the chance of re formation into more modern configurations, patterns and networks. Thus suppose our three emergency services (fire, police and ambulance) remain as they are today—huge and hierarchical—there is scant chance of any radical change. But if they were each to be broken up into increasingly specialist services then any number of permutations for reassembly might become possible.

I noted above how the ambulance service is being split into two different, specialist services; earlier I suggested that the police should break into specialist services; perhaps the fire service should too—maybe there should be a specialist chemicals section, a motorway section, a rescue section, or one for each major type of fire—traffic, domestic, tower block, and so on. But now see what might happen; re-formation might take place among all these services in a quite different dimension, free from previous patterns of thought. One could now envisage a lightly-equipped spearhead rapid response unit (neither fire, police nor ambulance) which reaches an emergency with extreme speed and then calls out any relevant portfolio of specialist services (all these would be autonomous specialist organizations

*The former Czechoslovakia became the Slovak Republic and the Czech Republic in January 1993.

YOUR ORGANIZATION: WHAT IS IT FOR?

assembled within a local, national, and later perhaps, an international federation).

This is what I mean by 'redesign the eco-system'—redesign not only a single organization but all those contiguous to it. Or again, at present in Britain, the Treasury regulates the entire economic system, including defending the value of our currency. In Germany the *Bundesbank* is responsible for this function, and is entirely independent of the government which nevertheless continues to manipulate the other levers of economic control. The point here is this: given careful thought, any system, however complex, however intricately woven (as a currency is within a nation's economic system), can be redesigned so that the functions of the organizations that operate it, or within it, can be reassigned. All complex systems can theoretically be disintegrated into any number of independent member organizations and reassembled in whatever patterns suits the circumstances better.

When the UK government recently handed over the distribution of social payments (child benefits, pensions, unemployment pay and so on) to agencies they were taking exactly this route—redesigning the eco-system by splitting the delivery of these benefits from the decisions as to their nature and amounts. They took a similar step when splitting the NHS into 'purchasing' and 'providing'.

The single-hierarchy monster

In other words, to get something done in society you do not necessarily have to form one huge national organization charged with dozens of activities; half a dozen small, specialized ones, or even local ones, might, acting together within a federation, do the job better (or even none at all—I am perfectly capable of saving for my own pension and do not need a massive government department to do it for me). It is not a message our politicians will like.

I am not here seriously suggesting solutions to these complex problems, merely thinking out loud about some of our social ills against the background of advice from the beneficiary doctrine which says: go to any lengths to make the quantification of corporate objectives possible—*we must be able to measure how well our organizations are working*. The criterion for the design of a system, and of all the organizations associated with it, is not cost or value for money, not management structure or efficiency; it is whether it is possible to see 'how are they getting on?' for each of the organizations in that system. So if the performance of the organizations within a system are not verifiable, you either re-form the organizations themselves within it or you change the structure of the system.

Is it going to be easy? I have no idea; the only considerations currently given to redesigning complex systems like our national health care are precisely these second-level concerns—cost, management, efficiency and so forth; I am suggesting that all these are irrelevant, or at least secondary, and that there is only one true criterion, which no one has even attempted to use before.

Finally, what happens if, in spite of their best efforts to re-form, an organization finds that it still cannot quantify its performance? Why then it should be privatized or closed down. Privatization is the ultimate solution because profit can be made from virtually any activity known to civilization. Alas, this solution is, as I have suggested before, entirely inappropriate in many situations—at least until companies have learnt to behave themselves with more consideration in society.

Summary

Organizations of whatever size or complexity—all the way from just a few people up to millions of members or employees—are essentially hierarchical. At the very top there should be the governing directors setting the corporate performance and conduct criteria to the chief executive who then breaks down these corporate targets into a small number of strategically important decisions—the corporate plan—and sets targets for the cascade of managers below. A number of well-tried systems for making these strategic decisions now exist.

Thus there is a hierarchy of managers in all large organizations, all moving through a set target, decide means, set target sequence. And this leads to a problem: in today's fast-moving world this sequential system of decision-making is too slow. The command structure now has to be broken down. One way is to flatten the hierarchy by cutting out all the advisers—the 'lean team' of executives only. Another is to delegate more decisions to better trained, and more engaged, subordinates. Another is to load more subordinates on to each boss.

But another, far more radical idea is to break down large organizations into smaller, autonomous units which, being small, have short, swift hierarchies. These may form into voluntary federations, like a mall and unlike a department store. This device accommodates another key trend in the modern world—specialization—which, by definition, demands smaller, niche-serving organizations which are inevitably more vulnerable than larger, more general ones. Both these requirements, size and risk-reduction, are neatly served by the federal concept.

Little is known of the management of federations and confederations; it is a major area of neglect by the management gurus who have hitherto concentrated on the study of large, prestigious, hierarchical organizations —the department stores of yesterday.

The concept of the federation will be most valuable to organizations wishing to become single-minded by shedding non-homogeneous intended beneficiaries. This re-formation may be achieved by simply splitting into two autonomous organizations each serving one beneficiary. Or by dropping one beneficiary who becomes an interest group. Or by splitting into several units in a federation, one of which may become the resource manager, the others using this resource to serve their respective, single, beneficiary. Or, if they operate within a system in which they have but partial control, and therefore cannot measure their performance, they could redesign the system so as to gain complete control of one or more parts of it.

The secret of the design of organizational structures and systems of organizations is just this: it must be possible to measure the performance of each constituent organization. 'Can you see if it is working?'.

CHAPTER EIGHTEEN

The consequences of the beneficiary doctrine

In this chapter I propose firstly to summarize all the salient points of the beneficiary doctrine. I then want to describe how it might influence certain aspects of society. What, for example, might be the main changes to companies and NPOs? How will the trend towards federalism modify the various types of organization? What will be the impact on the jobs of governors and managers?

I then catalogue the upheavals that the beneficiary doctrine will require of such organizations as the police, colleges, organized religions, government agencies and so forth.

Brief summary of the beneficiary doctrine

The beneficiary doctrine consists of three interlinked beliefs: that all modern organizations must quantify their corporate objectives and systematically verify whether or not these are being attained; that their behaviour in the community should engage all relevant interest groups and, at the very least, be non-harmful; and that we would be far better served by all our organizations if elected governance and executive management were explicitly separated.

Performance

One of the three central pivots of this theory is that organizations must learn to measure their performance from the point of view of the beneficiary. What matters is not the student/staff ratio or class-room utilization of a school, but the future earnings stream of its students. What is essential to an institution for the advancement of science is not how many learned papers its members have published, nor even how many members it has, but whether it can show that it is actually advancing science. To a company it is not what its market share is, nor the cost per unit of its product that matters; the crux is its long-term return on shareholders' capital.

Companies are well aware of their *raison d'être* and act with concentrated zeal to measure the returns they deliver to their shareholders. In startling contrast many NPOs claim their performance cannot be measured at all. This book suggests that this affirmation deserves to be challenged, ruthlessly, to extinction. The reason NPOs do not measure their performance is partly because it is admittedly very difficult, but chiefly because managers know that if it could be measured it might be seen as patently inadequate (recall how, when Weikart measured his organization, the return on capital fell away surprisingly sharply), and so they devise a number of spoilers to ensure that it cannot be assessed.

In my estimation *half* of all the NPOs in Britain are useless; and yet we depend increasingly upon just these organizations to solve some of the modern world's most distressing problems and to enhance the quality of our lives—crucial tasks which, very plainly, they repeatedly fail to fulfil.

Single-minded

The reason NPOs perform so poorly is not because they lack the stimulus of market forces or the profit motive, or that there is some mysterious defect that NPOs are heirs to, or because of underfunding or a lower quality of management—it is because they do not know exactly what they are trying to do for whom, cannot measure whether they are doing it and therefore, and rather obviously, cannot tackle it single-mindedly as companies do. Those NPOs that *do* know what they are trying to do, do it as well as, and sometimes much better than, companies.

The beneficiary doctrine states that any organization which cannot set a numerical BPI (the indicator which reflects the benefit the *beneficiaries* actually receive) should be re-formed until it becomes possible to do so. The problem of selecting a suitable BPI can only be solved by identifying one set of homogeneous beneficiaries and setting single meaningful, verifiable targets. This will allow NPOs to use, single-mindedly, and for the first time, all the modern techniques of top management, including corporate planning and quantified, single-criterion, project-appraisal procedures as already used in companies—and this, almost at a stroke, would vastly improve their decision-making and hence their performance. So long as they insist on serving several beneficiaries, and on setting multiple targets, they will continue to falter in everything they attempt to do; multi-purpose organizations are unmanageable by any modern standards.

Contrary to all current thinking, the problem of NPO effectiveness cannot be solved by, for instance, beefing up the management, or endlessly enforcing tighter inspection by watchdogs, or throwing more cash at them, or improving efficiency (especially as you cannot measure efficiency until you have measured output—exactly what most NPOs say they cannot do!). What NPOs need is what companies have got—single-mindedness. To be single-minded you need a single BPI.

Conduct

Unfortunately, companies defile their otherwise ample contribution to our civilization by their disgraceful behaviour; so single-mindedly do they act that they repeatedly and wilfully damage society. The last thing we want, as a by-product of part one of the beneficiary doctrine, is to exacerbate this by calling for absurdly ambitious targets from companies. For that reason the concept of a Tsat (above average) level of performance is recommended and, for the majority of companies, striving for some ideal, obtainable only by the very few, such as Tfan, or even 'excellence', is deprecated.

The rules which should guide corporate behaviour are the same for companies and for NPOs: the no harm principle and the principle of engagement. These should replace the deeply-flawed stakeholder theory. If organizations adopted the no harm principle society would be relieved of many of the damaging actions perpetrated by companies (and, let us not forget, by many NPOs too, who are by no means all as innocent as is 'often portrayed). If organizations adopted the principle of engaging the enthusiasm of all relevant interest groups this would enormously strengthen both their performance and their behaviour.

There is scant chance of either the performance or the behaviour of organizations being significantly improved by these measures, simple though they are, unless the third limb of the beneficiary doctrine is activated as well (failure to address these three aspects simultaneously lies at the root of the bankruptcy of all previous attempts to enhance corporate effectiveness), namely, the appointment of a governing board above the management of all our more significant organizations. One of the most potent reasons for poor performance and conduct in the past few decades has been the rise in the influence of managers. Their excessive domination stems not just from their abundant and formidable new technologies and their enviable skills, but from their unfettered freedom to determine the aims, strategies and disposition of the resources of their organizations, often diverting them to their own ends, sometimes perhaps decimating their value to their beneficiaries and even turning some into negative-sum organizations.

And all this at a time when we have come to depend upon organizations for almost everything our modern civilization values most. Managers have gained control of the controlling influences of all our lives.

Governance

It is these managers who have persuaded us to accept the stakeholder theory, which appears to license them to act in their own interests. It is managers who insist that 'it is not possible to measure our performance', it is managers who decide aims, set targets, monitor performance, determine behaviour. They have become judge, jury and executioner in their own case. Why, for example, does government continually take a larger and larger proportion of national income? Is it because government is such a splendid device for managing human affairs? No, it is not. No one on earth believes that. It is because there is no constraint upon the executive who, in spite of the so-called separation of powers, simply votes itself more of everything without hindrance from any form of effective governance. An unstoppable juggernaut. But government is just one example—albeit the most momentous—of what has gone so disastrously wrong with so many of our organizations; their system of governance is defective.

The appointment of a comparatively few, sensible people as professional governing directors (themselves trained, licensed and regulated by the 'Institute of Governing Directors') to supervise the management of our more influential organizations is essential. Alas, none of the present systems of governance is valid, not those for companies, nor schools, nor charities, nor Parliament itself; most of these call upon their governors to act as super-managers, forming an extra layer of amateur management over the professional one, interfering almost daily in trivial matters of which they are wholly ignorant, and, thus diverted, they fail utterly to attend their true duties—to supervise the performance and the behaviour of their organizations as corporate wholes *on behalf of the beneficiaries*. The last thing we want these people to do is to manage; we must prevent managerial power continually creeping upwards into their hands; what we want them to do is more faithfully to represent us, the beneficiaries, *to* the management, not to *be* the management.

Management

I hope I have adequately described the extent to which I believe management has gained control of the commanding heights of modern society. They distort the aims of most organizations: they select growth because it is in their interest; they claim 'independent survival' as the top corporate objective, regardless of whether this may suit the interests of their beneficiaries; resources are diverted to build their egos or their empires; strategies are formed for their personal fancy and vainglory (note their predilection for diversification, for example, in spite of mountainous evidence that it seldom works). I believe the mere fact of imposing the restraint of the governing directors upon managers will vastly increase the effectiveness of companies and NPOs alike.

But far from being cowed and stifled by the appointment of governing boards managers will welcome them for they will, at last, grant them what they have always wanted: BPI targets which allow the full exercise of their managerial skills and innovative ideas, instead of endless, trivial and often very silly, detailed MPIs. Managers will still astound us with their powers.

Their profession will flourish as never before. But they will be back inside the bottle.

For centuries we have searched for some way of encouraging managers to deliver their miracles of performance while at the same time constraining them within bounds. We have alternately granted them unique authority—as we do in companies—or have castrated them—as we do in NPOs—and we do both at once when we 'separate the powers' in our complex political systems. But the solution lies in none of these directions. It lies in simply separating elected governance from executive management.

This, then, is the beneficiary doctrine. It calls for three changes in corporate design: the setting of clear single-minded numerical corporate targets; the adoption of two new codes of corporate behaviour; and the application of true governance. The consequences of this tripartite approach will be dramatic.

The consequences of the beneficiary doctrine

I believe the adoption of the principles outlined above would yield a massive improvement for society. I list below some of the repercussions on some aspects of organizational life, starting with companies and NPOs, and I then summarize the effects of rising federalism.

The consequences to companies

The effects on companies would be felt mainly in the boardroom. Existing non-executive directors who hold executive posts in other companies would be asked to give way to a board of professional non-executives, elected by the shareholders, completely separate and senior to the managers, whose first act would be to elect a chairman—again, an entirely non-executive position.

A major change would be that these governing directors would appoint, dismiss and remunerate the chief executive, who, in turn, would appoint all the other executive directors (unlike the present practice, governing directors would not appoint, remunerate or dismiss any of these other executive staff).

Every year the governing directors would reset Tmin and Tsat for the next five (or more) years and would continuously monitor the company's actual and predicted progress towards these aims. It is possible, especially if they employ ROSC as their BPI rather than growth of EpS, that companies would place less emphasis on physical growth than they currently do, although certainly not less on growth of productivity and profits.

The governing directors would also set out a code of conduct for the behaviour of the company's managers and employees and would satisfy themselves that everyone understood it. They would account to the share-holders annually showing, in a standard double-page report based on the one on page 218, what the targets are, what the code of conduct is and whether they have both been met, and would confirm their confidence in the management's current long-term strategies. They would constantly review the changing needs of the various categories of shareholders and the shifting sentiments of the relevant interest groups toward corporate behaviour. They would have no other duties whatever unless Tmin was threatened, when they might first have to curtail the chief executive's bonuses, next to dismiss the chief executive and *in extremis*, dispose of the company.

Management by vainglory

Company managers would go about their duties as before except that they would neither set their company's targets nor decide its code of conduct. They would do what managers are supposed to do: determine the best means of achieving the aims. Moreover, because of the supervising influence of these governing boards, managers would be less inclined need-lessly to diversify or pursue other dubious red-herring strategies for their own entertainment and personal vainglory.

One thing companies would cease to do is to pretend they are acting in the interests of the community and the other stakeholders. They would feel no compulsion to offer their help to clean up city centres, for example, or to assist the economies of developing nations, although, no doubt, many would continue to do so where that is justified by the principle of engagement. The communal behaviour of companies would nevertheless improve beyond recognition as the no harm principle took root, thus substantially reducing the number of zero-sum and negative-sum com-panies in society, and, as the principle of engagement took over from the stakeholder theory, they would modify their conduct so as to engage their diverse interest groups more closely and enthusiastically.

There is a possibility, a small one in my view, that employees will revolt against so explicitly working for shareholders and, as a result, the company might decline as a form of human organization. Far more likely is that more people will become shareholders, or more employees will earn shares and that 'profit'—the corporate objective that dare not speak its name—will become ever more widely accepted. Contrary to the view of many well-meaning liberals, the vast majority of employees in companies know perfec-tly well that profit is the aim and are not perturbed by its morality; on the contrary, many take delight in seeing profits rise and rejoice in their company's success, even in firms owned by already-wealthy families (indeed surveys show that family businesses perform better than any other type of company).

The consequences to NPOs

It has been my contention throughout this book that most NPOs lag far behind companies in their performance although, mercifully, they do behave well in society. The reason for this dichotomy is simple: as a direct result of not being able to state their corporate objectives clearly many are decades behind companies in their management styles. Their huge committees, ranging up to many dozens of people, designed to obfuscate personal responsibility, the outrageous delays (excruciating in the case of the law), the inability to employ top-level quantified techniques such as corporate planning and project appraisal, their non-competitive, non-results culture—all these stem from their lack of goal-direction.

The defects are vast—and all because they *claim* they cannot measure their performance. It is not a question of whether these NPOs are managed well or badly; if their performance cannot be quantified they are not managed at all in any modern sense of that word. If they could measure their performance all these anachronisms would be swept away in their managers' headlong desire to demonstrate their professional ability to meet their shiny new targets. The growth rates of NPOs, currently on average far below those of companies, would at last begin to challenge them.

And so I would be exceedingly disappointed if most NPOs did not immediately respond to the beneficiary doctrine with a very substantial upsurge in performance. But also, as a result of being made to measure performance, I expect almost half of all our NPOs (including some very well-known ones) to have to face being re-formed or disappearing entirely, leaving only those which could demonstrate concrete, measurable achievements. The impact on society of concentrating on those organizations which work, and can be seen to be doing something thoroughly useful for someone, would be amazing. We will at last be able to see whether society should invest its next £1bn in ICI, Scottish Enterprise or Help the Aged. My guess is that, after the initial shake-out, the number and influence of NPOs in the community would soar. The return on society's capital would bound upwards, delivering a great surge in our wealth and welfare.

An exodus of governors

A massive effect would also be seen on their governing bodies. Today most NPOs can boast dozens of governors: 80 for the MBA, 62 for RIBA, 52 for the National Trust. A veritable diaspora would occur as these surplus governors retired, to be replaced in the main by a comparatively few sensible, experienced professionals with knowledge and commitment to the beneficiaries of their organization rather than to the organization itself. As with company governing directors they would need to maintain close contact with the beneficiaries to be quite sure they knew how the organization was performing and behaving from *the beneficiaries'* point of view. They would also be assisted by a team of specialists in beneficiary tracking, and by the auditors (two new and considerable costs for most organizations but paid for many times over by the fact that the governing directors would at last know what good their organization was doing its beneficiaries).

Thus the professional managers of NPOs would take great delight in their new-found freedom to determine strategies to achieve BPIs, rather than have to accept endless MPIs from the hands of governors who know little about the organization. They might be less enamoured of the jaundiced view that many governing directors might properly take of strategies designed purely for physical growth, or growth of membership or client numbers, a disappointment moderated, perhaps by generous bonuses based on a vastly more apposite ambition, namely growth of BpB, which would become the central aim of most NPOs, just as EpS is for companies (in this context it is significant that company managers, although obsessed by growth, do not aim to increase the *number* of shareholders).

An even more basic aim, to which all companies and NPOs should eventually graduate, not perhaps for several decades, is return on share-holders' or on society's capital (ROSC), but meanwhile how gratifying it will be for NPO managers to strive to place their organizations in the upper quartile of a BpB-based league table that really means something significant to their beneficiaries.

Single-function specialists

A great swathe of NPOs should specialize, aiming to serve just one benefi-ciary with single-minded vigour. All multi-purpose organizations, like RIBA, the BMA, the Royal Society, should drop the pretence that they are both extrovert and introvert at the same time, and honestly declare that their single purpose is to enhance the earnings of their members. It might challenge their ingenuity to phrase such a painfully truthful mission state-ment, but is it not just simply dishonest of these professional institutions to pretend they are anything but up-market, rather genteel, trade unions? Do we not all know, in our hearts, that that is what they are?

I believe that the highly focused, single-minded, specialist organization will dominate the next century; single-issue campaigns will supplant the present broad-spectrum charities, single-function agencies will replace multi-purpose institutions, and specialist companies will beat the diversi-fied conglomerates. I am sure that an organization with one set of homoge-neous beneficiaries will do better than the equivalent organization that is twice as large with two different beneficiaries; the sole reason we have such edifices today is to flatter the egos of their managers. The winners in tomorrow's world—that is, the organizations that we will find most effective at satisfying our needs—will be the ones that dedicate themselves to single intended beneficiaries and who do not attempt to play Father Christmas to all humanity.

Even those which already have only one beneficiary may have to reduce their spread. The Church of England has recently set up a nationwide unit to 'reduce the gap between rich and poor' on a budget of £4m per annum. This is ludicrous. It is inconceivable that this organization could have any measurable effect on anything whatever on a national scale. But, by concentrating on just one area—a small city, say—the picture might be very different; it might then have some visible outcome. The principle here is simple: organizations should do only what they can evaluate—doing something that has no measurable effect on anyone is a waste of money. Worse, it is sheer managerial vanity.

A kaleidoscope of variety

Many NPOs would, as a consequence of such specializing, become smaller—the TECs would, Scottish Enterprise would, along with hundreds of others which currently attempt to do several impossible things before breakfast. A few, however, will grow geographically, and those with proven records will expand both geographically and into a wider range of activities (the National Trust has performed well above Tsat for several decades and ought, surely, to be taking on some of the roles of its less successful rivals). A few organizations that are already large will need to beat the 'size-barrier' and become even larger.

I see a blossoming of competing types of organization as a result of this smaller, more specialist trend in NPOs. Some NPOs will turn to profit-making, companies will transmute into NPOs, the voluntary sector will compete with governmental (see below, where no less than four different types of organization are pictured running the prisons). We consistently fail to experiment with new types of NPO. They are stuck in the mud and there they will remain until we can measure their performance and see what difference each experiment makes.

The trend to smaller organizations would lead eventually to organizations serving just a few beneficiaries—or even just one! And why not? The very wealthy have always enjoyed their own private retinue of secretaries, gardeners, chauffeurs, cooks, pilots, financial and legal advisers, working together under a personal agent to serve just one person or family. As we all become more affluent this will become the ultimate introvert organization dedicated single-mindedly to one (very homogeneous!) beneficiary.

The federal tendency

One of the key conclusions from this book is the trend towards the federal structure that will become apparent as large organizations break up and small ones coalesce under the influence of four of the beneficiary doctrine's most potent precepts: the need to measure performance will lead to specialization; this specialization will lead to smaller organizations who will need an umbrella; the command structure involves too many delays in decision-making; and the principle of engagement works best in organizations employing only a few hundred people.

I see a kaleidoscope of new types of organization forming widely differing federal relationships, a rebellion of variety made possible by breaking out of traditional hierarchical management structures. Both by the process of accretion, then, and by the act of devolution, the same essential pattern will be formed—a cloud of small, specialist, autonomous units buzzing round the central nucleus, a mall, a federation. 'Split and specialize', if you like alliterative slogans. Or 'focus and federate'.

We will see organizations of every type falling to this vogue. We will see nations both breaking up and coming together as federations. This is exactly what we see today where the command structure of the former USSR is in terminal collapse while the European Community is crystallizing into a federation of states; one old-style command piston on its way down passing a modern federal design on its way up in the great engine of history. In nation after nation the demand for self-determination, for personal and minority recognition, for less intrusion into privacy and less government, will dominate social trends so that I expect to see innumerable ethnic and religious minorities breaking out of nations and joining or forming new federations.

License, franchise, devolve, federate

Not just nations—all organizations. We will see all the large charities and institutions federalizing. Barnardo's, for example, will fly into a dozen different regional and functional divisions, each employing a few hundred people, each dealing with a different type of childcare problem (young offenders, fostering, the disabled, and so forth) and each licensed to use the name 'Barnardo's' and use its central services so long as they uphold its standards, each of course with its own governing board, each able to measure its corporate performance.

Likewise, we will see the National Farmers' Union, say, splitting into specialist sub-cells—hill farmers, livestock, arable, organic—each with its own governing board and management set within a 'Farmers' Union Federation'. A whole string of ex-government departments will join the independent throng, their federal title no doubt including the words 'HM Government' or whatever.

We will see companies spinning off their branches; we may even have each local Sainsbury's branch, owned mainly by its managers and employees, permitted to use that name so long as they maintain the required standard and so long as they value the advantages of the central purchasing (or whatever service the resource-owning Sainsbury's then offers them), very like a franchise or licensing agreement. Moreover, while I am sure we will not see Sainsbury's branches joining a Barnardo's federation, we may see many differing types of organization within the same federation—all four types of prison (see below) would join the 'British Prison Federation', for instance. And we will see many different mall-managing organizations vying for the custom of potential members—Marks and Spencer will be there wooing the Sainsbury's branches to join them instead.

Two preferred types of organization

I have explained how I believe the project organization to be one of the most neglected forms of human system; its great advantage being that its aims are known with the starkest possible clarity, for, once they are achieved, it ceases to exist, a fact that should concentrate the mind most wonderfully but which, naturally enough, frightens the management (which is, of course, why this format is so neglected and why managers insist on claiming that their organization's survival is its top corporate objective). But these organizations would, I believe, serve us exceptionally well. They would serve the managers well, too, if they formed a federation of project organizations, for then, under its benevolent umbrella, the managers and employees could be re-engaged to tackle some new task as soon as the old one had been achieved. The return on capital of these throw-away, single-minded, professionally managed, transitory project specialists would be most impressive.

Again, I have suggested that introvert organizations might be more effective than extrovert ones because self-interest is a more powerful incentive than helping others. (Consider the family, an amazingly successful type of introvert organization, persisting almost unchanged over many millenniums.)

Imagine a local government which runs a bus service especially for its disabled population. Its cost is immense, as one would expect. But suppose, instead of being run as an extrovert organization by a management hierarchy of well-meaning civil servants, its facilities and know-how were handed to an introvert 'Disabled Bus Service Society' run by the disabled themselves? Would that service be more closely responsive to their needs? Cheaper? If you argue that it would be vulnerable to all the difficulties and dangers that small, amateur organizations are heirs to, then first give it a governing board (elected by and from the disabled users themselves, remember) and then form a protective federation to receive this and other, similar organizations. (The government of Niger has recently transferred the task of wildlife preservation from a large extrovert, civil-service dominated, organization to introvert profitmaking groups of local tribes.)

So, let us spin off some of the extrovert services that huge government departments provide, usually with scant sympathy, to more compassionate, introvert organizations within their own protective federations. It is wonderfully kind of people to run extrovert organizations for others but it is really not a very effective form of human endeavour. It is no coincidence that government organizations are unremittingly extrovert and that their performance is generally substandard.

These two organizational forms—introvert and project—seem to me to be absurdly neglected. They require two steps for rehabilitation to their rightful place: the appointment of governing directors to supervise them, and the formation of suitable federations to receive and protect them.

The impact on certain specific organizations

I illustrate below how the beneficiary doctrine might affect a small sample of well-known organizations. Similar modifications would be required across the entire range of NPOs and I present these below merely as a few examples of its multitudinous possible consequences. I have already described how the BMA and RIBA should become introvert, how Barnardo's should be federalized, how the Guides be retargeted, local government management be restructured and so on. As a guess, out of the, say, 2000 socially significant organizations in Britain, approximately half will disappear or be radically re-formed (perhaps along the lines described below) under the ordinance of the beneficiary doctrine.

Schools, colleges, universities

Under the beneficiary doctrine virtually all current school governors would be removed from their boards; teachers at the school and parents with children at the school (none of whom should ever have been deemed legitimate members) would be replaced by suitable governing directors (the head teacher is presumably the chief executive of the school and is also quite plainly not eligible as a governor). The new governing board would set Tmin and Tsat for performance on behalf of the students. Until the figures for salary progression of their ex-students, and those of comparable schools, become available—not for several years, obviously—they would have to make do with exam passes, entry into university, percentage unemployed or similar lamp-post proxies.

Instead of inspecting lavatories and designing school uniforms the new governing directors would spend their time making sure that the school was run for the students, and that their interests were not being sacrificed in pursuit of social equality, the speaking of Welsh, the development of a multi-racial intelligentsia or the enlivening of city centres, all of which I have quoted earlier as examples of how the stakeholder theory entices school and college managers down the path to perversion.

Adult colleges should be split into vocational and non-vocational, perhaps with the resources being held by a third, resource-owning or managing organization, which might then discover further uses for these,

perhaps in connection with local small firms, training organizations, dramatic societies, sports clubs, or whatever. The effect on students should be
remarkable: the curriculum would rapidly swing into the modern world of
work for the vocational college while the non-vocational branch would
begin to earn significant revenues from adults happy to pay the full cost of
their 'leisure learning'.

Universities are another double-beneficiary educational organization:
because they both teach and undertake research it is impossible to measure
their performance. While there is a link between teaching and research it is
tenuous: today most university researchers work at levels far beyond those
reached by most undergraduates; meanwhile, most researchers do little
teaching and not all teachers do research. Split these functions into two so
that measurement becomes possible. Those who both teach and research
can easily work part-time for each.

Perhaps we could go further: maybe there should be not just two or three
members of any given university federation, but a dozen; not just the
resource unit, the undergraduate teaching and the research organizations, but each faculty—medical, business, engineering, history, post-
graduates—could become an autonomous entity within a university
federation, each with its own governing board. Comparison of performance,
both across different faculties in the same university federation and similar
faculties in other universities, would then become possible.

The police

The police need to decide what they are for. Is it crime, or 'trauma', or a
social service? Whatever it is it has to be measurable. My view is that it is
crime and that everything else the police currently do should be hived off to
separate, specialist agencies. Road policing is one obvious choice, and the
traffic warden organization, suitably upgraded, is already there to receive
these duties (and then to be subsumed into a 'Roads Federation'—see
below). Missing persons is another area where the police are currently less
than agile; no doubt some company or NPO could be trusted to do that.

Many of their other activities are not additional to crime-fighting but an
integral part of it—helping old ladies across the road is part of the process
of engaging the community, for example. Indeed the beneficiary doctrine
suggests that the police have here missed an opportunity of vast dimensions: the citizen could play a far greater, perhaps decisive, role in policing
their own areas under the tutelage of the regular police (alas, I suspect the
police do not want such schemes as Neighbourhood Watch to work, lest it
robs them of some of their powers. Another police spoiler?).

The crime statistics are a disgrace. No evaluation of the above ideas, nor
of anything else relating to crime, can be made until we have proper,
professional figures, based on the cost of crime *to the citizen*. If ever the

main contention of the beneficiary doctrine required illustration—that every organization must be able to point to meaningful, verifiable figures to show how well it is performing *for its beneficiaries*—this is the worst case; the crime figures are an insult; they do not even measure what the police want to know, let alone what we want to know.

It is often suggested that the more efficient alternative to the present rather unsatisfactory disposition of police forces (that is, many small county-based bodies) is a national force. At once the objection to this is obvious: it places too much power over civil liberty in the hands of one management hierarchy. But there are many other alternatives. One of which, specifically predicated by the beneficiary doctrine, is to move in the opposite direction—from the current 52 county-based forces, each employing about 2000 police officers, to several hundred town-based forces each employing a few hundred (notice, incidentally, how the quest for 'efficiency' leads to one solution here—the wrong one in my view—while the beneficiary doctrine points in the opposite direction). These small local forces would be solely responsible for crime protection in their own local area, dealing with minor incidents themselves but calling in (and paying the full cost of) national specialist forces (fraud, murder, rape, art theft, and so forth) when they needed to. Perhaps we also require a new local community service—a second-level police-cum-accident force and court system to deal with minor local disputes and trauma.

Autonomous with governing boards

Each police unit—local and national—would be autonomous under its own small elected governing boards, entirely separate from government. Because these units would employ no more than a few hundred people that would ensure their full engagement and would encourage private and voluntary sector organizations to make a substantial contribution; it is time that relevant companies and NPOs moved beyond just providing support services and become more fully engaged in the core policing business, certainly for minor crime.

These five key strategies—very small autonomous local forces with governing boards who set the crime targets for their area; the formation of specialized national forces to deal with more serious crimes, also with their own governing boards; completely recalculating the crime figures on a cost-to-the-victim basis; discarding all non-crime activities; engaging the citizen and the private and voluntary sectors perhaps in a second-level service (especially relevant to the 96 per cent of crime that is 'minor')—all these strategies would double the effectiveness of the police within a decade. Adopting this corporate plan would turn the crime rate decisively down and keep it there until crime ceased to be the burning social issue it now is.

I see no reason why some of these specialist police forces should not be entirely introvert; for instance, a 'corporate fraud squad' could be funded, not by the state, but by companies; their governing directors elected not by the public, but by the participating companies.

We keep trying to tackle a huge range of problems with one vast hierarchical organization; split and specialize is a better way.

Prisons

One by one, over the next decade, the prisons should be rescued from the dead hand of Britain's most appalling government department, the Home Office. Some should be privatized, others should become self-governing NPOs run under contract and supervised by such organizations as the Howard League, the Prison Reform Trust, the National Association for the Care and Resettlement of Offenders, Women in Prison, the Prince's Trust—there are enough of these voluntary organizations to run a significant sample of our prisons. They have all been telling us how to do it for the past many decades, let them show us what results they can achieve. Judging by Barnardo's ITCs (page 128) several of our children's charities should be running prisons for young offenders.

In order to emphasize the task—which is to improve the lives of those criminals capable of release—I would like to place the prisoners themselves in the role of intended beneficiaries, not the public as the Home Office does (page 147):

Corporate purpose for the 'Federated British Prison Service'

The intended beneficiaries	Prisoners
The intended benefit	To help them lead law-abiding and useful lives in custody and after release
BPI	Their ability to earn an honest living

These would still be extrovert organizations of course, and the aim, reflected in their Tmins and Tsats, should be to improve the social behaviour of the inmates on their release as measured by their lawful incomes.

It is again imperative to stress that their governing directors should be drawn from the pool of professional governing directors, licensed by the Institute of Governing Directors, not fanatical liberals, but balanced, worldly people immune to silly idealism, concerned solely for the earning-power of the prisoners after they are discharged. It would be part of the job of these governing directors to supervise the tracking of their 'ex-cons' over the ensuing years. Most of these prisons would be small (little more than secure houses) and specialized (for remand prisoners, youngsters, drunk drivers, sex offenders and so on) with specialist staff and facilities. Expensive? Perhaps, but with, I suspect, a far higher return on society's capital than the Home Office's sterile concept of 'keeping them in'.

Finally, an experimental introvert organization should be formed to allow selected prisoners themselves to run their own prison with suitable safeguards. Thus we might have four different prison organizations: those run by the government, by the voluntary sector, by the private sector, and by prisoners themselves. The criterion in this race? Just one—the discounted cash flow experience of the prisoners, that is, the cash it costs to support them in prison and in the years after their release, less any legitimate income they earn. In the early years it would be the government which finances the contracts with these organizations but, gradually, their managements would discover new sources of income and, eventually, they might be cut adrift from the state entirely.

Churches and religions

The Church of England is in a long, slow decline which, in my view, is now accelerating with frightening speed. While the Synod is a fine debating forum it is useless as a governing body. What the Church needs is, first, to elect an entirely new, small, governing board, which then elects a chairman. Second, they must determine what the Church is supposed to be doing for whom and set targets—with special attention to what exactly represents Tmin for this organization so that it never again plumbs the depths of failure it has attained in recent decades. Third, they should select a strong autocratic chief executive who should temporarily transform the current loose assemblage of bishops and deans into a centralized traditional command hierarchy of executive managers.

Of all the more important British organizations, the Church of England most needs a 'turn-round man' to cut back to its core business (what is it, by the way?). As soon as that task is completed (not for at least a decade, one assumes) the governing board would gratefully replace the chief executive with someone more in line with its traditional culture and the organization would revert to its decentralized format from which point it might well adopt a federal form.

As for the other religions: I am sure they do the world much good, but I can also see much that contravenes the no harm principle. The taboo on birth control, for example, is partly responsible for the starkest plight that faces humanity in the next century—overpopulation—far more basic than 'global warming'. The role of women in society, while belatedly and rapidly unfolding in the developed world, is crushed everywhere else by religious precepts. The progress of technology is still inhibited, even in that bastion of science, the United States. As for the poor, many churches seem to use their best endeavours to keep them so in every way they can devise. It would be pleasant to believe that this huge volume of deliberate harm, surely unmatched by any other type of organization in the modern world, could be swiftly reduced. World public opinion could do the trick within a single decade.

Government agencies

Unnoticed by either the press or the public the present British government is energetically spinning off a number of its activities to 'autonomous' agencies. Unfortunately, most of these still answer to their sponsoring department of state and, having no governing boards, are very far from being autonomous. While they have been given a handful of top targets, especially for service levels, in accordance with the 'next steps' (Fraser, 1991), this is quite inadequate as a *corporate* target, as I have explained, and so they lack anything resembling a BPI.

Perhaps this is the place for a reminder: 'service levels' are either MPIs or CPIs for they measure how well a department or an agency is doing what it *does*. A BPI measures what that service is *for*—such as the extent to which 'child benefits', for example, improve the lives of those who receive them. The former—service levels—are easy to measure; the latter is difficult but far more meaningful.

Nor is there anywhere the variety of design for these agencies that would be available under the beneficiary doctrine—introvert, extrovert, project, specialized, company, and so on—nor has any use been made of the concept of federation.

I would like to see the beneficiary doctrine applied liberally to all government departments, especially in view of the enormous span of activities still to be devolved. Thus the entire legal system—complete with all the judges, the Law Commission, Crown Courts, the Lord Chancellor, the Lay Observers, the Prosecution Service and Legal Aid should each be hived off as separate autonomous units (each with a small governing board) within a self-financing federation under the generic title the 'British Justice Federation' or whatever (also with its own governing board), whose independence from government would be guaranteed under a written constitution.

Likewise, the Bank of England and all its various regulatory duties—the supervision of UK banks, the licensing of financial institutions, even printing, auditing and so on (plus, of course, regulating the money supply to stabilize the currency)—should also be floated entirely free and separate. Each of these sub-duties is worthy of a unit with its own governing board within the 'Bank of England Federation', each with its own numerical targets.

Again, a fully self-funding 'Roads Federation' should be formed, also quite separate from government, to design, build and maintain the road system of Britain—and to police it by means of the traffic warden service upgraded to become the 'Traffic Police Service'. No doubt its governing board would examine 'long-term rate of improvement in door-to-door journey times including all delays' as a possible BPI.

Government to spin off almost everything

The entire education system, the NHS, the emergency services, the Civil Aviation Authority, libraries, museums, the Equal Opportunities Commission and other commissions, registrars—almost every activity now performed by government (dozens and dozens of them)—could be devolved to autonomous federations of companies or NPOs (or mixed), most of them self-financing, with their own governing directors. I realize that it took two centuries for Western governments to gather all these activities into their hands, but I sincerely hope it would take less than a century for them all to be disposed of again. What would be left for government to do in the end? Defence of the realm, foreign policy, control of the economy, legislation; not much more, I imagine. The rest would have been devolved to specialist autonomous units with their own governing boards acting within their own relevant, independent federations. Or handed over to similarly autonomous units in Europe.

And, of course, it will be necessary to re-form all those absurd Training *and* Enterprise Councils into Training Councils; to drop the 'environment' from Scottish Enterprise; to split UNESCO into three—and so on for all the world's myriad local, national and international governmental organizations which currently have more than one single aim.

Many of these agencies and other NPOs are natural monopolies; we do not require more than one British Standards Institute, for example, nor more than one British Medical Association. The beneficiary doctrine has two substantial contributions to make to mitigate the problems of monopolistic behaviour; first, the proposed governing boards will maintain close control over their conduct and second, the technique of setting targets will keep them up to scratch in spite of the lack of competition (as noted on page 87, a professional manager striving to hit a valid target is like an athlete competing against the clock; he or she does not need a competitor to maintain high standards).

I believe a gigantic amplification of our liberties as well as a vast lift to our well-being would follow as each governing board in all these myriad organizations applied their sensitive antennae to the needs of the citizen, without the necessity for the current endless escalation in the number and powers of watchdogs, legislators, statutory regulatory bodies and artificial markets to protect us from their arrogant managerial disregard. And, in response to clear corporate targets, the performance of these agencies would soar.

Finally, government agencies are particularly poor at engaging their interest groups—they rely on their 'authority' to get people to cooperate, a technique of inducement thoroughly unpopular with the modern citizen as every person with experience of our tax or social services regimes will know. I am sure the quality of engagement will improve beyond recognition as more and more governmental activities are spun off to smaller, specialist agencies. As noted before, I would expect few of these units to employ more than a few hundred people, many would be deliberately split into regional and functional sub-units specifically to drop below this threshold so that the quality of management, especially in the practice of engagement, would immeasurably improve.

Summary

I began the chapter with a summary of the beneficiary doctrine with its three interconnected components: performance, conduct, governance. I then described some of its consequences upon companies, NPOs, on the rise of federations and what it would mean for governors and managers.

The consequence for companies, I suggested, would be seen mainly in the boardroom where the present non-executive directors would be ousted by the new governing directors with almost immediate effects on their performance, due to the managers at last being set sensible, long-term profit targets at the Tmin and Tsat levels. Corporate behaviour would vastly improve as a result of adopting the no harm principle.

NPOs would experience an even greater surge in performance for they have so much further to go than companies. A massive exodus of so-called governors would revolutionize the governance and management of all our major NPOs as they specialized single-mindedly to serve just one intended beneficiary. I envisaged them breaking down into smaller, specialized units, each able to quantify its aims, and then realigning as independent autonomous organizations under the protection of a federation.

As for governors and managers, they would each delight in the new clear-cut definitions of their tasks, the governors setting BPI targets and monitoring, the managers free to exercise their skills in developing strategies to achieve them.

I recommended a number of corporate plans; for the police, for colleges, for prisons, for the churches. As for government agencies, I would like to see them split into smaller, specialist, autonomous (i.e., with their own governing boards), self-financing, units each inside a relevant federation. This applies to the whole of our legal system (the 'Justice Federation'), the CAA, museums, roads (the 'Roads Federation'), the NHS, education (the 'Primary Schools Federation', the 'Secondary ...'), emergency services, the railways and on to infinity.

Companies and NPOs will become so effective, and so well-behaved, that our standard of living and our quality of life will soar. We will eventually deem them capable of carrying out virtually all the sensitive tasks that we currently require to be performed only by government.

I now wish to turn to the effects that the beneficiary doctrine would have on parliamentary government itself.

CHAPTER NINETEEN

The governance of nations

Government, whether local, national or supranational, is just another form of organization; I see no distinction, other than size and power, between an organization called the 'Government of Great Britain' and one called 'ICI', say, or the 'Institute of Dental Hygiene'. They each have their intended beneficiaries who demand a satisfactory benefit, they each come into contact with an array of interest groups; each are managed by executives. The beneficiary doctrine should apply to this form of organization just as effectively as any other.

To attempt to reconstruct all our centuries-old Western systems of constitutional government at the tail end of my final chapter is an amusing challenge which I do not propose to accept. Yet I am convinced that our parliamentary processes should be redesigned along exactly the same lines as for all the other organizations I have discussed above—power should be separated into elected governance on the one hand and executive management on the other.

Quite simply, I believe the reason that all our Western political systems are seen by the average citizen today as fatuous, ineffective and irrelevant to the needs of the modern state is that, all those centuries ago, our ancestors separated the wrong powers!

The separation of powers

The design of all current Western constitutional government stems from such distant historical events as the anger of the English barons with King John in 1215 and Simon de Montfort's then eccentric concept of 'parliament' in 1295; both these milestones resulted in the devolution of the political power of the monarch into the hands of lords and later of commoners.

Up to the middle of the seventeenth century it was customary to question whether ordinary citizens should be granted any political power at all; they were seen as mere servants of the state. Hobbes, for example, an English philosopher, wrote in 1651 that princes should reign over us by Divine Right—a view maintained in Japan even up to recent times. As late as the nineteenth century Hegel still believed that the citizen existed for the state and not the other way round. It is almost unbelievable that any sane person could hold such a topsy-turvy view of the world, yet it was orthodox in the civilized world in that not-so-distant age. The idea that the state should serve the citizen, and not vice versa, is a notion of almost unimaginable modernity.

In 1689 however, Locke, another English philosopher, published his *Treatise on Government* in which he introduced the idea of the formal 'separation of powers' to protect the freedom of the ordinary citizen. He was worried about the enduring power of the king, and to preserve our liberty from this potential tyrant he proposed that the legislative power of Parliament should be separated from the executive power of the king (notice that it was then the monarch who wielded executive power, not the government — completely different to today).

Then, in the 1730s, a French sage, Montesquieu, fearful of the growing influence of government (for the power of both the Church and of the individual citizen were then in decline in France) declared that a further safeguard was necessary, namely separation not merely into two powers, but into three: the legislature, the executive and the judiciary. So acutely was the threat to the liberty of the citizen perceived in those distant days that it was this three-part separation that was later written so decisively into the American constitution. (Incidentally, Machiavelli, contrary to his black, autocratic reputation, held that princes, nobles and commoners should keep each other in check — so his was another, quite different, but still essentially democratic, version of a three-part separation of power.) Later writers proposed yet a further split to safeguard our liberties — into local as well as central government.

The concept of separation

So this was the concept then: power should be separated to protect our liberty. The powers that should be separated were: the judiciary, the executive and the legislature. Moreover, because the legislature was the most powerful of the three, it should itself be further subdivided into two dissimilar chambers (Lords and Commons). A further devolution should take place to the local level. And this is still the basic concept of the separation of powers today, with such minor variations as, for example, in America where the Senate and the House of Representatives in Congress are both elected (each by a different voting system over a different period), while in England the Upper House remains hereditary.

The reason for my whirlwind excursion into 700 years of constitutional history is this: all the systems of government we know today evolved in an age when the world was *unrecognizably* different. Divine Right? Princes and nobles? In which developed nation today does the citizen lie awake tormented by these political perils? And yet all our systems of government are as they are today because, and solely because, of these far-off concerns and worries—our own, and most other European parliamentary systems implicitly are and the more recent American one explicitly is.

So far as I know no one has propounded any alternative division of powers during the past two centuries of political thought in spite of the mountainous sea-changes that have occurred in society. We have become inured to this particular division, dazzled by it, mesmerized, unable to break its spell. It is the only meaning we know of the phrase 'separating the powers'.

And how odd it now seems to have split the legislature into two on the grounds that it was the most potent of the three powers, for is it not clear that, today, it is the executive whose domination needs to be constrained? (And anyhow, one might ask, what company would split its management team into two on the grounds that it was 'too powerful'?)

It does not work and it does not protect liberty

I question whether this separation has ever worked either in the sense of achieving satisfactory results or of protecting the liberty of the citizen.

In Chapter 1 I reviewed the quite appalling failures of the British system of government—education, police, poverty, health, prisons, the debasement of our currency, the railways, justice—wherever you look you see levels of managerial failure that would not be tolerated in a modern company for 10 minutes. It works? One would have to be a fanatical parliamentarian to believe that.

Nor are the governments of other nations blessed with any greater success. The American constitution hog-ties their entire system of government; because their president is both chairman and chief executive (as I use these terms, see Glossary) and has to be constrained by such an elaborate panoply of checks and balances that only the lobby system, liberally oiled by dollars, can break the jam—hardly 'democracy' as anyone ever intended. Does it work? Have a glance at America's inner cities, at the drugs, crime, education, racial tension, budget deficits, poverty, etc.

As for protecting our liberty, Germany and Italy enjoyed systems of separation very similar to ours in the thirties but both Hitler and Mussolini smashed through them to rule supreme—once may be regarded as a misfortune, but twice? And, in spite of all those much-vaunted democratic defences, did not McCarthyism come within a whisker of destroying freedom in America itself in the fifties? In France they no longer make any attempt to follow the original concept: under the Fifth Republic their president has the power to dismiss not just the prime minister but parliament itself, which has become little more than a rubber stamp, legislation being forced through without a vote by means of Article 49-3 (rather like our 'guillotine' which, of course, is not what the French call it). Ironically, then, in this land of Montesquieu, the president is the effective head of the executive, the legislature and the judiciary! That which was separate is now joined.

In Spain, Greece, Mexico or wherever, it is different again. I am not complaining of this diversity, certainly not; diversity is experiment, experiment is learning, learning is progress—or it should be. But here we do not seem to be learning *anything*; in spite of all this variety, no consensus exists anywhere on earth as to which system is best—not even whether we need a two-way or a three-way separation of powers. That is why I say they must all be wrong; we have learnt no useful lessons at all from this 300-year experiment; none of us has adopted any other nation's system on the grounds that it was manifestly getting better results. I suspect they are all defective for the same reason: that they all sprang from political theories that emerged in Europe in the seventeenth century to address socio-political conditions wholly unrecognizable to us today, and because the traditional ceremonial and rituals have locked these systems into rigor mortis.

Meanwhile, all across the world, in nation after nation, the average citizen sees government as a worthless monster, totally incapable of tackling the problems of today, even a threat to civilized life, of value only to those who have learnt to milk it. Disillusion, disappointment, even anger, with all our political processes, local, national and international, is world-wide.

Separating whose powers?

That a separation of powers is an absolutely essential element in the design of any organization in order to prevent abuses of power by its executives, whether it be the Northtown Gardening Club or the European Community, is unquestioned—it is a central theme of this book. But my thesis is this: the device that we require is not a split between three arms of the constitution, none of which is a recognizable entity today, but a governing board, composed of people elected by, and responsible to, the intended beneficiaries, to sit above the executive team of managers.

That is the separation that we need, as between elected governance and executive management, not the one proposed by Montesquieu for purely parochial and ephemeral reasons relating to social conditions in France centuries before the appearance of anything remotely like modern democracy.

Upper and lower houses

I want to separate governance and management here, then, just as for all those other organizations. Exactly how this should be done in the case of a national government is far beyond the scope of this book. I believe, however, that governance should be carried out in what is now the Lords, where elected representatives ('senators'?), led by their elected president, would carry out the duties of my governing directors—that is, they should set suitable GNPH targets (as suggested on page 158) for the nation and determine what code of conduct the administration should adopt towards the nation's various interest groups. That they should also monitor progress towards these targets on behalf of every category of citizen, rich and poor, young and old, black and white, Jew and gentile, male and female, north and south, is quite certain—remember how insistent the beneficiary doctrine is on tracking equitable benefits for all classes of beneficiary.

The professional executive managers of the nation's affairs—the Cabinet, junior ministers, even some very senior civil servants—should sit in the Commons and, in the interests of open government, publicly discuss their proposed actions and legislation designed to achieve the targets set them by the upper house. The government will be led by a prime minister appointed by the president and, should performance slip towards Tmin, the prime minister will be dismissed, thus bringing down the administration— exactly as described above for any other organization. (And notice how the upper house is here superior to the lower; in all our Western democracies this logic has become reversed, thus emphasizing, yet again, how management everywhere has toppled governance.)

Would all the members of this lower house be appointed or some elected? Would there be a formal Opposition in the lower house as well as the upper? And, in this lower house, would a bill designed to improve GNP by £20bn take precedence in the parliamentary programme over one that was expected to deliver an extra £10bn—thus for the first time permitting a sense of priority in the work of this chamber? I hope so.

Also, presumably, these managers would devise the actions and legislation to protect citizens from harm and to engage them fruitfully in society— all in accord with the no harm principle and the principle of engagement.

Thus, I foresee two strains of professional politician: one who represents his or her constituents and one who manages the nation's affairs. It all sounds very foreign. There are no precedents. And yet we do need a more responsive form of representation today and we do need our representatives to remain faithful to us, to monitor that we are each receiving our just deserts, and not to turn their backs on us while they go off and manage the nation. Equally we need professional managers to concentrate their minds on today's complex and difficult executive decisions, and to enshrine them in sensible and effective law, in order to achieve a higher growth of GNPH and attain a better society for us all.

Is it radical enough?

What I am proposing goes far beyond other reforms of our democratic procedures, such as the much-discussed introduction of proportional representation in Britain; changes to the voting system are almost irrelevant to the central problem of our democracy for, whatever the stripe of the party in power, or the coalition of parties, or how they gain power, the central issue today is that the executive is out of control. We suffer from an elective dictatorship.

What has happened is that the traditional three powers are no longer separate; government today is a huge, interlocking, overweening, executive hierarchy, consisting of millions of employees, topped by the prime minister. Any idea that there is some kind of break in the sequence, any concept of a meaningful interface between legislature and executive, between ministers and civil servants, is pure make-believe; they are all managers in one vast seamless, classic, outdated pyramid command structure. All our Western governments have marched a similar route. My separation of powers would tame this pyramid by the simple act of recapitation.

What about the third power, the judiciary? But I want to take that out of government entirely, into a 'Federation of British Justice' (see page 269), whose autonomy from government is guaranteed by a written constitution. This federation would be required to interpret the law as handed down by the lower house, to supervise the mechanical workings of the law and to update the nuts and bolts of the legal system.

No, a two-way separation is all that is required; but it must be a governance-management one, not an executive-legislature one. Because of the logic, clarity and authority of the former separation it will be safe and practical to abandon the latter.

In the upper house we need the diversity that comes from an accurate representation of the electorate; in the lower we want the single minded achievement of Tsat.

Local government: the same story

Turning to local government, it is the same but worse. My local representative, whom I thought was going to fight for my interests, is actually running the town (along with the professional local authority officers, all in the same command pyramid), so he or she is hardly in a position to address my concerns about some of the management's decisions. From the moment of election, a local representative is appointed to one or other of innumerable management committees and I am promptly disenfranchised! (At least in the Commons only about one-third of our so-called representatives go off and run the country as ministers.)

Moreover, any ambition that Montesquieu and his successors may have had that local government would provide some further separation of powers is completely vitiated in Britain by the fact that central government pays 70 per cent of the local bills (it is not so high in the rest of Europe). The person who pays the piper, calls the tune; the power that was separate has now been joined and bang goes the last fig-leaf of the separation of powers.

The government of Europe

Much is amiss with the European Community: its voting system, the 'Buggin's turn' presidency (what would we think of IBM appointing a new chairman every six months?), its exorbitant agricultural policy, and on and on; yet towering far above all these problems (and from which they spring) is its tricameral separation of powers. In spite of the fact that it was designed and developed within the past three decades, and thus presumably represents the latest thinking on democratic system-building, it is fundamentally flawed.

And so what a splendid opportunity for reform presents itself in the European Community where the relationship between the three arms of government—the Commission, the Parliament, the Council of Ministers (not to mention the Court)—are quite beyond comprehension and entirely undemocratic in that the Commission (effectively the management) has been deliberately endowed with greater powers than the Parliament and, together with the Council of Ministers, easily outguns it. No wonder Brussels continually cleaves to itself more and more power in defiance of the principle of subsidiarity!

Many experts agree that this concept is defective. However, while they merely wish to tinker with the balance between the three power centres, I want two chambers only: an upper, the stronghold of the representatives of the people of Europe, headed by a chairman (or president, whichever you prefer); and a lower, to consist of the senior management team headed by a chief executive.

We should get performance targets, conduct and monitoring from the upper house; ideas, action, strategies and legislation to achieve these from the lower—all exactly as for all the organizations I have discussed throughout this book (the Council and Commission should obviously be subsumed into the lower house). I cannot imagine what madness was in their heads when the Europeans designed this monstrous constitution; it sums up, as well as anything I can say, the profundity of the ignorance most of us display, even so-called experts, in the workings of organizational machinery.

Simplicity and transparency

Another reason for separating governmental powers into two chambers, governance and management, rather than between the generally accepted executive, legislature and judiciary, is this: democracy, like justice, has to be seen to be done. It is crucially important that ordinary people understand who represents them, who makes the laws that affect their lives and are able to verify that all is transparent and above board. This must be especially so where, in Europe, we are moving towards a profusion of local, national and supranational layers of government; sorting out who is to do what among a federation of 300 million people in 40 nations, and thousands of increasingly autonomous provinces, *Länder* and cantons, not to mention tens of thousands of towns, cities and *arrondissements* (plus approximately half a million of my 'parishes'), is going to require exceptional organizational skills.

It is not only that government will be strangled by the checks and balances provided by the traditional triple separation of powers at several of these levels in this monstrous hierarchy of government, as it already has been in America (where, remember, the formal triple separation occurs at both state and federal levels), it is also that being able to understand who is doing what is going to be crucial for our confidence in the new systems.

Government in the Third World

Not only does Europe require a simple, comprehensible system of power; many of the nations of the Third World who are emerging from dictatorship also yearn for it. I note that, out of the 50 ex-British colonies that make up the Commonwealth, only half have followed the design of the 'Mother of Parliaments'—the others are single-party autocracies, some of a particularly unpleasant character. We should not be surprised that so many have been unable to emulate our system for it is complex beyond belief. No wonder autocracy is so welcome an alternative; at least everyone understands how it works and who is the boss. No; let us devise a system that might also work for the less developed, one that is not buried beneath centuries of Western European socio-political history.

And here is another reason for keeping it simple: all studies show that simple products work best; the fewer the components, the less often do the products fail. We are never going to see zero defect government, I am afraid, but simplification into two houses, each with crystal-clear and wholly distinct functions, one plainly senior to the other, would be a splendid start.

The United Nations is another case where we have failed to separate governance from management and where, consequently, its performance has been disappointing.

Wherever you look the gamekeepers are also the poachers, the players also the referees, the judges are the jury and the lord high executioners. It is the same old story in every human organization.

Diversity, individualism and government

The European Community (EC) provides a splendid instance of one of the main themes in this book; that as an organization grows—and the EC is moving from 12 nations to perhaps 40 by the inclusion of the EFTA and the swiftly-fragmenting Eastern European nations—it touches not just more people, but a wider selection of peoples; just look at the ethnic, religious and economic diversity these new nations will bring with them—it is like creating a new India.

But not just more diverse; improved education, greater purchasing power and a growing sense of our own individuality all conspire to form an overwhelming case for a more vigorous, truly democratic, system of representation that can more effectively convey the views of this seething modern electorate to, and keep control of, the management.

While it must be management's task to increase the size of the cake it must be the job of governance to ensure that each of us, in this kaleidoscope of human diversity, gets a fair slice of it.

The future: corporate democracy

I see 'corporate democracy' as the end point of all the centuries of democratic development we have so far enjoyed. A corporate democracy is a society in which the intended beneficiaries of all its socially significant organizations (including, critically, the various forms of local, national and international government), gain full and final democratic control by means of the separation of elected governance from executive management. This might indeed be 'the end of history'.

This is the sequence of events we need to see over the next several decades to ensure that organizations become truly the vehicle of their beneficiaries' needs rather than the playthings of their managers. First, each nation should set up an Institute of Governing Directors to launch and oversee the whole project. Then legislation would be required to enshrine the statutory duties of governing directors and to enable intended beneficiaries and interest groups to elect a governing board should they feel their organization requires one.

Hordes of old-style governors and non-executives would then be invited to step down in favour of these new, slimmer, professional governing boards and, overnight, this would begin to change the behaviour of managers. Proper, quantified corporate targets would be handed down to them along with a code of conduct, and they would at last bring to bear their remarkable skills to tailor their strategies specifically to hit Tsat and avoid Tmin. (I suggest these first and second laws of social development: the rate at which a society evolves is proportional to (1) the number of organizations supervised by elected governing directors, and (2) the rate at which its most significant organizations quantify their corporate objectives.)

I would like to believe that after a couple of decades our political masters might be so impressed by the effect that the beneficiary doctrine had wrought on these organizations that they would be moved to bring in a reform bill to apply it to government itself, by creating an elected upper house which would promptly set GNPH targets to an executive lower house (and, in Britain, complete the job with a bill of rights).

Corporate democracy is for people

I see each person's life as a stream of events. An organization is a group of people working to improve the balance of events for its beneficiaries, augmenting the pleasant ones and mitigating the traumatic, while at the same time taking care not to damage anyone else's stream. I believe the effect of many of the deeds of these organizations, perhaps almost all of them, can be—indeed should be—measured in terms of cash flow.

Thus a government should be striving to improve the GNPH of each of its citizens; every company should be developing strategies to raise the return on shareholders' capital; my local college should be offering to enhance my earning power; your local police protecting you from loss—and so on. I noted, much to my own surprise, how important income and salary are as indicators of performance for many of the NPOs I discussed in Chapters 9 to 12. I am not ashamed of using money as the central tool of target-setting and tracking for all our more important organizations, as many liberals apparently are. I positively welcome it. It is the key to performance, not the route to perdition.

I see the standard of living in even the mature nations of the world doubling every generation so that many people's earnings will equal those of their parents' boss's boss's income! Think, just think, what those people's standards will then be, what will be their demands on organisations! But this higher standard of living, coupled to the huge rise in the population of the world, will generate unprecedented threats as well as opportunities.

If this is how the world moves over the next century or so then every organization is going to have to listen ever more closely to what we want and to act ever more effectively to deliver it. To make sure they hear us more accurately we are going to have to elect a governing board of sensible, professional people to represent our views; to yield the necessary results they are going to have to employ highly professional executive managers. And the governance must be placed very firmly on top of the management.

Glossary

Aarrog

The average annual real rate of growth. The average compound rate of growth over and above inflation at which any factor, such as EpS, grows over a given number of years.

Auditor

In general use the word describes a qualified accountant who verifies the accounts for companies and NPOs. It is used here also to describe a future professional specialist who is expert in the design and verification of corporate performance indicators (CPIs).

The beneficiary doctrine

A tripartite theory which holds that organizations should concentrate on providing a verifiably satisfactory benefit to their intended beneficiaries, while observing a certain code of conduct, under the supervision of a governing board.

Beneficiaries' performance indicator (BPI)

A corporate performance indicator (CPI) which specifically measures the benefit delivered by an organization to its intended beneficiaries.

Beneficiary tracking

The act of carefully and deliberately studying the long-term effects that an organization has on its intended beneficiaries and measuring these in order to estimate the benefit per beneficiary (BpB) or the return on capital of these beneficiaries individually and of the organization as a corporate whole. Beneficiary tracking should be the responsibility of the governing directors but will increasingly be performed by independent organizations specializing in this activity.

Benefit per beneficiary (BpB)

The NPO's equivalent of EpS (earnings per share). It calls for more benefit per beneficiary each year—greater safety for motorists, for example, higher cure rates for patients, and so on. It is the second most fundamental BPI—the ultimate being return on society's capital (ROSC).

Chairman

The person who heads the governing directors on a governing board. He or she is elected by the governing directors and is essentially non-executive. (Many other titles are used elsewhere, such as president, mayor, executive chairman, but the title 'chairman' is used throughout this book to refer quite specifically to the unique job description in Chapter 16, the essentially non-executive, elected leader (male or female) of a board of governing directors).

Chief executive (CE)

A 'chief executive' is the most senior executive officer of any autonomous organization. He or she stands at the apex of the management hierarchy and reports to the chairman of the governing board by whom he or she is appointed, remunerated and dismissed. The CE is responsible for devising the strategies and actions required to achieve the corporate performance and corporate conduct laid down by the governing board. (Other titles such as general secretary, principal, vice-president, CEO, chief operating officer, managing director and so on may or may not meet this unique job definition and are not used in this book.)

Company

A 'publicly quoted company' is an organization whose sole intended beneficiaries are its shareholders and whose sole intended benefit is a satisfactory return on their capital (ROSC). 'Private companies' may add whatever other beneficiaries and benefits the owners may agree.

Corporate conduct

How an organization behaves in society. The beneficiary doctrine recognizes only two codes of conduct: the no harm principle and the principle of engagement. Conduct is largely independent of purpose; it is determined by the mores of the society in which the organization operates. (Other terms used elsewhere include ethos, social responsibilities, corporate culture, code of ethics, standards of behaviour, social conscience, etc.)

Corporate democracy

A society in which the majority of organizations—including, crucially, its various forms of local, national and supranational government—have adopted the separation of powers into elected governance and executive management.

Corporate objective

Used in this book to mean corporate purpose. (It is also, most confusingly, often used by others to mean any aim, goal, mission, whether corporate or partial, as well as corporate conduct and corporate strategy.)

Corporate performance indicator (CPI)

A unit which measures the success or failure of an organization as a corporate whole. They are designed to help top managers plan and control their organization as a corporate whole. All BPIs are CPIs but not vice versa. Some CPIs break down into MPIs and some of these build into CPIs—but seldom into BPIs.

Corporate perversion

The act of diverting the aims, strategies or resources of an organization to an interest group (often the managers themselves). The beneficiary doctrine holds that virtually all organizations which have defective systems of governance (i.e., virtually all modern organizations) will have been perverted.

Corporate plan

A simple set of statements describing the corporate purpose and corporate conduct for an organization, together with the key corporate strategies required to achieve the performance targets.

Corporate planning

A systematic process for deciding what are those key decisions that an organization, seen as a corporate whole, *must* get right in order to achieve its performance targets over the following few years. The process that leads to a corporate plan.

Corporate purpose

Corporate purpose is the reason why any organization is formed and why it exists today, the justification for all its strategies, all its actions, indeed, everything it ever does in its entire life history (except actions related to conduct). It is its *raison d'être*, the sole criterion by which one judges whether an organization is successful or a failure. It is the aim or end as opposed to strategy or means. Any definition of corporate purpose must include the identity of the intended beneficiaries and the benefit they expect.

Corporate strategies

Strategic actions are those which are taken because, and *only* because, the management believe they will improve the organization's ability to achieve its purpose or its standards of conduct; if they believed such actions would not help to achieve these they would not take them. Strategies are means, not ends, their sole justification is their effect on achieving the purpose or conduct. A *corporate* strategy relates to actions that affect the organization as a corporate whole—as distinct from strategies which affect only parts or sections of it such as market strategies, manpower strategies, and so on.

Executive chairman

A post, common in companies and NPOs, but unthinkable in the beneficiary doctrine, in which the functions of governance and management are combined in the person of one individual (male or female) at the top of the management hierarchy.

Extrovert organization

An organization whose intended beneficiaries are not the same people who founded it, own it, work for it or have effective control over its resources (for example, a government, a hospital, a charity all aim to benefit groups of people outside the organization itself). While NPOs generally may be either introvert or extrovert (no organization may be both) all government NPOs are extrovert.

Forecast

A forecast is someone's opinion of what will happen in the future. Most forecasts are quantified. All forecasts are liable to error, the further the horizon of the forecast the greater the errors may be and the more irresponsible it is not to show the range of possible error. Not to be confused with a target; a target is what you want, a forecast is what you expect.

Gap analysis

A technique for comparing targets against forecasts over a period of several years. Essential for the effective monitoring of strategies designed to achieve corporate targets.

Governance

The act of deciding and monitoring the required standards of performance and conduct of an organization.

Governing board

The group of governing directors who form a board at the top of any organization to carry out the duties of governance. In smaller organizations this can be as few as just one person; in international organizations hundreds may be required.

Governing director

A person, normally elected by the intended beneficiaries, who exercises governance. Governing directors are strictly non-executive and not to be confused in any way with the traditional so-called 'governor'. They are legally responsible to the intended beneficiaries for the performance of the organization and to the interest groups for its conduct.

Governors

Not a word recognized in the beneficiary doctrine. It connotes a group of people who act not only as governors but also as managers, thus precluding any possibility of performing either task effectively.

Intended beneficiary

The person or group of people for whose benefit any organization exists. They are its *raison d'être*.

Interest groups

All those people who are affected by an organization including the intended beneficiaries. (These are often called 'stakeholders' but this implies that they actually have a stake in, or a right to, a benefit from the organization. While not recognizing these rights the beneficiary doctrine accepts that many people do have an interest in organizations which affect them.)

Introvert organization

An organization whose intended beneficiaries are the same group of people who founded it, work for it, own it or have effective control over its resources. For example, a club, a society, a cooperative. All companies are introvert.

Managers

Those employees who receive instructions from a superior, who decide how best to achieve them and then give further instructions to a subordinate.

Manager's performance indicator (MPI)

Any performance indicator designed to help managers plan and control that part of an organization for which they are responsible, including any equipment, activity, people or other resource, often in the form of 'efficiency' ratios. Not to be confused with CPIs or BPIs.

Monitoring

Continually testing one's confidence in current strategies. It is thus more than merely 'checking results'. In the beneficiary doctrine both the governing directors and the managers monitor their confidence in their strategies by means of gap analysis.

The no harm principle

The moral precept which requires that, while in pursuit of one's objectives, one should never cause significant harm to others. If any significant harm is caused it must either be neutralized or full compensation should be made. Applicable to individual people as well as organizations.

Non-profitmaking organization (NPO)

A non-profitmaking organization is any organization that is not a company—that is, any organization which does not seek to make a profit and whose beneficiaries are not shareholders who expect a return on their capital. NPOs are often referred to as either non-governmental organizations or governmental—a distinction not made here.

Organization

An organization is a group of people working together to yield a satisfactory benefit for its intended beneficiaries while causing no significant harm to any interest group. Organizations may be introvert or extrovert, project or permanent and either a company or a non-profitmaking organization (NPO).

Performance indicator

Any figure which measures the performance of any organization, or part of one, or of equipment, people, resources. (See MPIs, CPIs, BPIs.)

Permanent organization

An organization set up to yield a continuous benefit to the intended beneficiaries for an indefinite period into the future. See its opposite, project organization.

Plan

A plan is a set of actions that one proposes to take to close the gap between what one wants to achieve (a target) and what one expects to achieve (a forecast).

Pressure group

A group of people who press their claims as members of an interest group with zeal.

The principle of engagement

An overall rule which, together with the no harm principle, should regulate corporate conduct. The principle of engagement says that managers should seek to engage the enthusiastic participation of all interest groups to increase the benefit the organization delivers to its intended beneficiaries.

Project organization

A 'disposable' organization set up to achieve a certain effect by a stated date and then, when this has been achieved (or when it becomes clear that it will not be), is disbanded or re-formed.

The purpose sequence

A catechism of five questions designed to ensure that an organization can answer the apparently simple question 'how are you doing?'. The first two questions define the corporate purpose and the remainder form the target sequence.

Return on society's capital, or on shareholders' capital (ROSC)

A technique for measuring return on capital which includes costs, income and capital by using DCF (discounted cash flow). ROSC is the most fundamental form of BPI for companies and NPOs, the ultimate criterion of success for any human organization.

Separation of powers

The principle of splitting authority between the various actors in any formal system of management in order to safeguard the liberties of the individual, especially in governmental and parliamentary systems. The beneficiary doctrine maintains that the only split required in any human organization is between elected governance and executive management.

Spoiler

A spoiler is any device which, when inserted into a purpose statement for an organization, renders its meaning unverifiable or unquantifiable. Typical of such devices are many mission, vision and value statements, multiple intended beneficiaries, complex benefits, MPIs masquerading as BPIs, etc.

Stakeholder

A person deemed by the stakeholder theory to hold a stake in the future prosperity of an organization and thus entitled to some consideration from it. They may include employees, customers, shareholders, suppliers, the state, the local community, society, bankers, special interest groups, the environment and technological progress. The stakeholder theory is rejected by the beneficiary doctrine.

Strategy

A strategy is any large-scale plan or overall principle to guide managers in devising actions to achieve targets. Note the distinction between a strategy, which is for a part of an organization, and a corporate strategy, which is for the organization as a corporate whole.

Strategy neutral

Any target which does not predicate or predetermine a strategy. True BPIs do not; many CPIs do, as do all MPIs.

Target

A corporate target is a quantified statement of a verbal corporate objective (or corporate conduct). It identifies levels of performance which the organization would, or would not, like to see. Not to be confused with a forecast; a target is what you want, a forecast is what you expect.

Target sequence

The second part of the purpose sequence, designed to quantify the purpose, in which the BPI is defined, Tmin and Tsat are set and then monitored.

Tfan

A level of performance far above average—fantastic, challenging, exceptional. The beneficiary doctrine deems this a highly inappropriate target for all but a few very successful organizations.

Tmax

A level of performance above which penalties for success may be applied—as when a monopoly might be penalized for making 'excessive profits'.

Tmin

Tmin is the minimum acceptable level of performance. At this level the management should undertake a major shift in strategy otherwise the beneficiaries might consider dismissing the management, in particular the chief executive, or even, if it persists, closing down the organization. Significantly below average performance. A Tmin growth target might be defined as 'barely perceptible growth over a period of some years'. Tmin for 'return on capital' is a level perilously close to the cost of capital.

Tsat

Tsat is a level of performance which the beneficiaries would regard as satisfactory and where they might award performance bonuses to the management. At this level the management might expand the organization beyond its current activities. Tsat for growth would be 'a significant annual rate of growth over some years'. Tsat is deemed to be 'well above average' or 'in the upper quartile' of comparators.

Total strategic situation

All the strategic factors taken together (target, forecast, gap, strengths and weaknesses, threats and opportunities). It describes the organization's present overall strategic situation as it is currently seen within its present and future environment.

References

Argenti, J. (1976), *Corporate Collapse*, McGraw-Hill, London.

Argenti, J. (1989), *Practical Corporate Planning*, Unwin Paperbacks, London.

Brownlie, K. (1988), *Yniscedwyn Intermediate Treatment Project: What happened to the 1980–83 Intake?* Barnardo's, Ilford, Essex.

Cheshire, P. (1990), 'Explaining the recent performance of the European Community's major urban regions, *Urban Studies*, **27**, (3), pp. 311–313.

Drucker, P. F. (1990), *The Management of Non-profit Organizations*, Butterworth Heinemann, Oxford.

Fraser, A. (1991), *Making the Most of the Next Steps: The Management of Minister's Departments and their Executive Agencies*, HMSO, London.

Hatten, M. L. (1982), 'Strategic Management in not-for-profit organizations', *Strategic Management Journal*, Vol. 3, pp. 89–104.

Klemm, M., S. Sanderson, and G. Luffman (1991), 'Mission Statements; Selling corporate values to employees', *Long Range Planning Journal*, **24**, (3), pp. 73–78.

Smith, D. and S. Tomlinson (1989), *The Schools Effect: A Study of Multi-racial Comprehensives*, Policy Studies Institute, London.

Webber, C. U., P. W. Foster, and D. P. Weikart (1978), *An Economic Analysis of the Ypsilanti Perry Preschool Project*, Monograph No. 5 of the High/Scope Educational Research Foundation, Ypsilanti, Michigan.

Wilson, D. C., and R. J. Butler (1986), 'Voluntary organizations in action: Strategy in the voluntary sector', *Journal of Management Studies*, **23**, (5), pp. 519–542.

Index

to track, 144, 216, 267
Government bonds, 97
Governors, 22, 49, 145, 186, 203, 216, 221,
   224, 256, 259
Greenpeace, 14, 15, 18, 28
Gross national product per head
   (GNPH), 157, 158, 160, 161, 162,
   172, 173, 281
   growth target, 160, 276
Growth, 25, 42, 78, 97, 108, 122, 124, 140,
   171, 172
   comparative, 107
   list of rates, 173
   of benefit, 124, 174
   of GNPH, 159
   only a CPI, 155
   targets, 85, 108

Hanson Group plc, 24, 195
Hierarchy, 211, 222, 230, 232
   government as huge, 277
   management, 120, 245, 266
   of aims and means, 43
   of autonomous organizations, 243
High/Scope, 130
Home Office, 7, 67, 147, 267
Howard League for Penal Reform, 150,
   171, 175, 267
   a BPI for, 152
   a CPI for, 151
   corporate purpose, 151
Human Development Index (HDI), 157
Hurdle rate, 101, 150, 175, 185

Imperial Chemical Industries plc (ICI),
   4, 19, 59, 75, 133, 189, 195, 259
   break-up value, 24
   ROSC, 102, 130
Imperial Group, 24
India, 227, 249
Inflation, 42, 55, 77, 98, 161, 168, 229
Institute of Directors, 24, 74, 206
Institute of Governing Directors (IGD),
   23, 223, 230, 256, 267
Intended beneficiaries, 35, 97, 194, 196,
   214, 215
   and interest groups, 199
   as raison d'etre, 36
   as stakeholders, 179
   final arbiters, 37, 82, 197, 280
   identity of, 3, 46, 121, 150, 151
   represented by governing directors,
   214, 223

rules for defining, 50
sole, 20, 35, 246, 260
versus incidental beneficiaries, 36
Interest groups, 20, 188, 196, 199, 214
   and engagement, 21, 137, 245, 270
   and governing directors, 217, 228
   and no harm, 188
   no legitimate claims, 50, 200
Introvert organization, 32, 33, 170, 260,
   261, 263, 264, 267, 268

Japanese companies, 81, 91, 185, 190
Joint projects, 48
Judiciary, 152, 273, 275, 277, 278
Justice, 8, 151, 163, 229, 274, 278
   Federation of, 269, 277
   system of, 6, 83, 151

Lamp-post figures, 71, 111, 138, 156, 167,
   264
Law Commission, 8, 269
Law Society, 46
Laws of social development, 280
League tables, 8, 61, 69, 141, 199, 260
Legal Aid Board, 4, 269
Local Community Service, 266
Local government, 129, 153, 210, 263
   a BPI for, 155, 156
   corporate purpose, 154
   management of, 277
Local Management of Schools (LMS),
   208
London, 70, 76, 77, 163, 173
Longitudinal research, 130

Mall management, 51, 231, 240
Management, 10, 225, 232, 256
   and governance, 26, 106, 174, 203,
   210, 216, 230, 235, 236
   books on, 11, 28, 33, 43, 84, 110, 204,
   225, 251
   in NPOs, 76, 120, 210, 259
   modern, 11, 62, 80, 221, 225
   professional, 14
   task of, 20, 24, 41, 82, 106, 181, 194,
   223, 280
Management performance indicators
   (MPIs), 97, 111, 144, 153, 158, 164,
   216, 233, 256
   and efficiency, 150
   and physical growth, 123, 173
   and service levels, 269
   extensive use of, 174